The Survival Handbook

Michael Allaby is a writer, lecturer and broadcaster on the
environment and the world food situation, and has been managing
editor of the *Ecologist*. He is the author of *The Eco-Activists*,
Who Will Eat ? and *Ecology*, and co-author of
A Blueprint for Survival.

Marika Hanbury Tenison has written many books and articles on food
and cookery and is cookery correspondent of the *Sunday Telegraph*.
Her publications in Pan include *Deep-Freeze Cookery* and
Deep-Freeze Sense.

John Seymour has farmed all his life and for most of it has grown all
the food for his family and himself. His books include *Self-Sufficiency*,
On My Own Terms and *The Fat of the Land*.

Hugh Sharman has a wide experience of energy problems and of
alternative technologies. He is the publisher of the magazine
Resurgence and also runs his own company promoting conservation
tools and alternative technology.

Michael Allaby

with Marika Hanbury Tenison
John Seymour and Hugh Sharman

the
survival
handbook

Self-sufficiency for everyone

Pan Books in association with Macmillan London

The publishers thank the following for providing drawings:
Brian Morgan, Jacqueline Small, Sally Seymour, Osborne Marks Associates,
First Impressions, Berry/Fallon and Bryan Ledgard

First published 1975 by Macmillan London Ltd
This edition published 1977 by Pan Books Ltd,
Cavaye Place, London SW10 9PG,
in association with Macmillan London Ltd
© Macmillan London Ltd, Michael Allaby and John Seymour 1975
ISBN 0 330 24813 8
Printed and bound in Great Britain by
Richard Clay (The Chaucer Press) Ltd, Bungay, Suffolk

Contents

Introduction

We are members of the most sophisticated society the world has ever seen. We pride ourselves, justly, on the technology that has sent our envoys into space and that can tear minerals from beneath the ocean floor. Our agriculture feeds populations larger than those at any time in the past, our food technology enables food to be transported over thousands of miles to sustain the populations of the largest cities in history, and our medical services ensure that people live for longer than man has ever lived before.

Yet as individuals we are helpless. We depend entirely on our complex technologies. Without them even the most elementary needs cannot be supplied. We cannot light our homes on dark winter evenings, or cook our food – far less produce it – or clothe ourselves. Should our power stations close or our transport systems fail we would be plunged into chaos almost at once.

Machines can and do fail and our industrial, urban societies are machines of the most elaborate kind. As we have become more aware of the degree of our dependence on this machine, so we have begun to feel vulnerable. People feel threatened and nowhere more so than in Britain, where our technological dependence has led us to rely on the export of manufactured goods to pay for the import of the food we need to keep us alive.

We are vulnerable because our technology is vulnerable. The world is changing and while the changes will affect the lives of all its peoples in time, they will be felt first and most acutely in the industrial nations and, perhaps, in Britain in particular. As world prices for essential foods and raw materials rise, our industry finds it more and more difficult to produce and sell sufficient goods to finance our imports. People are coming to believe that our present way of life cannot be sustained for much longer, while at the same time many people feel revulsion at the extremes of materialism that provide us with our aims and values. Whatever the future may hold, of one thing we may be certain: it will be very different from the immediate past.

We cannot know the future, of course, but there are many possibilities that are plausible. Will the riches of the world be distributed more equitably among its peoples, so that the disparities between rich and poor grow narrower? In such a world, would the quality of life deteriorate? Food and manufactured goods might become more standardized, to ensure that everyone has an equal opportunity to share in the general high level of consumption. Everyone might have access to the countryside and beaches, as well as to amenities and recreations of all kinds, but only as members of organized parties whose visits were arranged by rota and whose stay was limited. So might we all grow rich in a world grown cheap. Or the inhabitants of the industrial nations might grow steadily poorer as the wealth of the nations with food and mineral resources increased. Little by little our way of life would be eroded. Electricity, post and communications, transport and other services would become erratic. There would be frequent shortages of consumer goods and particular items of food, while prices rose much more rapidly than incomes. When at last the situation stabilized, the British might find themselves as poor as many citizens of Latin America, Africa and Asia are today. We might struggle bravely to maintain our living standards, borrowing heavily and consuming more rapidly than we produced until we precipitated a total economic collapse. The country would be bankrupted as its currency became worthless, with overseas investors trying to withdraw what remained of their capital and creditors trying to present their unpaid bills. We would be unable to import the food and goods we need and inevitably there would be social chaos, leading eventually, and probably after considerable violence, to national poverty.

These are the 'gloomy' scenarios, but how much better are the 'optimistic' ones? If our economy should begin to grow again we may find we must become even more ruthless if we are to maintain our position in a world whose balances of power are shifting. We will need to become even more materialistic and so our material wealth will be accompanied by spiritual impoverishment.

These are visions of the future. The facts on which they are based are, or should be, familiar to us all. We live in a world whose population is increasing very rapidly and in which already countless millions of parents must watch helpless as their young children die slowly, uncomprehendingly, from malnutrition, starvation, or diseases associated with or exacerbated by hunger. It is a world in which competition for fuels and minerals grows keener almost daily and a world in which the personal choices, desires and eventually the welfare of individual human beings must be subordinated to abstract concepts of 'national sovereignty' or 'progress' or 'development'. It is a world dominated by states with the immense power to destroy smaller nations; a power they might exercise at any time out of greed, jealousy, fear or simply miscalculation as they pursue their rival policies. It is the world into which most of us were born, in which we grew up, into which we must bring our own children.

It is a world that is rejected by many people who are seeking to devise alternative lifestyles for themselves based on values they find more human, more real. It is for such people that this book has been written.

The book began as an attempt to answer a single, simple question that gives it its title: if the society in which we live were to collapse, if its industries and services ceased to function so that shops ran out of supplies, mains services became unreliable and communications difficult, how could we survive as individuals, as families, as small and possibly isolated groups? In other words, how may we reduce our dependence on technologies over which we have no control? Could you build a house? Could you grow your own food? If there were no tea or coffee, could you find substitutes growing wild? Could you spin, dye and weave your own cloth, make your own furniture, build a boat, make a crossbow for hunting or defence or provide yourself with such mundane but necessary items as brushes? Could you generate electricity, heat your home in winter, or provide a constant supply of hot water? Could you make your own soap, starch or bleach? We found answers to these and many other questions. We can tell you how to deliver a baby, how to treat common ailments and administer first aid. Yet this is only scratching the surface. We are interested in a total way of life, and this cannot be based merely on a few technologies: indeed, it is from this naive assumption that we seek to escape.

We need to know how to live in peace and harmony with one another, as well as with the natural world around us. The ecological literature can tell us much about the latter, but little about the former.

8

So we have looked at communities to try and discover why some succeed and others fail. What are the emotional and psychological problems that may arise? What role, if any, should religion play as a unifying force that provides a community with a purpose? Is a successful community run as a democracy or as a dictatorship? We have looked at the way monasteries are organized, since they are the only examples we have of voluntary 'communes' that have endured over centuries. Against this we describe the actual experiences of a modern secular community. Nor have we forgotten that art and entertainment are important, if not essential. Could you make your own musical instruments? We describe the life and work of one of the many theatre groups that lives communally and tours its immediate locality.

A book of this kind is not written by one person alone. The principal authors are well known. Marika Hanbury Tenison has written many books and articles on food and cookery, but she is also the wife of an explorer and has 'lived off the land'. John Seymour has farmed all his life and for most of it has grown all the food for his family and himself. Hugh Sharman has a wide experience of energy problems and a profound knowledge of alternative technologies.

Most of the information on building and handicrafts was supplied by Trevor Lawrence, a skilled craftsman who is also a smallholder. My wife, Ailsa, supplied all the information on spinning, dyeing and weaving. Philip Brachi, of BRAD (Biotechnic Research and Development) provided descriptions of his own experiences in a community dedicated to alternative technologies and lifestyles, Fr Thomas Cullinan, OSB, supplied information about monastic life and Dr Michael Ash, who has been a ship's medical officer and has run a psychiatric practice, gave advice on psychiatric and medical matters. Information about brush-making comes from Mervyn Jones. In addition I am grateful to Brian Morgan, who provided many of the line drawings, to Colin Taylor and Michael Wingate of the Architectural Association School of Architecture, to Andrew Mann of the Children's Rights Workshop who explains the law regarding the education of children, to Stephen Lawrence of the Foot's Barn Theatre, to David Stickland of Organic Farmers and Growers Ltd, which helps market organically grown produce, to Hugh Coates, a farmer who also sells hand mills for grinding cereals, and to Lesley Hoskin, who checked the textiles section. MICHAEL ALLABY, Wadebridge, Cornwall

Land

Ownership or stewardship ?

The question you should ask yourself if you are intending to practise self-sufficiency on a small farm is, 'Will the land I own be put to a better use or a worse one than before ?'

There can really be no such thing as 'ownership' of land. Trustee-ship is a far better word, and has more meaning. My neighbour Tom Brithdir may accept that I 'own' Fachongle Isaf, but I can see a jack-daw from where I sit trying to make her nest in the chimney of what I call my house and *she* doesn't think I own it. Though, no doubt, she would defend 'her' territory – the bit of land she thinks she 'owns' – very vigorously from any other lady jackdaw.

But in terms of our human convention of 'ownership', or trustee-ship as I prefer, it is reasonable to say that no man has the right to change the use of a piece of land without standing to account before the rest of his fellows as to whether he is improving the land or making it worse. Orthodox commercial farmers have a perfect right, when they see the fifty-acre farm bought by some man from the cities so that he can become 'self-sufficient' falling into disrepair and un-productiveness to say, 'That man should not have that land. It should be taken away and given to somebody who knows how to use it.'

But what is a good use of land ? An orthodox farmer would say a good use is a use which makes the land produce a lot of food. If a farm was producing thirty hundredweight of wheat to the acre when you bought it and you make it produce two tons, that is a good use. If the yield falls to a ton under your management, then you ought to get out.

Where we decentralists would differ from the orthodox farmer here, though, is in the matter of *input*. For decades now the orthodox farmer has only been concerned with *output*. If he can get another half ton of wheat per acre by putting in another hundred units of nitrogen (fixed from the air with enormous expenditure of electrical power), making large applications of herbicides, fungicides and insecticides (all derived from oil) and using oil to drive his machinery (plus making a great capital outlay on machinery), then he will do it and call it a good use of land.

He has been encouraged in this attitude by the existence of almost free power – the cheapest source of power that there ever has been or ever will be on this planet. No other power source – atomic, coal, wood, solar, water, wind – will ever come bubbling out of the ground in millions of tons, practically for free. The modern farmer's undeniably high output has been achieved by *oil* and substances derived from oil.

It is conveniently forgotten by apologists for modern agriculture that yields just as high as those achieved now with enormously high inputs of chemicals were achieved in the past without any chemical input at all. Arthur Young (who was Secretary of Agriculture and knew what he was talking about) found many yields of two tons an acre of wheat in his travels through England in the last decades of the eighteenth century, and so did Cobbett a couple of decades later. I worked on a farm in Essex over forty years ago on which the farmer used to boast that he brought nothing at all in over the farm boundaries except store cattle for fattening, a ton or two of linseed cake for its 'kindling' effect on the beef, and occasionally fresh seed – and he *never grew less* than two tons of wheat an acre. The miserably low yields of the years between the wars, which are often quoted now, were from a depressed agriculture; in the days of High Farming before 1850 they would have appeared ridiculous. My Essex farmer achieved these yields without a drop of oil (he did not have a tractor), with no herbicides (selective weedkillers had not been invented), with no insecticides or fungicides (he did not need them because he practised a proper rotation of crops) and with no – or only very little – imported fertilizer. He did not need fertilizer because he had the dung from a hundred fattening bullocks every year for his hundred acres of good land, plus the dung from six horses, a herd of breeding sows and several hundred poultry. What did he feed these animals on ? On hay, straw, barley, wheat offal (bran and middlings), oats and mangolds that he grew on the farm. There was one very big input though: on his hundred acres he employed six men, and they worked very hard indeed through all the hours of daylight. The hoe was his herbicide, the horse was the tractor and the dung of the horses went back into the land.

Now, as the oil wells begin to run dry and we have to look in more expensive places for the golden liquid, oil and oil-derived chemicals will become more expensive. The process has only just begun and in a year or two the price of oil has doubled and the price of nitrogenous fertilizer has quadrupled. What if this trend goes on? The farms of the agribusinessmen will produce no food at all. I looked over a farm in Essex the other day which is 2,600 acres and is run by five men! One of them told me that the wheat (it is a monoculture wheat and barley farm) is sprayed *seven times* (including a spray of paraquat after the straw is burned before direct drilling). That farmer has never yet achieved two tons of wheat an acre. He gets the yield he does get (about thirty-six hundredweight) by enormous applications of fixed nitrogen. What if the herbicides dried up? What if the supply of fixed nitrogen dried up? Where would he find the hundred men and women he would need just to hoe the root crops that he would have to grow to kill the weeds on that 2,600 acres? Where would he get the thousands of bullocks or other animals that he would need to provide dung to take the place of power-derived sulphate of ammonia?

The land needs people

The time is going to come on this planet when we will have to get back to good husbandry again and away from the mere brute application of power and chemicals. And this needs people. Now, either people are to come back to the land again as landless labourers or helots, or they are to come as free men, farming their own land for themselves and their families.

But if they do come back as free men then they must come as *trained* men – knowing what they are doing (see page 284). Our land is too valuable to allow any of it to be used by the ignorant for learning on or making silly experiments. Would-be husbandmen should work for established farmers, preferably organically minded ones who are not completely hooked on 'NPK and power' (N=nitrogen, P=phosphorus, K=potassium), for long enough to know what they are doing when they take over their land. Nothing does more harm to the decentralist movement than the sight of a little farm going to rack and ruin while a lot of pallid ladies and gentlemen sit about twanging guitars and talking about high philosophy and the influence of the stars.

Back in the Middle Ages in Holland the cultivators had what was called 'the law of the spade'. When a farmer felt he could no longer keep up the gruelling toil that was necessary to keep the dyke in repair to keep the sea out, he would stick his spade in the dyke and walk away. This was an admission of defeat and somebody else would thereupon take out his spade and take over his land – and with it the obligation to do his share of work on the dyke. And so it should be with us.

The aim of the good husbandman should be to establish a beneficial cycle of energy: soil – plant – animal – soil again. He should imitate nature herself in as many ways as he can, only changing or interfering with nature when he needs to serve the high purpose of creation. Nature is never a monoculturalist. That is, she never grows one crop and one crop only for years on the same soil. Why ? Because one crop always takes the same things out and puts the same things back, and this is bad. Also, monoculture invariably leads to a build-up of diseases. So we must not practise monoculture. We must never grow the same crop twice running on the same piece of land. Like nature, we must introduce variety. The more kinds of plants we can grow, the better. We must keep animals (no land is really healthy without the dung of animals), and we must keep a variety of animals. The plants must feed the animals and the animals must feed the plants. On a good farm or holding, everything is complementary.

For example, we keep cows to give milk for the house. They give us much more milk than we need, so we make butter and cheese. A by-product of butter is skimmed milk; a by-product of cheese is whey. These we feed to the pigs. The pigs produce dung which we put on the root land. The roots that we grow we feed to the cows. The dung of the cows may go on potato land. The big potatoes we eat or sell, the little ones go to the pigs. Grain (grown on land manured with the dung of cows and pigs) helps to feed us and also the chickens. The chickens eat tail grain (small), scratch through the chaff after thresh-ing, improve grassland by scratching, and pick up waste grain on the stubble after harvest. Their eggs and carcasses feed us. On grassland, hens not only manure the land themselves, but they peck out any undigested grain in cow or horse droppings, and also spread the dung so that it does more good.

All waste vegetation goes to the pigs or the poultry. They compost it better than any compost heap by eating it. What they do not eat they tread into the ground; it mixes with their manure, rots and fertilizes the land. Straw from grain crops is either eaten or used as bedding. In either case it is turned into good manure and put back on the land. Straw used for thatching eventually comes to the end of its life, is then used as bedding and ends up as manure. Nothing, but *nothing*, is wasted. Everything contributes to the wellbeing of everything else. We work at all times with nature, never against her.

Nothing comes on to our land from outside except very occasionally lime, even less often slag (to correct a phosphate deficiency) and seed (far more of which we should grow ourselves); if we have to buy in animal feedingstuffs as, alas, sometimes we do, it is an admission that we have too few hands trying to look after too much land. We should never have to. We could easily feed a resident population of thirty people on this little farm, fuel ourselves with waste wood and have quite a lot of very high-quality food to sell to other people, and that with an *input* of practically nothing from outside. But to do this we would need the *labour* of the adults among those thirty people, and we would have to be allowed to build houses for them. If we could do this, no agribusinessman in the world would have the right to look at our farm and say, 'That land is not being properly used.' As it is, with our wretchedly small labour force (for most of our twelve years here on these sixty-two acres it has been farmed by two people working half-time), we still produce perhaps ten times what the land was producing when we took it over.

There will always be towns, there will always be cities. Without these, civilization is impossible. But we need *many more* of the people in the world to live on the land, producing most of their own food, selling a surplus to the towns and cities, and working, too, at professions, industries or handicrafts that contribute to the wellbeing of everyone. The present system of huge conurbations supported by chemical- and power-hooked agribusiness, with 3 per cent of the population trying to feed the other 97 per cent (as in England), is sick and carries within it the seeds of its own destruction.

How to find land

The search for land to grow food on in the British Isles as well as in other countries is becoming intense. During the great land boom of

1973, people were actually going round knocking on the doors of small farms in my area offering ridiculous prices for the land; land for which people like myself paid £60 an acre ten years earlier was being sold for £600 an acre, although in most cases it was unobtainable anyway.

The position now that a kind of slump seems to have set in is that very small holdings – five to ten acres, say, with a house – are holding their value, while large farms, or agricultural land with no house attached, are now selling at from £350 to £450 an acre in marginal areas like Pembrokeshire. If you want to buy a smallholding you may well have to pay £1,000 an acre (but it is the *house* you are paying for). But if you bought a 500-acre farm you might well get it for £350 an acre, with only one house, of course, but probably with extensive farm buildings.

The apparently obvious solution, therefore, is for a group of would-be self-sufficient people to get together and buy a large farm and cut it up between them. The trouble with this is that if they do they come up against Britain's repressive planning laws. Created between the wars to stop ribbon development in the Home Counties, these laws are now strangling all good development in the countryside. They do not seem to be able to stop an oil refinery being built in a national park or a hundred hideous 'holiday chalets' from appearing on the most conspicuous site on a beautiful coast, but they *do* stop the man who wants to return to the country, take his share of it, make it more fruitful and productive and beautiful than it was before, and help reverse the disastrous flight from the countryside. However, much might be done by converting existing farm buildings into dwellings. It is very difficult for the planning authorities to prevent one from building *new* farm buildings and anyway most planning 'officers' are very overworked! And there *are* still smallholdings to be found in Wales, Scotland and the north of England, away from centres of population, the sea, or the sort of grand scenery that attracts the second-home owner, for sale at reasonable prices – but one must search for them oneself. They are not worth the while of the estate agent.

Eire, too, is an obvious country to search in, for, again, if you get away from the sea and the beauty spots there are plenty of small farms for sale at low prices. A complication here is that according to law a foreigner cannot own more than five acres without special permission. There is nothing to stop him from buying his house and five acres and renting the rest, though. And of course, the United States, New Zealand, Canada and other sparsely populated countries have a great deal of good land, some of it almost free.

How much land do you need?

The question of the amount of land you require is a most complex one. Half an acre in the Black Fens will produce more than a hundred acres on top of the little mountain I can see from my window, so all talk of acreages is ridiculous. It also depends on what you want to do with the land. If you take a big allotment in a city and *really know how to farm it* you can grow an awful lot of food – certainly you would never have to buy a vegetable again. If you have a large cottage garden in good countryside, and access to some road verges, common or rough land nobody uses, you can keep two or three goats, and if you know about goats you can have your own dairy produce and a little meat, though you will still have to buy some concentrate from outside. At any rate, you will be getting your dairy produce *almost* for nothing. If you buy a couple of weaner pigs every year (say at £12 each) and feed them your waste garden produce, household scraps, cheap spoiled carrots or 'stockfeed potatoes' that you buy from farmers for nearly nothing, swill (perhaps from a nearby pub) – go to a great deal of trouble, in fact – you will get not free, but very cheap, bacon, ham, pork and sausages. If you do not want to go to all that trouble, you can buy barley 'off the field' when it is harvested, mill it if you've got a mill (see page 88) or soak it if you haven't; your bacon will be slightly less cheap, but still cheap. If there are only one or two of you and you fatten two pigs thus and sell one of them, you have the other pig for free. And the pigs will give you a lot of manure.

If you want to go one rung further up the self-sufficiency ladder and get a cow – or two, because two are more than twice as useful as one – then you need at least an acre of *good* lowland for each cow, unless you are prepared to buy in a lot of fodder. You will get lots of manure, some income from the sale of calves or surplus stock, and all the milk, butter, buttermilk, cheese and yogurt that you can consume, plus a lot to sell (see page 287) or give away, plus whey or skimmed milk to fatten those pigs on – it is better than anything you can buy.

When you have reached the cow rung of the ladder, you are still having to buy corn: in Britain, that is wheat, barley and oats; in America, 'corn' means maize. However, you are getting all your dairy produce, most of your meat, all your vegetables and all eggs and poultry meat free for your land and labour. If you intend to ascend another rung of the ladder and grow your own corn, too, then you have a big jump to make. The best land will produce two tons of corn an acre (wheat or barley) with plenty of muck but no bought-in chemicals. Two tons of wheat, barley and oats are probably ample for a large family plus two cows, two fattening pigs and possibly a sow, enough poultry to supply the family (say twenty), provided there is plenty of grass, hay, roots and dairy by-products as well. However, you are more likely to get one ton, or thirty hundredweight.

But unless you are an agribusinessman prepared to buy large quantities of imported chemicals and see your land deteriorating in your generation, you cannot grow corn on the same acre every year. Therefore you should have at least three acres so that you can rotate your land. A holding on very good lowland, therefore, capable of supporting a couple of cows, fattening pigs, poultry, wheat for the family and perhaps some malt for brewing could not possibly be less than five acres. Worse land, or marginal land, will have to be in even larger units.

It is a mistake for the self-supporter to have too much land. It is far better to have five acres and *really farm it* than to have fifty and scratch over it. It is unforgivable for someone to buy land and not make it produce *more* than it was producing before. Self-supporters must set an example of husbandry – it does great damage to the de-centralist movement when traditional farmers can point to a holding and say, 'Look what a mess those ignorant townsmen have made of that little farm!' And it is wise to consider very carefully before you plan to grow *all* your own food. Suppose you produce all vegetables, dairy produce, poultry produce and pig meat, but have to buy corn. Even at today's high prices, you are still in a very strong position. You are saving a lot of money on food and you will almost certainly have a surplus of produce to sell, too. If you try to farm even five acres of arable land you will be letting yourself in for buying a lot of equipment, either a horse (needs feeding) or tractors, and a lot of work, too.

And if you live on land which won't very well grow wheat, for example, surely it is better to grow oats and trade them for wheat? Or you might grow just grass and trade cattle or sheep for wheat. Generations of people in the Celtic Fringe lived very well *without* wheat at all.

In grass-growing areas it is very nice to have a larger farm, leave most of it down to grass as it probably was when you bought it, and farm intensively just, say, five or six acres near the house or where you will. You will be able to run a flock of sheep on the unimproved grassland which will keep you in mutton and wool and give you a surplus to sell, and maybe a single-suckling herd of beef cattle (i.e. each cow has one calf a year and brings it up and you sell it). All that takes very little work and is quite profitable. The small acreage you grow most of *your* food on, though, will take a great deal of work.

But probably you could say that half an acre of good land, an acre of medium, or two acres of marginal, if very well farmed, will provide ample, varied, good food for one person.

Soil

The question of how to tell good land when you see it is also very complex.

The soil, as a rule, is derived from the rock beneath it. The mineral constituents of the soil, which plants require, came from that rock. My own particular soil, though, like a lot of other people's north of the Thames–Bristol Channel line, was dragged there by ice and has nothing to do with the rock beneath it at all.

Plants need loose, friable soil, firm enough to keep them up, rich in minerals, well drained but not too dry, and deep enough for their roots to go down unimpeded. Soil varies in 'heaviness' from pure sand, which is the lightest of all, to heavy clay which is the heaviest. Some crops, such as Jerusalem artichokes, lucerne (alfalfa) and asparagus, will grow well in fairly light soil. Others, such as oak trees, wheat, potatoes and grass, will grow well in fairly heavy soil. But nearly all crops do well in a medium soil: that is, a loam or a mixture of sand and clay. The best soil in the world is the peat soil of the Fens of East Anglia, for that is almost pure manure: it is the composted remains of plants of the past. It will grow anything, retains water well and yet is well drained; it can be worked at practically any time and it needs no manure because it *is* manure. It is a wasting asset, though, and the peat of the Black Fens gets thinner every year. In any case, it would cost you £1,000 an acre and you would be very lucky to get any even at that price.

Drainage is another important factor. Some soil is naturally well drained; some soil is not but can be drained quite cheaply by man. Other soil cannot be drained at all except at prohibitive cost. So don't buy a bog, or soil with many of the weeds of wetness, such as rushes, kingcups, flag irises, moss or other marsh plants which indicate that it is certainly wet. Unless you can both drain it *and* buy it for the price of good land, don't have it. If it is drainable, though, it may turn out to be very good land. The Black Fens had to be drained.

Very sandy soil will probably be too *dry* and also 'hungry': that is, it will need great quantities of manure or green manuring (growing crops just to plough them in) to keep it fertile. Soil on chalk, such as downland soil, is similar. Soil that is acid will be seen to grow such plants as may-weed, sorrel and spurry. The acidity may be corrected by liming, but this costs money or time.

Take a spade and dig down into any land you intend to buy. If the spade goes in easily and reveals nice, friable, darkish soil to a depth of, say, 25 cm, and then a well-drained subsoil, that is good. If the spade hits rock at 12 cm, think twice. If the spade reveals water at 25 cm, think three times. If the spade reveals heavy (but not water-logged) clay, reflect that although you may have a fertile soil it will be one that is hard to work, impossible to work in wet weather and impossible to run pigs or other livestock on except in a dry summer. If it is very sandy, on the contrary, it will be easy to work at all times, capable of bearing pigs or other stock at all times and of improvement therefrom, and warmer in the spring (clay is cold and therefore *late*). However, it will dry out in droughts and unless you can irrigate it, or put great quantities of organic matter into it, you will not grow much in dry years.

'There is gold under gorse, silver under bracken, and copper under heather,' said the old commons enclosers – and they might have added, 'not much copper'. Good land grows good weeds. I like to see plenty of vigorous, hungry weeds, such as fat hen or tall nettles, on a piece of land. A blind farmer wishing to buy a new farm had his boy drive him to it in a horse and cart. 'Tie the horse to a thistle,' said the farmer when they got there. 'There's no thistle big enough,' said the boy. 'Then drive home again,' said the farmer.

Altitude matters. If you buy a smallholding 250 metres up in Britain, you will not grow very good crops (except of such things as kale, oats, perhaps, and moderate grass) which can stand altitude. You *can* grow seed potatoes, though, which you can't at sea level. Or you can put up a glasshouse.

Drainage

The draining of land is a fascinating subject. The aim of the drainer is often not so much to draw the water out of the land, as to stop water coming down the slope on to it from above. Thus a ditch dug across a contour will *not* drain the land above it, except for a few metres, but it will drain the land below it. The water in the land above it does not know there is a ditch there. But when it percolates slowly down to the ditch it is carried away and therefore does not make sodden the land *below* the ditch.

Thus you can often improve enormously a wet field on a slope, no matter how slight the slope is, by digging a contour ditch above the field. Don't bother to dig one below it, unless you own the field below or wish to be very kind to your neighbour!

Ditches may be dug by hand – a good countryman may dig a chain (20 metres) in a week – or by a mechanical digger. You can buy a power arm for a tractor for some £600 which is quite capable of digging a ditch, or you can hire a man with a digger for about £3 an hour – and a good man can do a lot in an hour, depending entirely on the nature and condition of the ground. If you are a registered farmer you can get a government grant for draining which will cover around fifty per cent of the cost. It is useful, in any case, to send for the council's Drainage Officer and get his advice. He will prepare plans which will cost you a few pounds if you do not use them, but nothing if you take the government grant and do the work, or get it done.

He may well advise 'tile draining' as well as ditching. This is digging narrow slits in the earth, placing either earthenware 'tiles' in them (small bits of pipe, 30 cm long with 7.5 cm diameter for side branches and 10 for main drains) or the new, and much better, plastic perforated lengths, then in-filling the slit with loose stone and covering. This is, as it sounds, expensive, but it does the job and it

7.5-cm pipes

10-cm pipes

plan of drainage system

section of underground drain

earth fill

stone filling

drain pipe

will last centuries. The underground drains have to debouch into an open ditch, of course. In clay soils do not put them too deep – from 60 to 90 cm is enough; in sandy soils they may go as deep as 1.2 metres. In clay soils they should be from about 3.5 to 6 metres apart – in light, sandy soils perhaps 12 metres.

Mole draining works very well in heavy land which has no boulders in it. The procedure is to drag a torpedo-shaped steel cylinder, which is carried at the bottom of a steel blade, through the earth. The cut made by the steel blade fills up but the hole left by the 'mole', or steel cylinder, stays open. The moles can be cut in from a ditch, in which case a length of plastic pipe or a couple of earthenware 'tiles' should be forced in to act as a collar to the hole, or they can be cut across an underground draining system and work in conjunction with it. Often in fairly heavy land where the moles will 'stand up', moles are all the draining that the land needs, and they cost a fraction of what tile draining costs. In very good circumstances they may last for fifteen years. Eight or ten years is more normal, though they may last even less time than this in light land.

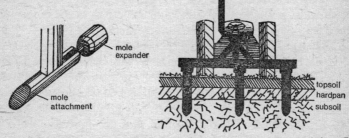

mole expander

mole attachment

topsoil
hardpan
subsoil

Chisel ploughing is another way of opening up soil for draining. It is the dragging of long knives through the soil so as to break up any 'plough pan' – an impervious layer that forms at the depth of ploughing – and to create pervious slits through the soil. On heavy boulder clays it is sometimes necessary in conjunction with underground drains or open ditches to get the water out of the land at all.

It will be realized that moling and chisel ploughing are high energy-using techniques. It takes a very heavy tractor to pull either and you needn't think you are going to do it with a horse. But in the past moling *was* done with horses – perhaps six or eight big shires or Suffolks – and although six horses are theoretically only six horse-power, it is surprising what they can pull. I have seen subsoiling done in South Africa with a span of twenty oxen. Another 'alternative

21

technology' way of dragging heavy implements through the earth is with windlasses of some sort at the edges of the field. 'Steam tackles' were, for a short time in history, an application of this method, but a 'gin ring' with a horse walking round in a circle, or a capstan with either horses or men walking around to turn it, suitably geared down, can exert enormous power. But if you don't want to use heavy machinery, or can't get it, you can do all the draining in the world with a pick and shovel.

One thing to remember is that underground drains, although they cost a lot in both materials and labour – you've got to cart a lot of small stones from somewhere for 'back-fill', remember – don't need any maintenance. An open ditch does. Every so many years someone has got to get in it and dig it out again, for it will silt up. And nearly every winter you *should* 'flash it out', which is the countryman's way of saying slash out the growth – the brambles and so forth which are in it. Also it should be fenced to prevent cattle from breaking it down.

Now, if you want to create underground drains but don't have, or can't get, any tiles or plastic pipes, you can do it by digging the drains as usual – as narrow as you can, but of course you've got to stand in them while you're working – and building drains in the bottom of them with whatever material you can get. Thick slates are ideal. Place slates along each side at the bottom of the slit and then lay a horizontal slab over these to form a roof. Then in-fill with small stones as usual, before putting back some of the earth on top. Bush drains were used by the Romans. You lay bushes, or small sticks, in the bottom of your trench, back-fill and cover. These will last until the sticks rot. I have experimented with sticks at the bottom, then half sheets of old, holey corrugated iron on top, then back-fill. This works if you knock a lot of holes in the corrugated iron to let the water down. You can easily split a piece of corrugated iron down the middle with an axe (somebody else's if possible) or a mattock. It's a good way of getting rid of rusty old corrugated iron. How long it lasts I do not know – I am like the old lady of ninety who, when asked at what age you give up sex, said, 'I don't know.'

Hedges and fences

Hedges and permanent fences must also be considered. In bygone ages (and even today in some countries) small children were the fences. They wandered out with the cattle and sheep in the morning and played, hunted and fished while the animals grazed, and kept them out of the growing crops or other people's land: a duty in which Little Boy Blue failed so lamentably. Then they brought them back at night.

Nowadays, though, we have to have fences, for various reasons. The first is obviously the boundary fence: if you can't keep your stock off your neighbour's land, or his off yours, you will soon be enemies. Good fences make good neighbours. Secondly, fences will keep stock off growing crops, particularly hay crops. Thirdly, fences will enable you to enjoy the benefits of rotational grazing. The grass or clover plant does not give of its best if nipped off very frequently, so that it never has time to grow to any size. It gives a much better yield per acre if it is allowed to grow to the flowering stage – thus being able to push its roots well down into the soil – is grazed right down to the ground and then rested to recover again. You will be able to keep more and better-fed stock if you confine them to part of your farm until they have grazed it right down, then move them on to another part, and don't bring them back to the first part for a period of months. Then, again, it is good to follow one species of animal with another over the land. Grazing animals void the eggs of internal parasites. If they or other animals of the same species then ingest them, you can get a bad build-up of parasites; if animals of another species ingest them, the worms die. Thus if you follow cows with cows you will get a build-up of parasites; if you follow cows with sheep you will not. Cows like longish grass, so put them into new pasture first. Sheep, horses and geese can crop short grass, so put them in afterwards. But all this entails fencing.

In the Open Field days of the Middle Ages, fences were movable affairs of hurdles made of withies (see page 59), split chestnut or ash (see page 204), thorn bush or other material. With the Enclosures came the quick-thorn hedge. This hedge has to be established within the protection of two temporary artificial fences for at least three years, otherwise the stock will simply eat it. You can buy quick-thorn (whitethorn or may) plants by the thousand quite cheaply. When established, it needs periodic attention: *splitting back* (cutting back the side growth) and *buck-heading* (cutting off to a certain height) every two or three years, and *laying* maybe every five to ten years, depending on how it grows. Laying consists of half cutting through each major branch near its base, bending this over at the cut so that it lies nearly horizontal, and pegging it there with stakes driven in.

Generally the stakes can be cut out of the hedge itself as you work. This fills the gaps and allows the hedge to grow up thick and strong again. If you neglect a thorn hedge, it grows up high and straggly with plenty of gaps below.

Nowadays we are lazy and impatient and we buy wire. There is barbed wire, high-tensile plain wire, sheep netting and pig netting. Pig netting, strangely, is actually what you use for permanent sheep fencing. It has oblong holes in it and is very expensive. Sheep netting has six-sided holes, is lighter, and less durable, but is for movable fences such as you use when you are folding sheep over roots. Hurdles, if you make them yourself, are not only cheaper, but free.

Colonial box anchor

All wire should be strained. A loose wire is useless. Good anchors at each end of a fence are essential – see the drawing of the 'colonial box anchor', which is by far the best. Straining can be done with a wire strainer which works on a lever principle and costs about eight pounds; with a block tackle; with a tractor or Land Rover; with a horse or a horse and cart, or with an improvised lever. There is a temptation to staple wires to, or strain them round, growing trees. We all do it, but remember that if you do you may ring-bark the tree and kill it, and also that sawyers will hate you after you are dead. A tree will grow and swallow the wire, and a broken piece of wire long lost within a tree can play hell with a circular saw.

Barbed wire is much used for reinforcing a neglected thorn hedge, but will make a fence of its own or, better, reinforce a fence of high-tensile plain wire. Five strands of the latter, if really well strained, will stop cattle but not sheep. Eight strands will stop sheep, but it is more expensive than pig netting for this purpose. I am tempted to say that nothing will stop pigs but a good wall and – here is the let-out – even one strand of electric fence.

As for posts, chestnut is best, heart of oak pretty good – the outer sapwood rots within a few years – thorn, holly and other very hard woods are fine for small posts or *droppers* (posts stapled to the wires but not forced into the ground). They space the wires, prevent cattle from forcing them apart, and do not rot because they don't touch the ground. Of softwoods, larch is good if creosoted, but not otherwise. Most other softwoods are pretty useless unless they are pressure-creosoted and the creosote meets in the middle.

To creosote posts, put them in an old drum of creosote, bring it to the boil and then let it cool. When it is cool, take them out. The boiling forces the air out of the posts and when they cool they draw the creosote in. A better, and cheaper, way to preserve posts is to soak them for several months in old sump oil which you may get free from a garage.

Fertilizing

Having bought your land, and drained it – but let's hope it didn't need it – how do you know if it is too acid and requires liming? Well, if it grows acid-loving weeds like corn marigold and sorrel, it needs lime. In any case, unless your soil is derived from limestone or chalk, it almost certainly needs lime to give you the best results. You can be pretty sure that from 500 kg to a tonne of ground lime (which is ground quicklime) or double this of ground limestone or ground chalk, will do good and not harm, and that thereafter, in a garden at least, say 200 to 250 g of lime per square metre should be put on the surface of the ground, after all cultivations have been carried out, before members of the cabbage tribe are planted, and perhaps 100 to 150 g similarly before peas or beans or other legumes are planted. This, with a proper rotation, will mean liming about once every other year. If pasture lacks clover, lime it. This will help the clover at the expense of the grass. If it still lacks clover, it needs phosphate.

The acidity or alkalinity of soils is expressed in terms of pH, which letters derive from some incredibly complicated computations of hydrogen and hydroxyl ions, but for our purposes we may take it that a pH reading of 7 is neutral, anything over that alkaline, and anything under, acid. Wheat, barley, sugar beet, mangolds, turnips, the cabbage tribe and clovers like a pH from 6 to $7\frac{1}{2}$. Oats and rye can suffer more acidity – say from 5 to 6; same with swedes; potatoes and celery like it from about 4.8 to 5.7. And how do you measure pH? Either you can send a sample of your soil to the nearest Ministry of Agriculture advisory officer, or you can buy one of the little acidity testing kits in the nearest gardening shop and follow the instructions exactly. If these resources are closed to you, just use your common sense as generations of husbandmen have done since Adam. If you never put any lime on at all you will still grow crops. Potatoes and celery dislike lime. Rye and oats don't need much.

How to make lime

How do you make lime if you can't ring up the lime merchant? You can make it by burning limestone or chalk, either in a kiln or in a structure built from alternate layers of broken stone and firewood,

chimney
mud casing
alternate layers of limestone & wood
opening to windward
section through improvised lime kiln

with mud plastered on the outside to keep the heat in, and you slake the resulting quicklime (which is dangerous) with water. You then put it on your land or plaster your walls with it. One thing to remember is that even on limestone some soils require liming. Another is that the more organic matter you use, muck or compost or green manure, the less lime you will need. A garden worked with plenty of compost may need one good liming to start off with and then no more for decades.

Phosphates and potash

Phosphates and potash (P and K) are the other two chemicals that soil may be short of. Both of these occur in muck or compost, but both can also be bought. Grassland can well receive a quarter of a ton of basic slag per acre (0.6 tonnes per hectare) every five years. Slag is the lining of blast furnaces. It begins as limestone but becomes impregnated with the phosphorus burnt out of the iron ore. Slag will encourage the clover at the expense of the grass, which is a good thing. You should, however, begin by getting the soil of a new farm analysed (a job you cannot do yourself without elaborate equipment and training), then repair the deficiencies by fertilizing, and thereafter rely on the natural cycle to return all animal and vegetable wastes to the soil. The man who burns his straw is robbing posterity.

Nitrogen

Nitrogen (N) in the soluble form of nitrates, which plants can use, is also necessary, but should come from muck or compost, or the nitrogen-fixing bacteria of legumes such as clover, or the nitrogen-fixing bacteria of the soil. You can increase yields dramatically by the heavy application of 'bag nitrogen' (mostly sulphate of ammonia in which the nitrogen is derived from the air by massive expenditure of power) but this is expensive and land becomes 'hooked' on it because it destroys the natural nitrogen-fixing power of the soil. It is far better to leave 'bag nitrogen' to the agribusinessmen and put on plenty of muck and encourage clover in your grasslands.

Implements

If you cultivate less than a quarter of a hectare, you can probably manage it with a spade, hand rake, hoe and fork, but with more land you will have to start thinking about either horse-drawn or tractor-drawn implements. You will need a plough (whatever the 'no ploughing' boys say, you will still need a plough – you cannot cultivate grass turf unless you either plough it or dig it, or poison it with paraquat or other toxic substance, and if you do that, this book is not for you).

horse plough

You will need some form of harrow. Thorn bushes dragged across the land will surface-harrow it, but you can generally pick up old

a horse~drawn disc harrow

horse harrows at sales. Disc harrows are particularly useful for breaking up old turf *after* it has been ploughed. Spring-tine harrows are
very good for breaking up clods in heavy ground.

spring-tine harrow

You can drill seed with a drill or you can sow it by hand in the
biblical manner. Corn (wheat, barley, oats and rye) can be broadcast
very effectively, but if you broadcast it you will need more seed, say
360 kg per hectare instead of 270 kg. To broadcast, you split an old
sack so that it can hang over your shoulder and under the other arm.
You fill this with seed and walk backwards and forwards across the
field scattering it. OMCS (Old Mother Common Sense) must be
brought into play here, as she must in so many other farming tasks.
If you want to sow 360 kg to the hectare it's no good getting to the end
of the hectare with a few kilos left or, worse, finishing your seed after
you've done three quarters of a hectare. If there are wheel marks on
your land, dividing it visually into parallel bands, it is easy to see each
band, but if not you must place a white rag on the fence at each side
of the field and use these white rags as marks, changing them after
each pass. Try if you can to get someone to show you; if not just call
on that Old Mother which lies deep down inside every one of us
although we may have forgotten it.

A seed drill has pipes going down into the ground, which are dragged along, and the seed is dropped down them at about the right spacing. There are many methods of dropping the seeds; revolving wheels with cups round the edge are most commonly used. Drilling is a good idea because it saves seed and puts the seed at just the right depth; however, broadcasting is surprisingly effective.

Row crops (fodder beet, mangolds, kale, cabbages etc) can be sown with a drill (even a single-row drill like a Jalo, which you push by hand, will do small acreages). Or you can draw out furrows with a hoe and laboriously sprinkle the seed thinly into them. You will then need a horse-hoe, or a tractor-hoe, to kill the weeds between the rows. A horse-hoe is a simple implement, on wheels, and covers a lot of ground very quickly. It is just as quick, in fact, as a tractor-hoe and far pleasanter to work. A horse-hoe is a good and simple implement for horse-hoeing, but it does only one row at a time.

Power

What you pull your implements with is up to you. Horses or oxen are fine: oxen have the advantage that they are growing into meat all the time. The method in most ox-power countries (except India) is to break them to the yoke at eighteen months, work them until they are three-plus, then kill them for beef after a few months' fattening in a yard or on good grass. By then they are very heavy animals and the beef is prime.

A horse is faster (it takes two good horses to plough old pasture, though) but they must be well fed. They should have 4.5 kg of oats a day on light work, and up to 9 kg a day for a very big horse on heavy work (even better would be less oats, but with some maize or wheat bran added). In both cases they need good hay – 3.5 kg a day for light work and 7 kg for heavy work. When they're not working give them only hay and grass – no oats. Some swedes are good for horses and so, of course, is grass. Two good horses plough roughly an acre (0.4 hectare) a day.

A tractor, bought new, nowadays costs a king's ransom. If you have that sort of money you don't need to farm. Even old tractors can be expensive, but you should be able to get one for approximately £200. Small rotavators (which do the work of ploughing and harrowing) are not too expensive, but they wear out.

Harvesting

Harvesting corn (wheat, barley, oats, rye) can be done with a sickle (laborious and slow), a scythe (a man can do an acre [0.4 hectare] a day), a mechanical mower, a reaper-and-binder or a combine harvester. With all but the last two, somebody has to come behind and bind the corn up into sheaves. The last two machines need great power to tow them – either a tractor or several strong horses. For the self-supporter, possibly the scythe is a good way – if you can mow a ton of grain in a day you are not doing badly, with your family and friends following up to tie the sheaves and *stook* them – that is, lean them up against each other in short rows, to dry.

a sheaf of wheat

After a week or two (three with oats), when the green grass at the base of these sheaves is dry, put the sheaves into *mows* of about fifty sheaves each, starting in a big circle and coming up to a point; or cart them to the stackyard and build ricks which you thatch; or store them

circular corn ricks
thatched with reeds

under cover. In due course you will have to thresh and winnow. Thresh either with a flail (a long and a short stick linked together loosely with leather thongs), by bashing the sheaves over the back of a chair, or in a threshing machine which has a drum in it going round fast, which knocks the grain out of the straw. The threshing machine will winnow – that is, blow the light chaff away and leave the heavier grain. You can do this yourself by letting the grain trickle down from a height on a windy day. If grain has been dried well in a field and rick, you can store it in a heap on the floor. If it has been combined, though, and is thus wet, you can store it in sealed plastic bags. The carbon dioxide it generates prevents it from going mouldy.

Hay can be cut with a scythe (but this is difficult and skilled work – more difficult than corn), by a tractor mower, a horse mower or a motorized scythe. It must be turned about, whether by hand, horse tedder or tractor tedder, until it is dry. The aim of 'tedding' is to aerate the hay by lifting and throwing it, so that it lands in an open, fluffy condition. If you wish to stack it loose, then *cock* it – that is, pile it into tight heaps about two metres tall. Thus it is safe from rain for a few days. If it is still too green, or it gets wet, spread it about again the next dry day. If rain threatens, then cock it again. And so on. If you bale it you will probably hire a baler and then it is (one has to admit) a lot quicker to handle. And you need a cart, wagon or trailer to carry both your hay and corn in.

If you wish to put a field down to a *ley*, which is a mixture of grass and clover, it is generally best to sow the grass and clover seed mixture at the same time as you sow spring corn and harrow it in. The ley will grow at the same time as the corn, protected by it, and you will have a good sward ready to graze when you cut the corn.

Row crops

Row crops are anything like turnips, swedes, potatoes, cabbages, mangolds, carrots and kale, which are drilled in rows. However, you can broadcast kale if your land is *clean* enough. ('Clean' means weed-free.) Drilling can be done either with a seed drill or (in a small way) by hand. Potatoes you drop behind a plough and plough in. (A ridger plough is useful, but an ordinary plough will do.) The advantage of row crops (and the disadvantage, you may say, with an aching back!) is that you have to hoe them. They are thus a 'cleaning crop' and you should grow one of these at least every four years on arable land to keep it clean. Most row crops, except carrots, like plenty of muck.

Fodder beet is the king of cattle and pig food, in my opinion, for it is high in protein and far more nutritious than, for example, mangolds. Mangolds, though, crop very heavily (fifty tons to the hectare or much more) and are very good for milch cows. For all roots (except carrots), dung heavily in the autumn, plough deeply (whatever the 'no-ploughing' school says), work down to a fine seed bed in the spring and drill your seed in the last week of March or early in April. As soon as you can see them, *horse-hoe* between the rows if you have a horse-hoe, when the plants have about four leaves, and *single* them by cutting out gaps and leaving just single plants with the hand-hoe. Leave about 30 cm between mangolds (with rows about 50 cm apart) and 20 cm for fodder beet, turnips etc, with rows 50 cm apart. Then continue horse-hoeing whenever you see weeds; hand-hoe at least once and, preferably, twice. Lift by hand and *clamp* – that is, make a pile, cover with straw or dry bracken and cover this with earth well banged down with a spade. Roots don't like frost.

Protein is your big problem, therefore experiment with beans, peas and high-protein foods. Field beans can be sown at the end of October at 225 kg of seed per hectare. Sow them fairly deeply – you can even drop them behind a plough and plough them in. Hand-hoe them the next summer if you can, or hand-weed. Cut with a sickle, scythe or binder, and thresh. But try other sorts of pulses. (We have tried soya beans without success – back to the drawing board!) Protein is important.

You should not have any bad crop diseases if you rotate your land properly and muck it heavily. If you grow, say, potatoes, year after year on the same land, you will get an eel-worm infestation; similarly with cruciferous plants you will get club root. If you do have problems with crop disease, you can always call the advisory officer.

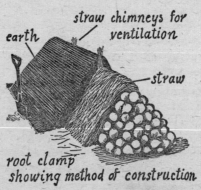

root clamp
showing method of construction

Rotations

The old 'Norfolk Four-Course Rotation', as a base to start off with, was a very good one, but it might be better to have even fewer 'white straw' (i.e. corn) crops. The 'Norfolk Four-Course Rotation' begins with roots, heavily dunged, of course; barley undersown with a ley; then the ley. After a year of grazing, the ley is ploughed up and wheat is planted; then the land is put back to roots again. The roots are a cleaning crop, the ley puts fertility back into the soil, and the wheat and barley take it out again.

Jerusalem artichokes are a fine crop on fairly light land if the rainfall is not too heavy. Just plough them in – they will come up and smother everything – then turn pigs into them to feed. They are a marvellous cleaning crop and you do not have to hoe them.

The self-supporter, particularly if he is one of a community, will wish to produce cloth, rope, cordage and wool. You can grow flax or linseed in Britain. If you let the plant go to seed you can harvest it, like corn, thresh the seed out and crush it for oil. Flax seed is very small, so plough your land in the autumn, work it down to a very fine seed bed as soon as you can in the spring, sow at about 80 kg per hectare if you drill, and more if you broadcast, as soon as you can get it in – i.e. as soon as the land is dry enough. Harrow it in. The land must be clean and the seed bed firm, and you may have to hoe or hand-weed it. It grows best on medium loam or clay soils and if you are growing it for fibre, it should not receive too much nitrogen. If you harvest it green, after flowering but before the seeds are fully ripe, it makes linen, or flax canvas, string or rope. Pull the crop by hand, stack it, bound in sheaves like wheat, until it is wanted, then *rett* it (lay it to soak in water for a week or so), haul it out and *scutch* it (comb it to scrape the retted flesh away from the fibres), dry, spin and weave it (for the processing of flax in more detail, see page 109).

Hemp is another textile crop – it makes the best rope in the world and can be recycled to make the best paper – but we are not allowed to grow it now because people smoke it and it makes them high. It was once much grown in America to make paper.

Flax and hemp are hard to harvest, because they have very tough stems. A combine harvester will harvest the mature flax for seed production, but of course the stems are not much use for fibre. A binder will harvest the green flax or hemp for fibre or for the ripened seed, but it is hard on the knives of the binder. It is difficult to cut with a scythe; a sharp sickle might be better. With fibre, though, you can pull the whole plant out by hand.

Livestock

It is possible to live off the land with no animals at all, but there are certain disadvantages to this. First, it is ecologically unsound. The animal and vegetable kingdoms are interdependent; it is very difficult to keep land in really good heart without animal manure, and grazing animals make use of herbage (such as grass, heather and scrub) which we cannot otherwise use. Secondly, it is doubtful if a satisfactory human diet can be obtained with no animal products – that is, without milk products or eggs, not to mention meat. There are indications that brain damage to children has been caused by a strictly vegetarian diet, probably for want of animal fats, and in any case the sustained hard manual work necessary for the self-supporter cannot be nourished on vegetable matter alone. And if you have milk and eggs, then you must have animals and birds; these will reproduce (they must, to give you replacements) and half the offspring will be male, and what will you do with them if you do not eat them or pass them on for somebody else to eat? The smaller animals are kept in check by predators. The larger animals, in Britain at least, have no predators but man, and if man did not control their numbers they would increase until they overcrowded the country and starved first us and then themselves.

Cattle

The cow is the keystone of sound husbandry. If you have milk, buttermilk, cheese and yogurt you cannot go very far wrong. Further, butter-making leaves a supply of skimmed milk, and cheese-making leaves whey, and these are the best foods in the world for both poultry and pigs. If you make enough butter and cheese you can do very well without any imported protein at all, for whey and skim supply everything that pigs or poultry could possibly need to supplement an otherwise vegetable diet.

Buy your first cow before she calves, so that she gets used to you and you to her before you have to start milking her. Get her used to coming into the cowshed every day to be fed and handled, massage her bag and teats, don't lose your temper if she kicks you at first (she won't break your leg!) and generally make friends with her.

Let her calve out in a clean field (unless the weather is absolutely awful). Leave her alone while she's calving, and don't interfere unless she has been straining unsuccessfully for several hours. Then, if the calf appears to be in the right position (forefeet first, then nose), put a cord round the calf's forefeet and pull very gently while the cow strains and not when she is not straining. Try a gentle pull first and if this does not do it exert more tension. I have never had to use a tackle (in practically a lifetime of having cows around) but sometimes people do. If it comes to that pass, send for a vet. If the calf is wrongly presented – i.e. you don't see the fore hoofs coming out – send for a vet anyway. Most probably you will have to do nothing.

Let the cow lick her calf for a few hours, then pick the calf up and get the cow to follow it, and you, to the cowshed. Let the calf suck for a week, then take the cow right away into another building, and start hand milking twice a day. The cow will bellow for a few hours, then forget all about her calf and settle down to being milked by a human.

Milk 'dryhanded'; don't strip-milk, which is dirty and inefficient. Grab a teat with your full hand, stop the milk from squirting back into the cow by pressure of your forefinger and thumb, then squeeze the teat downwards with your other fingers so as to squirt the milk into the bucket. Give the cow some food to nibble while you milk her – it keeps her quiet and helps her let the milk down. It is theoretically better to milk her at regular intervals spaced at twelve hours, but in my own experience it hardly matters. There is absolutely no need to get up at six o'clock to milk her and if you're enjoying an evening out and don't get back until midnight, you can milk her then. The milk will taste just as nice.

For feeding, grass is all a cow needs in the summer, if the grass is good and there is plenty of it; in the winter, as Bottom pointed out in *A Midsummer Night's Dream*, 'good hay hath no fellow'. But in winter a cow needs a little corn, too, and perhaps a mixture of rolled oats and rolled barley, with a teaspoonful of some mineral mixture thrown in if you can pay for it, or a double handful of proprietary 'dairy nuts'. If you grow linseed, a handful of the seed in her food would be much appreciated. It is the aim of the self-sufficient farmer to do without imported feedingstuffs as much as he can, and he should even be content with a lower milk yield if he can achieve this with home-grown as opposed to imported fodder. The time is rapidly coming when there will be no imported high-protein food and we will have to think in terms of growing our own or going without. A cow will give milk on nothing but good grass in the summer and good hay in the winter, with perhaps some roots such as mangolds, swedes or fodder beet, but her yield will be greatly increased by the addition of 'concentrates', as farmers call grain and high-protein food. A commercial farmer might give a big cow a 'maintenance ration' (sufficient to keep her on, but not to give milk) of perhaps 9 kg of good hay, and then a 'production ration', of 350 g of a mixture of barley meal, rolled oats and bean meal per litre of milk yield.

And what do we feed the calf on meanwhile? What about the skimmed milk that is left after we have separated the milk for butter? 'Skim' has half the energy value of whole milk, but contains all the vitamins and minerals, and whey contains about a third of the energy value of whole milk. If you add 50 g of finely ground oats to a litre of skim or whey it helps. It is better for the calf if you separate the milk immediately it is drawn with the cream separator, so that the skim is not stale when it goes to the calf.

In practice, what often happens is this: you find one cow is not enough (because she is dry for a couple of months every year) so you buy another. Then when the one you want to milk has a calf, you put that calf on the other cow, together with her own calf. If you are lucky she thinks that it is hers and that she has twins; then you can let them out on the grass and forget all about them. Or, if you like, you can sell your calf at a week old, or – dare I say it – eat it.

As for what breed of cow to get, Jerseys are fine in every respect except that their bull calves are worth very little, for they never put much weight on and have yellowish fat which doesn't look nice on the butcher's slab. If you eat them yourself, though, they are fine. The Jersey gives the richest milk of all, is hardy, quiet and loving, and very easy to manage. Guernseys are similar, but a little bigger. Welsh Blacks, if you can get a good milking strain, are said to be very good and are certainly hardier than the Jersey – which is very hardy. Friesians (called Holsteins in the USA) are enormous, give a lot of milk of poorish quality, but need copious feeding and good pasture. The bull calves are very valuable for beef, whether pure-bred or crossed with a beef breed such as Hereford or Charollais. South Devons are even bigger, but give a lot of very rich milk, with small fat globules which makes it better than Jersey for making cheese. Ayrshires give plenty of milk, only slightly richer in butterfat than Friesian, and are not in favour with the butcher, so your bull calves are not worth much. I have tried Dexters, with no success whatever, and would not recommend them. Kerrys might be better, though I have not tried them. For the beginner, I would plump fair and square for a pair of good Jerseys.

It is expensive to keep a bull for one or two cows. You may be able to make use of a neighbour's bull or you can telephone your local Ministry of Agriculture office and organize AI (artificial insemination).

Pigs

Pigs come next and are an essential tool for the self-supporter, for they dig his garden and manure it for him, and dispose of all his organic wastes, such as vegetable tops, small and misshapen spuds etc. If you decide to breed pigs, remember that you either have to keep enough sows (say six) to make it worth your feeding a boar all the year or you will have the bother of getting your sow or sows to a boar every time they need one, which will be twice a year. Instead of breeding, you can buy weaners (about eight weeks old) and fatten them for pork, bacon and ham. I would always keep pigs out of doors, on fresh ground, in a rough shelter and behind an electric fence. They are then much healthier and make better bacon, and furthermore before they do make bacon they are happier, which is important.

lop-eared pig

Feed them *anything*, but also feed them barley meal or, better, two-thirds barley meal and a third wheat meal, and as much skimmed milk or whey as you have to spare; always give them as much as they will eat up readily and still be slightly hungry. For perhaps a month before you kill them (probably at six months) keep them warm and confined, and give them more than usual to eat – however, you probably won't want them too fat.

Sows eat the equivalent of 1 kg a day of proprietary pig nuts when they are dry and from 2.5 to 3.5 kg a day when they farrow and are feeding their piglets. Fodder beet is excellent, and so are carrots and potatoes, which are better boiled but are also acceptable raw. Jerusalem artichokes, which pigs root up themselves, are fine, too. We had a sow last year who wandered off into the woods and we didn't *see* her, much less feed her, for three months. When she had eaten all the acorns she came back as fat as – well, a pig. When a sow is due to farrow, my advice is to see that she has a rough shelter and plenty of litter (whatever the books say) and is left strictly alone.

As for breeds of pigs, it doesn't matter what breed you get *so long as it has lop ears*. Do not get a 'prick-eared' pig. No fence on earth will stop it. Lop-eared breeds are Welsh, Saddleback (Essex or Wessex), Landrace and Gloucester Old Spots.

Sheep

Sheep present two problems. If you keep ewes, how do you get them served if you have too few to make it worth keeping a ram? You *could* keep a ram for a minimum of half a dozen ewes, but it would be barely economic. Secondly, sheep need a wide range to thrive. So on small, confined areas (perhaps two hectares) one should doubt the wisdom of keeping sheep. It might pay to buy half a dozen lambs that have failed to 'grade' (i.e. achieve the official weight) by the autumn, and are therefore going cheap, and to run them on grass or, better, roots (swedes, rape, kale) and kill them one by one during the winter. Any kind of sheep will do, but beware mountain breeds, such as the Welsh or Cheviot, because they escape so easily. The little Southdown is ideal because he is small and doesn't take so long to eat. If you are keeping them mainly for their wool (see page 105) this will affect your choice of breed. Merinos are not yet generally kept in this country. Coke of Norfolk did try them, but his tenants called them 'Whig sheep' and wouldn't take to them. Certainly the wool they produce is of poorer quality on English or Welsh grass than it is in the semi-desert conditions they are used to.

In the winter you can keep lamb or mutton a fortnight, if you hang it in the cool. So if you split a sheep with a neighbour, you can easily eat it, with or without a deep freeze.

Sheep need nothing but grass, winter and summer, but if you wish to fatten them in the winter crushed oats are best, or hay, which they must have if they are being folded on roots.

Shearing a sheep is something you absolutely must see somebody else do before you try it yourself. It is as simple as that.

Sheep are susceptible to a number of parasites – keds, ticks and blowfly maggots are the worst. You prevent damage to your animals first by keeping them clean. Shear off wool that is soiled with dung. Then, each year after shearing, dip each sheep in disinfectant. You can buy a proprietary sheep dip, which will be based on a modern insecticide, or you can make your own. To every 450 litres of water add 1 kg white arsenic, 1 kg washing soda, 3.5 kg flowers of sulphur and 4.5 kg of soft soap. You can dip the animals in a hand bath, made from wood, 1.8 metres long, 75 cm wide and with a sloping bottom that is about 90 cm deep at one end and about 70 cm deep at the other. Hold the sheep, turn it upside down and immerse it, making sure its head remains dry and that the dip mixture does not enter its nose or mouth. Handle pregnant ewes very carefully indeed or they may abort. If you have more than a few sheep, you can dip them more safely and conveniently by making a permanent dip, which is a trough sunk into the ground and lined with bricks or concrete or some other impermeable substance. The dip must slope at both ends so the sheep can run into it and climb out of it; it should be about a metre deep, so that the sheep swim along it; and the sides should slope so that it is about 50 cm wide at the top and about 30 cm wide at the bottom. It should be about 3.5 m long.

The rules for helping cows calve apply to ewes; but you shouldn't have to interfere.

Goats

I have had little experience with goats, and all of it bad; but I have met people who have had great success with them and would never keep any other milking animal. They *will* eat scrub and trees, they will *not* (by and large) eat grass; they need shelter from rain and bad weather; and they will not give very much milk without some concentrates (e.g. oats). In full production, a goat will give 3 to 4.5 litres of milk a day. The confession is wrung from me that they are very engaging – but, for God's sake, don't let them near your fruit trees.

Slaughtering and butchering

To kill cattle, sheep or goats, stun them (indeed, kill them) with a shot from either a humane killer or a .22 rifle (the latter is, in fact, much more humane), then cut the veins on either side of the neck to let them bleed. Skin the animal, saw through the breastbone as it lies on the ground, haul it up arse-first with a tackle, cut around the *bung* (or anus) with a sharp knife and tie off the rectum. Then cut carefully down the line of the belly, with your finger shielding the point of the knife so you do not stick paunch or bowels, disembowel, then haul out the 'pluck' (connected lungs, liver, heart etc). You cannot do this, though, until you have cut the windpipe and gullet: best just to cut off the head. Next morning, when the carcass is cold, saw or chop right down the backbone and joint as required.

To kill a pig, shoot it in the brain, then 'stick', by pushing a sharp knife into the front of the throat and back – at an angle of 45 degrees – towards the heart. This will bleed it. Then scald with near-boiling water (either pouring it on with a jug or immersing the pig bodily into a bath of water of exactly 65.6°C), scrape the bristles and outer skin off with some not-too-sharp, hoe-like instrument (see page 259), split the breastbone and then proceed as for other animals.

For bacon and ham, rub a pinch of saltpetre and plenty of dry salt hard into the side or the hind quarter, bury in salt, rub every day for three days, then leave sides buried for two weeks and hams for three. Hang in a dry place, preferably bandaging in cloth first. The bacon will be saltier than shop bacon, so cut into rashers and soak for ten minutes before cooking. Keep the ham as long as you can – up to two years – before eating it; but it is fine after six months. If you have a big open chimney, you can hang it in that for a week to smoke after it comes out of the salt, but you don't need to.

Poultry

Poultry are one of the lowest rungs of the self-supporter's ladder. They are easy to keep, require little space and little knowledge, give eggs and make a fine meal.

Chickens are ideally kept in movable arks (see page 58). Keep them shut in until after midday so that they lay their eggs before they go out, then allow them to range freely and shut them in again at night away from the foxes. They will come home by themselves when it starts to get dark. If the foxes eat them even during daylight hours, then you have too many foxes.

The best way to feed them is to suspend a hopper containing wheat or mixed corn (e.g. wheat, barley, maize) from the roof of their ark, and another of a proprietary high-protein food, fish meal, meat meal or other high-protein food. They will help themselves as they like and yet eat surprisingly little, for every afternoon they fill their bellies on grass and earwigs. They do marvellously in dry woodlands. If you don't give them any protein, they will still lay you eggs, but not so many.

rat-proof feeder filled
with corn or dry mash, with
pecking holes for chickens
and dish to catch
spilled food

If they go broody, just let them sit on their eggs and hatch them out.

You can shut up young cockerels for a fortnight while you are fattening them and give them as much barley meal and skimmed milk as they will clear up twice a day. Alternatively, just leave them outside to grow naturally and wring their necks when you are hungry.

Rhode Island Reds, crossed with Cuckoo Maran if you like very brown eggs, are a good breed for both eggs and meat.

Ducks should be treated much as chickens, except that it is inhumane to keep them without water to swim on, and it is better to get a broody hen to hatch out duck eggs than to let a duck do it. If you do the latter, confine the mother in the coop for several weeks –

41

so that the babies can get out but mum can't – to stop her dragging the little dears about in the wet grass and killing them.

To kill both ducks and chickens, hold the bird comfortably in the left hand, put the right hand over its head with the index finger down one side of the neck and the other fingers down the other side; then, catching the legs with the left hand, allow the bird to drop, and bend the head upwards with the right hand at the same time stretching the neck. As soon as you feel the neck stretch, desist – or you will pull the head off. Pluck immediately, while the bird is warm, and hang up by the legs. Next day, cut the neck where it joins the body, preferably with secateurs; remove the inside of the neck, cut the head off, push a finger down into the chest cavity from the neck and twist it around so as to sever ligaments, then cut out the anus and gut from the rear end, removing all the machinery without busting the gut.

Geese live on grass and that is that. But fatten them for the last fortnight of their lives by feeding them plenty of barley or oatmeal and grain. Kill geese (and turkeys) by holding the bird by the legs, upside down and with its back away from you, whereupon it will try to lift its head. Lower until the head is on the floor, get your good husband or wife to lay a broomstick over the neck, stand on the broomstick with both feet and pull the legs upwards until you feel the neck break. If you are clever enough to hold the wing tips at the same time as the legs, then they won't flap. All poultry flap their wings like mad for some minutes when you kill them, but it is just nerves and you must pluck away regardless before the bird cools and the feathers set.

Turkeys eat grass, too, but must also have a little grain. Both geese and turkeys are good mothers, but if you rear turkeys with chickens, then you must give the young turkeys a proprietary medicine in their food or they will get a disease called black head and die. Except for this, in twenty years of keeping poultry I have known of no disease in any that are allowed to roam out of doors and are kept on clean ground – in other words, if they are not confined for too many months on the same small piece.

Horses

Before you consider a horse or horses, remember that a working horse will consume the produce of more than three-quarters of a hectare of land – half, say, under grass and half under oats. A horse on good grass (or even poor grass if there is a good amount of it) will keep his condition the year through with nothing else, but if he is to work he needs hay in the winter and corn. Oats are the best corn; maize and barley aren't bad; wheat and rye are worse. A horse on grass in summer should get about 2.5 kg of oats for half a day's work and spend the other half day, and the night, on grass. In the winter, a horse doing light work should be stabled for part of the day and get roughly 5.5 kg of oats and from 4.5 to 9 kg of hay, depending on how much grass he is getting. Swedes are good, and so is oat straw if hay is short. For a heavy horse doing continuous heavy work (in other words, ploughing for six or seven hours), a ration might be: 7 kg of crushed oats mixed with chaffed oat straw or barley straw, and 7 kg of hay; but 4.5 kg of oats is more reasonable for a moderately worked horse. Feed half of this in the early morning, some in a nosebag at half-time and some after work, and leave plenty of hay for the horse to eat during the night. A horse wants *time* to eat – two hours for a meal – so don't rush him. If you want to start ploughing early, then get up even earlier, as the old horsemen did.

Two good horses will plough an acre (0.4 hectare) of heavy land in a day, and three will plough an acre and a half of lightish land with a two-furrow plough. Harrowing, drilling and row-crop cultivation are much faster – in fact, at these a horse is not much inferior to a tractor. One horse will pull a small one-horse plough, but not fast or deep, and not through thick turf. If you want to plough thick turf, but have only one horse, plough it with pigs (i.e. let them root it up – don't hitch the pigs to the plough!). But OMCS (Old Mother Common Sense) should tell you not to expect a couple of pigs to root up a large acreage. You must, of course, concentrate them.

Above all, do *not* feed your horse corn when he is not working, or he will founder and die. Horses out on grass for much of their lives very seldom get ill – if they do, send for a vet. If horses are working hard they must be shod, perhaps every six weeks. Fortunately, more and more boys are having the sense nowadays to apprentice themselves to farriers.

Harness is a problem. There are few good harness-makers nowadays, and any self-supporter should consider this trade as his money-income standby. You can get plenty of good harness in France and Spain, particularly the latter, and if you are lucky you can pick it up at sales, or you can get it made new at very high prices. You could, of course, make it yourself.

Incidentally, if you go to the Continent for harness, you could do worse than to buy a Brabant plough. These are very common there and are the best horse ploughs ever made. The French, Belgians and Spaniards also have many other excellent pieces of animal-drawn equipment.

Do not, by the way, be too worried about the amount of land that it takes to feed your horse. Reflect that, although only a small proportion of the food that goes into him is turned into useful energy, none of it is wasted. It stays on your farm – in the form of the most useful manure. This consideration applies to milk- and meat-providing animals as well. The people who say that only such and such a proportion of the food that an ox eats is turned into meat forget that the rest is not wasted. It goes back into the land to be recycled and grow more food.

Food

Bees

You do not actually 'keep' bees – you just have them around and rob them if you can. The modern beehive is now almost prohibitively expensive to buy new (about £40 for a complete one), so, unless you can make one yourself (and to do this you need to be a very good carpenter), buy one secondhand or are rich, you might do without.

Or you might consider that a capital outlay of £50 altogether spent on bee equipment should, with good management, bring you in perhaps 18 kg of honey a year (a wild guess – it can be anything or nothing!) and honey is at the time of writing worth up to 50p a pound (£1.10 a kilo). You therefore may get back £20 a year, and your whole capital in about three years.

Bees need cost nothing to keep. People who feed them with sugar are just greedy – they rob the bees of too much honey and so have to feed them on this inferior substitute – but if you leave the bees a fair share of their own honey they do not need feeding and will be healthier, and give much better honey, than sugar-fed bees. However, in a year when there is little honey made because of weather conditions and when the winter is a very cold one, the bees will need feeding to survive. The reason why commercially produced honey is so un-honeylike is that it is simply sugar turned into honey. Real flower-derived honey is far superior.

The secret of the modern beekeeper is the *bee-space*. If you allow bees to nest inside an old orange box or a hollow tree they will build there a big, shapeless lump of comb, filled with honey; each cell will have an egg laid in it, later to become a bee. After smoking the bees hard (which makes them think the forest is on fire so that they fill themselves with honey in preparation for swarming, and therefore cannot sting you), or after going as far as killing them with fire or sulphur, you can gouge the honey out, eggs, grubs, dead bees and all, and allow the liquid honey to drip through a strainer. This is how our ancestors used to get honey (even from those picturesque straw bee-skeps) and how Central Africans and the Veddas of Sri Lanka still do.

The discovery of bee-space changed all this. It was discovered that there is an exact, critical space between two boards, say, into which bees will crawl, make their comb in one storey, as it were, on the sides of each of the two boards, and *not* fill up the space in between. Thus you hang in a box vertical planes of beeswax (nowadays imprinted with the pattern of a bees' comb so as to show your little helpers exactly where to build) and with exactly the right space between them; the bees will build out their cells and fill them with honey, and you will be able easily to extract them from the top without killing the bees or even disturbing them much. You can then make a further refinement. The bottom compartment of your hive you call your brood chamber, and in there you allow the queen to lay eggs to her heart's content. Above this you place a queen-excluder, which is a wire mesh large enough to let workers through, but too small for the queen to pass. Above it you hang more 'frames', as you call your vertical planes of beeswax. The workers build on these and fill them with honey ready for the eggs, but the eggs are never laid because the queen can't get to them. These are the frames you pull out for the extraction of honey. The components of the hive above the brood chamber are called the 'supers', and you can pile super on super to make your hive ever higher and impress your neighbouring bee-keepers with your prowess.

To keep bees, or at least to have them around, you need basically one hive, consisting of a brood chamber, a minimum of two supers with their necessary frames and the wax foundations inside, a veil, a smoker and, most important of all, either a good book on the subject or a friend who will show you how. Further, it helps to have or to borrow a centrifugal extractor. But there is a lot to bees, and it would take a book as long as this one to describe half of it. You could, of course, as a matter of survival, go back to the Middle Ages or Darkest Africa and capture a swarm of bees (it hangs on a tree and the bees will not sting you, being loaded with honey), dump it in a straw skep

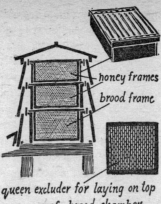

honey frames

brood frame

queen excluder for laying on top
of brood chamber

double-walled W·B·C hive

or any old box, allow the bees to make honey, destroy them at the end of the summer and rip out the honey. Incidentally, if you are not allergic to bees it does not matter much if they sting you, but you must protect your face. The psychological effect of angry bees dive-bombing your face is devastating: you *must* have a veil. Apart from the veil, wear clothes that cover the whole of your body – a jumper, trousers tucked into socks or boots, and gloves. Bees climb *upwards* if they alight on you. They will not climb down into your boots, but they will climb up inside your jumper if it isn't tucked in. For ladies, skirts are *not* recommended.

Game

You can kill any mammal or bird that lives in Britain with a shotgun, but bear in mind that the bigger the animal the closer you need to be. Alternatively, you can use a .22 rifle, for which ammunition is cheap, light and compact. and which will kill anything from a sparrow up-wards if used with accuracy and a knowledge of where to aim in order to kill outright with the first shot. But for all larger game a .303 is to be recommended, preferably using a soft-nosed bullet. Remember that in Britain and in most other countries there are strict licensing laws regarding the ownership of firearms, and you should acquaint yourself with them.

To kill a big animal with a rifle, shoot him just behind the point of the shoulder blade, but a little lower down. Do not try the head-on shot unless the animal is looking straight at you, very close and you are a very good shot. Then aim at the crossing of two imaginary lines that go from each eye to the opposite ear. If you wound an animal, sit down and rest for half an hour before you follow the blood spoor. If you follow immediately, the animal will keep moving for a day or so before he drops. If you wait half an hour he will lie down, get stiff, and you will come up on him quietly and get in another shot. But if you are humane you will not wound an animal.

If you haven't got a gun, or don't want to use one, there are a hundred ways of pitting your human brain against an animal's (see pages 215 and 217 for bows and arrows and crossbows). Here are some methods I have myself found successful.

Snares

Snares will catch anything from a linnet to a lion. To snare rabbits, make a noose of wire, with a smooth running knot, about as big as the circle you can describe with your thumb and fingers of both hands; tie the 'fall' of it (the other end from the loop) to a bush or stake, prop the snare up so that the lower 'limb' of the circle (the bottom of it) is above the ground as high as your clenched fist, and prop it over a run along which you know rabbits pass; in front of a rabbit-hole, if you like, but a good trapper imagines he is the prey – and anticipates its movements.

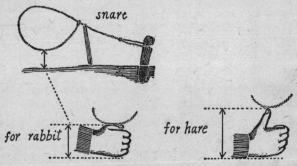

For a hare, make the loop slightly bigger and place it above the ground the space of the width of your hand plus your extended thumb. Hares make very definite tracks and also habitually use certain gaps in hedges.

Dogs

A good lurcher (a greyhound cross) will run down and kill a hare, but many a hare gets away, too. Some lurchers will kill rabbits, but this is difficult because rabbits are generally near their holes. Some lurchers will have a pheasant, grabbing these stupid birds before they can become airborne. We had a lurcher for eight years who kept us so well supplied with hares we used to have to give scores away. Incidentally, if country people tell you hares are no good to eat, know that it is because their parents were brought up on hares and therefore came to disregard them. You should hang them a week or a fortnight before cooking. Skinning and gutting them then is a smelly business, and they may look a bit green, but do not be put off: they are delicious.

All game (deer, hares, pheasants, partridges, wild fowl etc) is better hung – but if you are hungry it is delicious *not* hung, too. Rabbits are not game and should be 'hulked' (gutted) immediately and cooked within a few days.

Dogs are better used for driving ground game into nets. If you find a rabbit warren, go out quietly at night and set a long net, hung very loosely on slanting stakes, between the feeding ground of the rabbits and their holes. Then have an accomplice with the dog chase the rabbits into the net. OMCS might suggest you go out in the daytime and push in the stakes, so there will be less disturbance at night, but you can't do this in gamekeeper country. (But if it came to a survival situation we might be eating gamekeepers.) Small purse-nets can be set over holes in hedges hares use, and the hares bolted into these at night by a dog.

Partridges and ground-roosting pheasants can be netted at night by dragging a very wide net (maybe 46 m long by 9 wide) over the ground, holding the leading edge of the net up high with two sticks fastened to its corners. By the time the birds know it is there it is over them and they fly up and become entangled in it. Then drop the net on them. Nylon or the new monofilament man-made fibres are deadly for this job and don't rot.

Pheasants just lend themselves to the methods of the good poacher. By day they can be got with raisins with horse-hairs threaded through them. They swallow the raisins and then run around 'gagging' until you pick them up. But the poacher must hide nearby for this method. I have never quite believed in the whisky-soaked raisin method – and have never tried it. Or use little paper dunce's caps pushed down into holes in the ground, with some sticky substance inside them and a few raisins or grains of corn dropped in them, covered by a wire-netting box-trap with a funnel in the entrance like a lobster pot. Leave the funnel out a few days and 'feed' the trap to get the birds used to entering it. Then, one evening, insert the funnel and take the birds out in the morning. I once caught eight pheasants in one night by this method. At night, those pheasants that roost in trees can be taken by shooting by torchlight or against a moonlit sky, with an air gun or a .22. An air gun is quite adequate for this work and has the advantage, like a crossbow, of silence. Or there is the old trick of the sulphur candle on the end of a long cane put under a sleeping pheasant's nose (but I have never tried this), or the piece of burning rag with some sulphur rubbed into it.

Fish

Fish are always available to the hungry if they have initiative. The energy input-output ratio of fishing with a rod and line is wrong: you put more energy into it than you get energy in the form of fish out of it. But a night-line set for eel (the most delicious of all freshwater fish) or trout works well. That is a line laid along the stream with maybe twenty or thirty baited hooks on it. Slugs seem a good bait for trout, incidentally. Any man-made monofilament net of the right mesh to gill a fish set across a stream will take fish, particularly if you drive the fish into it from downstream. If you leave such a net across a river overnight you will take salmon or sea-trout. For salmon you need from 13- to 14-cm mesh, about six meshes deep. Hang it on the head line (which must have floats along it), four meshes of net for a length of line of two meshes (in other words, baggy) and about the same on the weighted footline. Monofilament is best but our old poachers used fine cotton. From 11 to 12 cm is the best mesh size for sea-trout.

Sea fishing

Without going into boat fishing (but see page 222) you can often catch dab or flounder or other sea fish by laying a long-line (a line with many baited hooks on it) out by the edge of the sea at low tide and inspecting it at the next low tide. It has got to be well anchored, of course. Lugworms, limpets, sections of herring or mackerel all make good bait. You must give a limpet a shrewd kick when he is not expecting it to get him off the rock. It is no good trying to dig for lugworms by pushing a fork in under their sand casts. You must notice that there is a breathing-hole 25 cm away from the sand cast, and it is mid-way between cast and hole that the lugworm is to be found. This is the lug-digger's secret. I knew an old man in Kent who used to catch a sackful of flounder with a long-line like this – and the hooks were made of blackthorn thorns!

Flounder can be 'pritched' at low water in estuaries with a flounder-spear, which is a multi-pronged spear with barbs on the prongs. You walk along the shallow water jabbing the sand or mud in front of you. Eels can be caught in ditches the same way – they lie dormant in the mud. In an estuary if you set a net up on stakes parallel with the shore, in such a manner that the tide flows under it on the flood and lifts it up, but closes it down on the ebb, flounder and other fish will get caught in it as they try to get out to deep water again when the tide ebbs. Such a net set as a barrier across the mouth of a tidal creek is effective, too. Eels in shallow water in muddy estuaries can be 'babbed'. This art consists of threading a bunch of worms – lug or earth – on knitting wool, bundling them up into a bunch, lowering the bunch into the water and very gently taking it out again. The eels will get their teeth caught in the wool. I have filled a tin bath in a few hours like this, but with a boat.

If you have a boat and a small amount of gear, you can catch herring, mackerel, plaice, sole, conger eel, skate, sprats and any of the other fish that teem in our coastal waters.

Herring are netted in a drift net. You will need about 45 m of net. Catch the fish in late autumn or winter; wait until other fishermen are getting good catches, so as not to waste your time hunting for fish that aren't there. Shoot your net where you think the fish are, so that it hangs like a wall in the water. Fasten one end of it to your boat and wait. From time to time you can unfasten yourself and row along the net to see whether there are any fish in it; if not, back you go to the end. If the shoal really hits your net you will know about it because the floats of the headline will sink. If that happens, haul the net up immediately. Pay it into the bottom of the boat, fish and all, and head for home. Spread a large sail on the beach, haul the net over it and shake out the fish.

Pilchards, which have returned to Cornwall after a long absence, are also caught in the drift net, and so are sprats (if the mesh is fine enough).

Mackerel, which come to the west coast in midsummer and end with the 'harvest mackerel' of September, are caught on lines or with 'the feathers' – long-lines with a dozen hooks or more, each with a tiny bunch of brightly coloured imitation feathers. You trail the line from the boat and haul it in loaded with fish.

A long-line (which may have a thousand or more hooks, though a hundred will be enough for you) will catch conger eel, hake, cod and codling, haddock and whiting. The usual thing is to shoot the line at night and collect it again in the morning. You will get the best fish in winter.

Flat fish are caught by trawling. You can buy little beam trawl nets suitable for use from a small boat.

Lobster, crab and crayfish are taken in pots; these are large baskets, weighted and marked with a float. The fish enter to take the bait but cannot find their way out.

Salt

If I wanted salt and didn't have any, I would go to the beach on a sunny day with a large container (not copper), prop it up on boulders, fill it with sea water – filtered to remove the sand – and light a fire of driftwood under it. The driftwood of today makes plenty of heat because it is always covered in oil. I would then lie down in the sun and ask my children to go on collecting driftwood, feeding the fire and pouring in sea water. At the end of the day there would be a quantity of salt at the bottom of the pot or pan.

Gardening

Gardening may be defined as the arable cultivation of land with the use of hand tools as opposed to animal- or engine-drawn ones.

The general treatment of soil is the same for gardening as for farming: draining, liming, possibly the application of phosphate or potash, and certainly the application of humus in the form of manure, compost or green-manuring crops, must be thought of. Perennial weeds such as couch grass, ground elder and bindweed must be attended to. If you have not got pigs to pig the ground (and what a lot of work they would save you!) you must fork and fork and rake and compost or burn the creeping roots that you get out, to rid your garden entirely of these perennial weeds. Annual weeds are no problem, for you must hoe and hand-weed your crops anyway, and you should look upon the annual weeds as a valuable source of green manure. Dig them in or, perhaps better, just pull or hoe them out and leave them on the surface to rot, or carry them to the compost heap. But you *must* get them out – do not think you can grow any crop satisfactorily in competition with weeds. The weeds got there because they were evolved to suit those particular conditions. Your crop got there because you put it there and it was evolved (by man) to be grown in controlled conditions. If you do not intervene, the weeds will win every time. I should make one exception here: Jerusalem artichokes on light ground. They will beat any weed I know – but beware that they do not become a weed themselves!

Crop succession in a garden can be endlessly complex and I know of no better writers on this subject than Lawrence D. Hills and W. E. Shewell-Cooper. But, broadly, crop rotation should be ruled by two considerations. One is that, in the family *Cruciferae*, brassica (cabbage tribe, which includes radishes) and turnips and swedes need lime (preferably two years before they are planted), and there must be the longest interval possible between plantings, because club root is the curse of the garden. The other is that potatoes, on which a man can live if he has to and which are the most reliable of all crops to grow, *do not* want freshly limed ground, and will suffer from eel-worm if grown year after year on the same land. Thus Hills recommends (and many gardeners have always practised) a rotation that starts with potatoes (heavily manured if possible), and goes on, after liming, to *Leguminosae* (beans and peas). When these are lifted early in the summer, brassica are planted (cabbage tribe). The next year (brassica are mostly harvested in the winter) the various root crops (*not* potatoes) are grown: turnips, swedes, parsnips, beet, salsify, carrots – and onions and pumpkins, which are not root crops. Lettuce, which is not a cabbage-tribe plant, can be fitted in on any odd scrap of ground, and so can radish (which *is* a brassica, but if you don't leave it to go to seed it won't get club root). Hills is a great advocate of *comfrey*, which is a deep-rooting perennial wonder-plant which gives an enormous crop of dark green hairy leaves every year for scores of years. Its virtue is that it sends its roots deep down and brings up potash and other minerals from below. It can be fed to stock in moderation (mixed with other food), and when the leaves are plucked young and tender it makes good 'spinach' or green soup. However, its chief virtue is that its mature leaves can be dug in with the main-crop potato seed to act as a potash-rich manure for them. We grew it with great success on deep, light land in Suffolk and I can thoroughly recommend it. It was called *knit-bone* by the ancients and was used as a dressing for open wounds. Dr Shewell-Cooper and his disciples might favour the rotation: potatoes (well mucked), other roots, peas and beans (lightly limed), cabbage tribe (well limed), then back to potatoes.

Potatoes

The 'seed' (which is just potatoes) can be the small potatoes of your own growing ('once-grown seed'), but if you go on planting your own seed for too long your potatoes will lose vigour and suffer disease. The reason is that the potato is a mountain crop which came from Peru or Colombia. Seed has to be grown high enough up not to suffer from aphids and the diseases that these spread. Therefore most of our new seed comes from Scotland or Ireland, although seed can be produced at a height over 250 metres in England or Wales, too. Get your seed early and *chit* it – that is, spread the potatoes out in trays very shallowly, allow light and air to get to them (but not frost), and shoots will appear. Plant early potatoes in mid-March and the main crop in mid-April (whenever you plant potatoes you will get a crop; however, frost cuts them off and they have to put forth shoots again). Dig earlies as soon as they are big enough to eat, as you want them every day. Dig main crops after the tops have all died down (we have sometimes left them until after Christmas). It is a good thing to *pig* the ground after potatoes, for the pigs will get out the ones you have missed and thus prevent the build-up of disease. When there is 'blight' about (in muggy warm summers) spray your main crop with Bordeaux Mixture. You can buy this, or make it by dissolving 2 kg of copper sulphate in 160 litres of water, then adding 1 kg of freshly burned quicklime, slaked in water to a cream. But even if you don't spray and get blight, you will still get some potatoes, though not so many. In this case, leave the potatoes in the ground as late as you can (i.e. until just before the hard frosts come), so that the blight spores from the haulm have all blown away and don't get on the tubers. Cut the diseased haulms off, too, and compost them in a hot compost heap. You can sometimes stop blight when it has appeared (the tips of the leaves go black) by using the stronger Burgundy Mixture – 100 g of copper sulphate in 4.5 litres of hot water, with 100 g of washing soda mixed in just before you spray it. (Incidentally, don't mix either the Bordeaux or Burgundy Mixtures in galvanized iron vessels.) These two sprays, as their names might suggest, were invented to combat mildew in grapes.

Peas and beans

Dig a trench about 20 cm deep, dump in compost (compost is just rotted vegetable or vegetable and animal matter) or muck (farmyard manure), sprinkle with lime, sprinkle with a little earth, sow peas fairly thickly (2.5 to 5 cm apart), cover with soil, and pray. If the mice eat them all, do it again, but with peas soaked in paraffin. You can get dwarf peas, but I prefer climbers, which should be given sticks to climb up. If your land is good, well limed and well manured, you don't really need to dig a trench – just score out a deepish furrow with the corner of the hoe, plant your peas, and cover. You will still get a crop. Runner beans are much the same, although they benefit even more from a trench with muck in it. A short row gives a huge yield. Slice them and pack them down hard in dry salt in crocks and they will last the winter. Both peas and runners (especially runners) need plenty of water, and spraying the flowers on runners with water helps the pods to set.

Broad beans are, in Britain at least, best planted in November. Thus they escape the horrid blackfly. I like to sow broad bean seed in double rows, the seeds 25 cm apart on the rows (and the two rows about the same distance apart), staggered, of course.

French beans and haricots can be sown successively from April onwards. In Suffolk we used to grow large blocks of Comtesse de Chambord, sowing early in May, with 30 cm between seeds and rows 45 cm apart and staggered. Earth them up a bit as they grow. Allow them to get quite ripe (if they grow well they are a good *smothering crop* – that is, they suppress weeds); harvest, hang in bunches in the wind but out of the rain, thresh (with a flail or over the back of a chair) in the winter, and cook as baked beans. (The only difference is that they are very much better!) Soak all dried beans or peas for at least a night before you cook them.

Cabbage tribe (brassica)

Sprouts and sprouting broccoli require very firm ground and plenty of space – roughly 60 cm both ways. Sow in seed beds in April and plant out in June, or in July if you are going to do that excellent trick of planting them between the rows of peas or beans, so that they will grow on for the winter after you have cut the beans and peas down to the ground. But if you leave them as late as that to transplant you should prick them out first into an intermediate plant bed with each plant about 10 cm away from its neighbour.

Cabbages don't need such firm ground. Spring cabbages should be sown about mid-July in a seed bed and planted out after the early potatoes, peas or beans in late September. They overwinter and give you fresh greens when they grow on again in the spring. You can cut them early as 'spring greens' or leave them to heart. Sow summer and autumn cabbage in March and plant them out when they are about 10 cm high (it doesn't really matter). Winter cabbage you sow in April or May, plant out in July, and eat all winter. Savoys are a very hardy winter variety.

Cauliflowers are not for the beginner, as they need much attention. They must be planted out carefully with a ball of soil on the roots, well fed with compost or manure and lime, and maybe top-dressings of nitrogenous manure, and always kept watered.

Root crops (not potatoes) and onions

Turnips, swedes, beet, carrots, parsnips: drill most of these in March (but parsnips in February, as they are slow to germinate). Draw out small furrows with a hoe corner and sprinkle seed in lightly *or* plant in stations – two or three seeds to a station. Single, when they appear, to the spacing you want. Common sense must be called in here. You know how big a turnip is – place them far enough apart so that they do not touch as they grow up. Onions can be grown as seed in August and transplanted in the spring, or in February if the land is dry enough. Thin in May or June. For the beginner I would recommend *sets*, which are little bulbs you buy from any seed merchant. Put these out in April. You must hand-weed onions very carefully, for they suffer badly from weed competition.

Pumpkins, marrows, gourds

I plant these big seeds in April where there has been an old muck heap and protect the young plants with upturned jam jars into May, when the jars are taken off. The plants will straggle for metres and produce a great crop of pumpkins. If you haven't got a place where there has been an old muck heap, then dig pits, fill with muck or compost, and plant in those. Pumpkins are best for food value.

Diseases and pests

Theoretically, there are many diseases and pests your plants could fall prey to, but only a few are common. Blight in potatoes we have dealt with. Club root in brassica you may prevent by not growing too many brassica breaks in your rotation, and by liming. If they do get it I should shamelessly use mercuric chloride – a tablet dissolved in a litre of water and dolloped down each hole at planting time, or some proprietary remedy. If you suspect your seed bed, soak that in the solution too, before sowing the seed. It's a poison, so be very careful with it. Lawrence D. Hills says a quarter of a mothball crunched up and dropped into each planting hole helps, as do a few pieces of rhubarb stem, though I haven't tried these. Cabbage root fly is also a common pest, and mercuric chloride stops this too. Hills recommends squares of roof felting with holes in them, through which the plants are threaded before they are planted. The cabbage root flies then lay their eggs on the roof felting, where they die. Calomel dust sprinkled around the plants when they are planted, and again a week or two later, also helps.

Cabbage white butterflies are another common pest. Their green caterpillars (which I am told are delicious fried) will ruin a crop in a few days. Nicotine, made by boiling 100 g cigarette ends in 4.5 litres water for half an hour, is what Hills recommends, and I know it works. Strain through nylon and mix one part to four parts of water when you need it. Derris works against very young caterpillars. Pyrethrum is better. You can also pick them off by hand if you have time.

Slugs can be killed in hundreds at night with a torch and a pinch of salt on each slug, or by picking up (ugh?) and dropping into salty water, or with proprietary slug bait, or Sluggit spray (*very* effective – but what side effects does it have?) or with deep plates sunk level with the ground with weak beer in them. Left to themselves, the slugs will completely clear a brassica crop in damp weather and do enormous damage to other crops, too.

Buildings

If you produce your own food you need plenty of space under cover. Dairy work needs a dairy – a light, airy, clean place with boiling water easily come by and clean cold water (although some of the best cheese in the world is made in dark, dirty, peasant kitchens on the Continent). You can milk cows out of doors – it is very hygienic, actually, because there is no build-up of germs – but it is more convenient to milk them inside. A concrete floor that you can wash is nice, with a gutter behind the cows for them to dung in, a trough in front of them for them to eat out of, and a cord or chain to tie them up with. Don't bother with a 'feeding passage' in front of the cows; it is a waste of space.

If you grow grain, you will need a floor to keep it on – perhaps a loft such as the grain loft you used to find on every farm – with a mill room under it. If you decide to bale your hay and straw, then you will need a large shelter such as a dutch barn to keep it in. If you don't bale it, you can stack it loose outside and thatch it. This is more labour, but is in some ways better.

If you work horses much and consistently, a stable is most useful. It is unfair to make horses work hard and long hours straight from grass, even if they are fed some corn out of doors. They need a proper stable, plenty of time to eat their corn, and the attention of being groomed and looked after. Their harness, too, takes up a great deal of room.

You will need a good workshop. Life is difficult without one. It is a bad idea to leave carts, implements and other tackle standing about in the rain, so you will also need good cart shelters.

Pigs are happier outside than in, provided they have dry, warm shelters with plenty of dry litter to sleep or farrow in. If you keep sows, each sow will need a warm, dry shelter to farrow in by herself. When you fatten pigs, they will need warm shelters. Such shelters can be movable, or semi-permanent. Pigs need moving often – if you keep them too long or too often on the same land they get worms. Pig shelters that can be dragged with a horse or tractor are good. Old corrugated iron sheets put on double with plastic fertilizer bags between them insulate well and keep all rain out. They will do for sides and roof, nailed on to a rough framework of green poles. Try not to buy anything if you can possibly help it. Two walls of wire netting stuffed with straw between them makes a fine wall, warm and well insulated. We have made mobile pig houses out of split pine poles, sawn down for us by the Forestry Commission, and with double old corrugated iron roofs.

The best way of keeping hens is in movable arks or houses which can be dragged around so that the hens are often on fresh ground. These have to be well made of timber, but you can often buy them second-hand. It is not permissible to keep hens indoors all the time (by the laws of humanity, though not the land) but it is permissible to have a winter house near the farm, lighted by electricity, oil, methane or what you will, but lighted, in which a chosen few hens are kept during the dark month or two of the winter when you would otherwise have to go without eggs. These hens will be put out into the fields as soon as your other, outdoor, main flock begins to lay again.

Growing withies

Withies are willows, or osiers, grown for basket and hurdle making. Once a bed is established it will need replanting very infrequently – there are withy beds that have produced steadily for eighty years or more.

The willows are grown from 'sets' – small plants that grow into larger ones. The most common varieties are Black Maul and Champion Rod. In willow-growing areas, you obtain your sets by buying at one of the annual auctions – these are still held in Somerset, for example. The rods you buy are intended for basket-making, but select the best of them and cut them into pieces 30 to 40 cm long. You will need between 45,000 and 60,000 sets for each hectare of land.

Prepare the ground well. It must be ploughed or dug deeply. In the old days they reckoned that with 'steam tackle' the land had to be cultivated after ploughing at least eight times. If no cultivator is available, it must be dug to a depth of two spits. Plough in the autumn or winter, and clear away all weeds and manure thoroughly.

Lay the sets in damp grass until late winter, which is the time to sow them. They are planted about 40 cm apart, in rows that are 60 cm apart, and so that about 20 cm of the set protrudes above the ground.

Keep the beds well weeded and watch out for insect infestations. Harvest the first withies in the autumn. These will be of little use, but harvesting is necessary to strengthen the roots. The full crop will be attained after three years, and it should be 5 to 7.5 tonnes to the hectare.

Harvest the withies by hand in autumn or winter, using a sharp hook. Cut the willow almost vertically, to leave a long cut edge at a steep angle, so that the rain cannot enter easily. Tie the withies into bed bundles, or bolts, each one a metre around its base.

The willow is now called 'green willow' and can be used for making hurdles and some baskets.

For wickerwork furniture or for baskets that will be exposed to damp, you need 'brown willow'. Sort out some green rods and steam them in a chest. Then stack them in the open for several weeks to dry. Do not strip off the bark.

For 'buff willow', sort green rods into lengths of 60 cm and tie them in bundles. If they are very dry, place them in cold water and bring them to the boil. If they are wet, plunge them into boiling water. Boil them for 5 hours and then leave them in the water for a further 24 hours. The tannin in the bark will stain them a rich golden colour.

Remove them from the water, stack them in heaps, and cover them with willow bark. Water the bark each day, and before using the rods, strip the bark from them.

For 'white willow' you must place the green rods, harvested in the autumn, in a few inches of running water as soon as they have been cut. Leave them there until the spring. Remove them and strip off the bark.

Rods for brown and buff willow should be stored, green, for at least six months before use.

See page 242 for basket weaving.

Compost making

Farm compost

Compost making is not, strictly speaking, necessary, but it can be convenient if the muck that could go on to the land directly is available at the wrong time of year. It will be available at the wrong time of year if animals are in-wintered, and cattle will be in-wintered if the land is too heavy and wet for them to graze without causing severe damage to the pasture – which does not grow in winter. The cattle will move out of doors again when the first grass is growing – the 'early bite' – and that will be the spring. Autumn, when the land is ploughed, is the best time for applying muck or compost. What do you do with the muck from the yards between the spring and autumn? You can compost it.

Aim to build long rows – 'windrows' – about two metres square in cross section, from muck and vegetable wastes, with a little lime. You can mechanize the operation using a tractor or horse, a muck-spreader and a 'mould'.

Make the 'mould' from sheets of any robust material – old corrugated iron is ideal – so that it looks like a small hut with only two sides and a roof and no floor. The three sections are two metres wide and three metres long. Mount the mould on skids (made from old railway sleepers, perhaps).

Hitch the muck spreader to the tractor or horse, and the mould behind it. Place all in position, the spreader fully loaded, and start to move. The muck spreader flails the muck into the air, outward and backwards, where it is caught in the mould and settles; eventually the mould is filled with a loose, aerated heap neatly shaped and proportioned. As the spreader works, throw vegetable wastes, weeds from the nearest ditch, any kind of green matter into it and, every so often, a few shovelsful of lime. As the mould fills, move forward, dragging the mould behind the spreader on its skids.

The heap will heat and steam may rise from it. When the temperature falls again the heap should be turned, using a front loader, if you have one or can borrow one for a few hours; otherwise use forks.

The compost will be ready by autumn.

Garden compost

Again, compost is not necessary in the garden, but it is a convenient way to store wastes and to accelerate the process of decomposition.

You will need a container that has holes or gaps in the sides to permit aeration. If you make one, the optimum size is about 1.5 m^3, and if the front can be opened or removed it will make life much easier for you later. For best results you should have two such containers or 'bins'.

Compost can be made from anything organic: if something has ever lived, it can live again! Paper should be shredded, though, fibrous material such as nettles will decompose faster if they are beaten to break the stems, and really woody material, including hedge trimmings, breaks down very slowly. Ideally you should have animal manure, green and other vegetable matter – including kitchen scraps – and a little lime.

Build the heap in layers about 15 cm thick – first manure with a sprinkling of lime just to whiten it, then vegetable matter, then manure and lime again, and so on until the bin is filled. Throw it in loosely, do not tread it down, and finally cover it with something waterproof. Watch it for a few days, and if it begins to look dry, sprinkle a watering can or two of water over it. It must be moist but not sodden. The temperature will rise, then fall. When it falls, turn the contents of the first bin into the second, so that the material from the top goes to the bottom. The compost will be ready to use in six to eight weeks. When you remove the compost to use it, any material that has not decomposed completely can be put back into another heap.

Cooking to save fuel

Electric and gas cookers waste as much fuel as they use, so make sure you get good value every moment the cooker is switched on. Solid fuel cookers are better value for the busy cook, but they burn up extra fuel when the top is being used, so in their case the oven should be used as much as possible.

In the oven

The aim is to conserve energy and to cook food with the minimum of power. Planning ahead can help here; if you plan to cook an economical meal using slow-cooking cuts of meat that need a long, slow cooking process, then make sure you utilize your oven space to its best advantage. Cook three or four slow-cooking main-course dishes at the same time and freeze two or three of them to use at a later date, or at least plan a meal that includes a slow-cooking main dish, a braised vegetable and a baked pudding. If the oven is to be used for any length of time, try to cut down on grill or ring cooking during that period. If a dish is to be covered during the cooking time, make sure it is *tightly* covered or sealed in foil, as this will shorten the cooking time as well as preserving all the goodness of the dish.

Make sure your oven is scrupulously clean. Layers of grease on the inside will cut down on the heat available.

Use dishes for slow-oven cooking that are good conservers of heat – earthenware is particularly good.

Try not to open the oven door more than is absolutely necessary. Use the oven, rather than the top of the stove, for slow-cooked recipes whenever possible, as the oven is a far more economical method of utilizing fuel. Tenderize meat by marinating it overnight in a little oil and lemon juice – this can make a difference of as much as 30 minutes' cooking time with cheaper cuts of meat. When freezing stewing meat, cut the meat and add the marinade before freezing. When cooking large joints of meat that have been frozen, allow them to thaw completely before roasting; a large joint of beef will require 2 hours per kg cooking time from the frozen state and only 30 minutes per kg from the thawed state – and thawing, after all, costs nothing.

On the hob

You would probably be surprised by the amount of heat that is lost when cooking on the hob of a cooker with the wrong sort of saucepan. Good, heavy saucepans that distribute heat evenly are an investment

– they heat up more quickly and utilize heat more efficiently. Always use a saucepan that covers the ring of the cooker to avoid heat loss and buy saucepans that have heavy, tight-fitting lids. Some saucepans work in a tier system so that they can be stacked while cooking is going on and one dish cooked over the heat rising from another.

When cooking vegetables, one variety can be cooked in boiling water and another steamed in a steamer above it. Use hot water from the tap to speed up the boiling process.

To economize on ring cooking, two or more vegetables can be cooked together in one saucepan. Wrap the vegetables in a loose foil parcel, prick each parcel with a pin to allow the water to filter through, and plunge them into a large saucepan of boiling, salted water.

Under the grill

Grill cooking is quicker, and therefore cheaper, than most other forms of cooking, and it can be speeded up by lining the grill pan with foil. Make the best possible use of the grill by combining foods that are to be cooked in this way – for example, grill mushrooms and tomatoes to serve with chops, steak, liver etc.

Other methods

Pressure cooking: Although the cost of a pressure cooker demands quite an initial outlay, the results are well justified by the fuel saved by cooking in this manner, especially as the pressure cooker is particularly successful in the cooking of cheaper cuts of meat and ingredients such as dried pulses and old fowls that require a long cooking process.

Normally liquids boil at a temperature of 100°C. This temperature is controlled by atmospheric pressure and cannot increase however long boiling continues. By enclosing ingredients in a steam-proof container and keeping control of the steam, cooking under pressure raises the basic temperature, cooking food more quickly.

Hay box cooking: The hay box method of cooking was invented a long time ago on the principle that food could be heated to boiling point and then transferred to a box insulated with hay to continue the remainder of the cooking process required. Now a similar box has been produced, using modern polystyrene as an insulator, with a fitted saucepan so that stews and casseroles that need a long, slow cooking time can be heated through on the stove and then transferred to the insulated box, so cutting fuel use to a minimum.

Cooking at the table: Cooking at the table over a methylated spirits or gas cylinder flame is fun and can also be essential in times of economic crisis. A small camping stove or fondue set is a real asset to any household as it can be used to make any number of quickly cooked dishes.

Barbecue cooking: Although charcoal is by far the best fuel to use for outdoor cooking, as it reaches a high temperature and the coals retain their heat, successful meals can also be cooked over the dying embers of wood fires. When building a barbecue, make sure that you have a good draught so that the fire draws well, and wait to start cooking until the fire has burned to red embers. Brush meat, poultry or fish with oil before cooking and keep the ingredients just high enough over the heat to prevent them from catching on fire.

Cooking to save nutrients

Meat and poultry: Do not rub meat with salt before roasting or grilling, as this draws out the blood. 'Seal' the meat by an initial cooking in a very hot oven.

Baste well during the cooking process to keep the meat moist, or wrap in foil to conserve all the juices. Do not overcook.

Use the juices in the pan to make gravy. Leave roast meat or poultry to stand for 5 to 10 minutes before carving. For casseroling and stewing, make sure the cooking vessel is tightly sealed before cooking. 'Seal' the meat by browning it over a high heat before stewing. For boiling, use as little liquid as possible. Save the cooking liquid to make stock.

Fish: Rub large fish with olive oil to prevent them from drying. Coat fish which is to be fried in batter or egg and breadcrumbs to keep in the juices. Never overcook fish. Do not attempt to grill thin white fish fillets as they are likely to dry out.

Vegetables: Choose young but mature vegetables and if they *have* to be peeled, peel as thinly as possible; the skins of many vegetables contain a high percentage of their nutritional value. Cook in as little water as possible and cover during cooking.

Only cook vegetables for just as long as it takes for them to be tender – all cooked vegetables should be crisp in texture and never flabby.

Use the water from cooking to make stock or gravy so that the full nutritional value and flavour are retained.

Preserving food without a deep freeze

Freezing food is the only method of preservation that keeps it in its original condition. With everything except root vegetables (which can be stored as they are – see page 67), alternative methods such as salting, smoking, drying etc are necessary and these alter the flavour of produce. That, however, is not always a bad thing – the new flavour can be delicious.

Canning

This is a complicated process and has to be done under ideal conditions with the correct equipment. It is not really to be recommended in the home as, unless the process is totally effective, there is a danger of bacteria, and unless cans are stored in a temperature of under 10°C in a dark place, much of the goodness and colour of the food will be lost.

Bottling

The containers must be completely sealed. Ordinary screw-top jars are not adequate and special bottles should be bought for the purpose. Bottles must be sterilized in a hot oven for 20 minutes before being filled. Pack the ingredients to within 1 cm of the cover and boil in a pan of water or heat through in 1 cm of water in a slow oven (150°C, 300°F, gas mark 2). Store filled bottles in a cool, dry, dark place.

Fruit is the most suitable produce for bottling. All fruit should be covered with a sugar syrup to prevent loss of colour and flavour. Choose freshly picked, firm, ripe fruit; wash if necessary and remove hulls or stalks. Peel and core apples and pears; pack blackberries, raspberries and loganberries with dry sugar (one part sugar to four parts fruit); cook rhubarb in sugar syrup.

Peel, quarter and pack tomatoes with 2 teaspoons salt and 2 teaspoons sugar to each kg of fruit.

Pickling

Fruit and vegetables can be preserved by combining them with spiced, sometimes sweetened, vinegar.

Spiced vinegar: 1 litre malt vinegar; 1 blade mace; 7 g stick cinnamon; 7 g cloves; 7 g whole allspice; 7 g black peppercorns; 14 g bruised root ginger.

Combine all the ingredients in the top of a double saucepan over water and cover tightly. Bring the water to the boil and cook over a very low heat for 1½ hours. Strain the vinegar through muslin.

Pickling vegetables: Wash vegetables, removing any damaged or bruised produce, and prepare them in the usual way. Cover them with a brine made from 100 g salt to 1 litre of cold water, weigh them down with a plate and leave them in a cool place for 24 hours. Drain well, pack into jars to within 2 cm of the cover and fill with either cold or boiling-hot spiced vinegar.

You can pickle: Beetroot, red cabbage, cauliflower, cucumber, green tomatoes, marrow, onions, French beans.

Pickling fruit: Add 1 kg sugar to 0.5 litre of spiced vinegar. Stew fruit in the sweetened vinegar over a low heat until tender. Drain and half fill warmed jars or bottles. Boil syrup until reduced by half and pour over fruit. Tap the jars to remove air bubbles and screw down caps tightly.

Salting

Salt, dry or in brine, prevents the growth of destructive micro-organisms and preserves meat and fish. The only vegetables that respond well to salting are French beans, which should be picked when young, as the salt tends to toughen them. Cheaper cuts of meat, such as brisket, respond well to salting. Use coarse salt, not the free-flowing kind.

Salting pork: Pack fresh, chilled joints of meat in a sterilized earthenware crock with a glazed lining. Cover with a solution of 1 kg pickling salt, 225 g sugar, 14 g saltpetre and 6 litres water. Cover with a plate, heavily weighted (the meat must be submerged in the brine), cover the crock and keep in a temperature of less than 3°C. At the end of each 7 days, remove the meat from the brine, stir the brine well and return the meat. Allow 8 days' curing time for each kg of meat.

Salting beef, lamb and mutton: Use tougher cuts with some fat. Allow 500 g of salt to 11 kg of meat. Place a layer of salt in the bottom of a glazed earthenware crock, cover with layers of meat rubbed well with salt and covered by more salt. Cover and leave for 24 hours, then cover with a solution of 4.5 litres water mixed with 500 g sugar, 14 g baking soda and 25 g saltpetre. Put a weighted plate over the meat to keep all of it below the surface of the liquid; cover tightly and store below 3°C. Cure for 4 to 6 weeks. After that the meat can be stored, in the brine, in a refrigerator.

Salting fish: Salt only freshly caught fish. Remove the head and gills, gut the fish, wash well and remove blood and cut out the back and rib bones, or fillet the fish. Scale and put into a brine made from 700 g salt to 4.5 litres of water for 20 minutes. Drain well and coat the fish with pickling salt, using one part coarse-ground salt to four parts fish, by weight. Place on wooden racks and weigh down heavily. Dry out of doors when the humidity is low and leave for up to a week or until all the brine has drained away. Hang the fish in a dry shed with good ventilation to remove all moisture. Wrap dried fish in waxed paper and pack in wooden boxes. Store below 10°C.

Drying

Unfortunately, the British climate is not well suited for drying. Apple and pear slices, and mushrooms, however, can be dried until leathery in a very slow oven, and herbs can be dried by hanging them upside down in a cool, dry place.

Smoking

A home-made smoker can be built in a garden – from a barrel or an old fridge, for example; or small smokers can be bought from some kitchen shops. Use only hardwoods for smoking, and do not light the smoking fire with chemical firelighters. The smoking must be sustained; it will take about 72 hours' smoking for a large ham. The temperature of the smoke should be between 21° and 32°C. Fish should be salted in brine before being smoked and the smoke heat should be kept below 21°C.

Storing root vegetables and fruit

Beetroot, carrots, turnips etc: Do not wash, but brush off excess soil. Leave 1 cm of crown on the roots and pack in boxes between layers of moist sand. Store in a dark, cool place (a cellar is ideal) and water the sand if it becomes too dry.

Potatoes: Store potatoes in a cool, dark place. Cover a mound of potatoes with a good layer of straw and then with a thick layer of earth (see page 32).

Apples and pears: Store on wooden racks in a cool, dry place, not near vegetables (an attic is ideal). Make sure the apples are not touching each other, and check them frequently so that apples that go bad can be removed.

Substitutes for tea and coffee

We consume more tea and coffee than any other beverage, and the tea or coffee break provides not only a restorative effect but also a time to be sociable. Both tea and coffee are imported, are relatively expensive and are likely to become even dearer in the future, so it is well worth exploring the possibility of any alternative beverage which can be made with natural resources available in this country.

It is surprising to learn how many forms of hot drink there are. Most of them are based on the principle of infusing fresh or dried flowers, and have been in use for centuries; many have medicinal properties that make them highly acceptable to the digestive juices as well as to the palate. Most herb or flower teas are made from common wild flowers and therefore they cost virtually nothing to produce. Coffee substitutes are harder to find and, on the whole, the main ingredient has to be processed by being roasted and ground in some manner.

Alternative teas

On the whole, flower and herb teas should be drunk without the addition of milk or cream. Sugar, on the other hand, can be served with the tea, although the plants or flowers themselves usually make a naturally sweetened beverage. When flower or herb teas do need sweetening, honey makes a very good substitute for sugar. All the teas should be strained before serving. To dry flowers or leaves for making tea, pick them when the flowers are in full blossom, early in the morning on a warm day. Remove any insects or dirt, but do not wash them as this will spoil the taste and texture. Spread them out on a wire mesh tray and leave them to dry in a warm, well-aired place.

To infuse flowers or leaves, place them in a clean, wide-mouthed jug, pour boiling water over them, stir gently and leave them to stand for a few minutes before straining.

The strength of these alternative teas depends, to a great extent, on individual tastes – as it does with ordinary tea. Experiment until you achieve the strength required.

Excellent teas can be made by combining the leaves and flowers of more than one plant in the same way that high-quality China and Indian teas are made by blending. Try combining marjoram with mint, for instance, or clover with chamomile – the results can be most refreshing.

Borage Dry the flower heads only. Add 2 teaspoons of dried flowers to half a litre of boiling water and leave to infuse for 5 minutes before drinking.

Burnet Dry the leaves, crumble them lightly and use like ordinary tea leaves. Serve with sliced lemon and sugar or honey.

Calamint Use fresh or dried leaves. Infuse a handful of fresh leaves or 3 teaspoons of dried leaves in half a litre of boiling water.

Catmint Infuse a handful of freshly picked leaves in half a litre of boiling water.

Chamomile Gather the heads before the petals begin to droop and use either fresh or dried. Infuse a handful of fresh flowers or 1 teaspoon of dried flowers in half a litre of boiling water.

Clover Dry the flowers of red clover and infuse 3 teaspoons in half a litre of boiling water.

Corn mint (apple mint) Use fresh or dried leaves. Infuse a handful of fresh leaves or 2 to 3 teaspoons of dried leaves in half a litre of boiling water.

Elderflower Use fresh or dried flowers. Infuse 1 head of fresh flowers or 1 tablespoon of dried flowers in half a litre of boiling water and leave for 2 minutes before straining.

Gorse Sweet and rather heady. Infuse 2 tablespoons of freshly picked gorse flowers in half a litre of boiling water.

Heather Infuse 3 tablespoons of fresh flowers or 2 tablespoons of dried flowers in half a litre of boiling water and leave to stand for 4 minutes before straining.

Hollyhock Use fresh flowers. Pour half a litre of boiling water over a handful of freshly picked flowers and infuse for a few minutes before straining.

Lime Pick the flowers while they are in full bloom and dry them. Add a heaped tablespoon of dried flowers to half a litre of boiling water and infuse for 3 or 4 minutes before straining. The heady scent of lime flowers has a tranquillizing effect and the tea has often been used as a mild sedative, so perhaps this is not the ideal beverage for a break in a working day.

Marjoram Pour half a litre of boiling water over 1 heaped tablespoon of fresh or dried leaves and infuse for a few minutes before straining.

Meadowsweet Use leaves and flowers. Pour half a litre of boiling water over 30 g of fresh or dried leaves and flowers and infuse before straining.

Nettle Use the dried flowers of the white nettle. Pour half a litre of boiling water over 2 teaspoons of dried flowers and infuse for 2 minutes before straining.

Rosemary Use fresh or dried leaves. Pour half a litre of boiling water over 1 heaped tablespoon of fresh or dried leaves and infuse for 3 minutes before straining.

Roses Add a quarter of a litre of rose petals to half a litre of water, simmer gently for 10 minutes and strain before drinking. The taste of the tea will vary with the scent of the flowers used.

Saffron Use ¼ teaspoon dried, powdered saffron to flavour half a litre of boiling water.

Sage Add half a litre of boiling water to 30 g of dried sage leaves and infuse for 3 or 4 minutes before straining. A little orange or lemon juice added to the tea gives it a delicious flavour.

Strawberry Use the fresh or dried leaves of the wild strawberry. Pour half a litre of boiling water over a handful of leaves and infuse for a few minutes before straining.

Tansy Add half a litre of boiling water to 1 heaped tablespoon of dried leaves and flowers and infuse for 2 or 3 minutes before straining.

Thyme Add half a litre of boiling water to 1 heaped tablespoon dried leaves and flowers and infuse for 3 or 4 minutes before straining.

Violet Add half a litre of boiling water to 2 teaspoons dried flowers and infuse for 5 minutes before straining.

Woodruff Use fresh or dried leaves and flowers. Pour half a litre of boiling water over a handful of leaves and flowers and infuse for 3 or 4 minutes before straining.

Yarrow Use fresh or dried leaves and flowers of the young plant. Pour half a litre of boiling water over a handful of leaves and flowers and infuse for 3 or 4 minutes before straining.

Alternative coffees

During the war years the French, probably the greatest coffee-lovers of all time, were forced to simulate the taste of this drink by substituting alternative ingredients which were dried, roasted and then ground in the same way as coffee beans. Three main substitutes were found – dandelion roots, chicory and acorns – and although none of these gave a very close resemblance to real coffee they at least had the advantage of being (except in the case of chicory) free from the stimulative caffein.

Coffee made from roots or acorns tends to have a bitter taste and usually needs to be sweetened in some way. To give a nutty flavour to the drink, some roasted and ground sunflower seeds can be added to the basic mixture.

Dandelion Dry young roots. Clean them, roast them in a moderate oven, cool and grind. Pour boiling water over the grounds, stir well, leave to steep for 10 minutes, then strain.

Wild chicory (Cichorium intybus) A native weed of Britain and Europe, which has pale blue flowers and rather ragged leaves. The leaves can be eaten in salads and the root contains both starch and sugar which is changed, when roasted, into a caramel-type substance. Wild chicory has been used since 1722 as an additive to coffee, giving a slightly bitter taste, and the dried roots can be roasted and ground to give a complete coffee substitute. Dry the roots, clean them, then roast in a moderately hot oven; cool and grind finely. Pour boiling water over the grounds, stir well and leave to steep for 5 to 10 minutes before straining.

Acorns Chop the nuts roughly and roast them in a moderately hot oven. Cool and grind and return to a moderately hot oven until the ground nuts are well roasted. Place the required amount of ground acorns in a wide-mouthed jug, pour boiling water over them, stir and leave to steep for 10 minutes. Strain before drinking. Whenever possible, the acorns should be freshly roasted for each brew of coffee.

Goosegrass (Galium aparine) Roast the seeds in a moderately hot oven, cool and grind. Pour boiling water over the grounds, stir and leave to steep for 10 minutes. Strain before serving.

British wild foods

Shellfish and crustacea

One of the greatest sources of free food in Britain is the sea shore, where rocks, sand and estuaries can provide a varied treasure trove of good food to be had for the picking or digging. Most shellfish are high in protein and minerals as well as being delicious in taste and texture, but they do have to be treated with respect and caution. Always avoid shellfish which are living near jetties, piers or sewage outlets of any kind.

The old rule that one should eat shellfish only in a month with an 'R' should be respected within reason, but not, as is generally thought, because the other months happen to cover the breeding season of molluscs. All fish lose some of their flavour during the breeding season, but this does not, in itself, make them dangerous to eat. Caution in gathering and eating shellfish in the summer should be exercised because of the possibly high temperature of the water. All shellfish and particularly bivalve molluscs like mussels (which sluice water through their shells in order to filter out food) are susceptible to the action of bacteria; if the bacteria are there and conditions are ripe, germs can multiply at a frightening rate. Provided, however, that you collect shellfish when the weather is cold, that you gather them from a clean, unpolluted area of coastline, and that the shellfish are scrubbed clean and are alive at the moment of cooking or eating, there should be no danger. Bacterial action starts the moment the shellfish dies, so any shellfish that are open (or not tightly closed) should be discarded at once. A bad shellfish has a decidedly 'off' smell and flavour which can be detected instantly, so that the offending ingredient can be spat out immediately, thereby preventing the advent of 'toxyphobia', which is experienced by those who have eaten and digested a 'bad' oyster.

When alternative forms of cooking are not available, most shellfish (provided they have been well cleaned) can be cooked on an open fire of wood or coals. Let the fire burn until the ash is glowing and either place the shellfish directly in the hot ash or cover the burning embers with a layer of seaweed, place the shellfish on the seaweed and top with another layer to keep the steam in. Leave for 10 minutes. In America this is done by making the fire in a pit and covering the shellfish with canvas or tarpaulin.

Cockles (Cardinum edule): Among the commonest shellfish, cockles are all too often soused in quantities of malt vinegar, which has the effect of destroying the deliciously fresh and subtle flavour of these underrated shellfish.

Cockles were, and still are, plentiful around the more muddy shores, though in some areas they have suffered from over-picking or from pollution. They are found between tidelines, lying on top of or just under the surface of the sand, and their position is often determined by a muddy vein through the sand or a thin layer of green plantain filming a muddy area. Cockles grow up to 5 cm wide, have a thick, ribbed shell, and vary in colour from a bluish white to a whitish grey.

Usually when you find one cockle you will be on or near a whole bed of them, and the easiest way to gather them is to scoop up the shells with a garden rake. Return any shells less than 2.5 cm wide to the sea bed, and throw away any shellfish that are broken. Gather the shellfish in a sack or bucket. Do not let the shells stand for any length of time in direct sunlight. Because cockles feed by sluicing water through their shells, they are inclined to contain waste sand, grit and mud when you pick them. This can be eliminated by scrubbing the cockles, placing them in a bucket, covering them with clean, cold water and leaving them in a cool, dark place for 6 to 8 hours. During this time all the waste will be exuded and the shellfish will be clean. Seaweed can be placed over the shells to keep them cool and fresh.

Place the cleaned cockles in a large, heavy pan and cook them over a medium high heat, shaking the pan, for about 3 minutes until they are opened. Remove the cockles from their shells and serve as a salad with a shellfish mayonnaise, in a white sauce flavoured with chives, or as a soup with the cockles served in their shells in the same way as a mussel soup. Cockles were extremely popular with the Romans and are still the main ingredient of the popular Italian dish, *spaghetti con vongole*, for which a sauce made of oil, finely chopped shallot and garlic, snippets of bacon and freshly cooked, shelled cockles, is served over spaghetti.

Clams (Mya arenaria): Caught by surprise, clams, which are larger than cockles, can be rather off-putting to look at, as the searching, weaving, pinky proboscises emerge from their shells to syphon up food. Like cockles, they live in mid-tidal sand and sandy mud; they can be up to 15 cm wide. Their shells are grey-brown in colour, fairly smooth and often have a purple tint inside. They tend to be below the

surface of the sand or mud. The flesh is succulent and rich and they make really first-class eating if you can find them. Gather clams like cockles, scrub the shells to remove mud and leave them to clean, covered with fresh, cold water, for 6 hours.

Steam clams to open them, in the same way as cockles, or drop them into boiling water and cook for 5 minutes until opened.

Like oysters, clams can be eaten raw with lemon juice, but they are difficult to open as their hinge muscle is of prodigious strength. To open, plunge a sharp oyster knife into the hinge muscle with a quick jab, turn the knife to cut through the muscle and then slide it along the shell to loosen the meat. Serve on the half shell with buttered slices of brown bread.

Steamed or boiled clams can be removed from the shell and served like cockles, or they can be served in a rich milky soup flavoured with onion and parsley.

Limpets (Patella vulgata): Limpets cling tenaciously to rocks along our coasts and removing them by hand is often difficult. The meat tends to be tough and has not nearly the flavour of cockles or clams, but it is nourishing and if enough are gathered they can be used to produce an acceptable meal.

Avoid gathering limpets near jetties or sewage outlets. Prise them off the rocks with a sharp knife; cover the limpets with cold water;

leave them to stand in a cool place for 6 hours and then plunge them into boiling water. Cook until the meat comes free of the shell, drain well, fry or stew until tender and serve like cockles.

Mussels (Mytilus edulis): Probably the best and most easily gathered shellfish to be found around British shores, mussels are rich in flavour and nourishment. Unfortunately, they are particularly susceptible to the action of bacteria and great care must be taken to gather mussels that have grown on an unpolluted stretch of coast. Mussels should never, on any account, be picked near to drains, waste outlets, above the tideline or in places where the water is discoloured.

Gather mussels at low tide, from cleanly washed rocks. Select the large shells, scrub them clean with a wire brush and leave them to stand in cold, fresh water for 6 hours before cooking. Discard any that are open before cooking and, after cooking, remove the wiry beards that protrude from the mussels.

Mussels can be steamed (like cockles) to open, baked in a hot oven or put into boiling water. They are delicious as a soup, flavoured with onion, garlic and parsley, or they can be left on the half shell, stuffed with garlic and parsley butter and reheated or grilled. Shelled mussels, wrapped in thin rashers of bacon and grilled until the bacon is just cooked, are delicious with a squeeze of lemon.

Scallops (Pecten maximus): These distinctive fan-shaped shells usually grow too deep for easy picking but sometimes, when the tide is very low, it is possible to find the occasional exposed bed. Pick large shells

that are firmly closed, scrub the shells with a scrubbing brush and stand them in cold water for 6 hours. Place the shells in a large, heavy saucepan and steam over a high heat until they are open. Cut the meat away from the shells, remove any black veins and slice the flesh if the scallops are large. Scallops can be cooked in a cheese-flavoured white sauce; brushed with oil and lemon juice and grilled; wrapped in bacon and grilled, or dipped in beaten egg and breadcrumbs and deep-fried. Like mussels, they can also be cooked in a garlic- and parsley-flavoured butter.

Razor shells (Ensis siliqua): These are delicious and often plentiful when the tides are exceptionally low but, unfortunately, they are extremely difficult to catch (as anyone who has tried to do so knows).

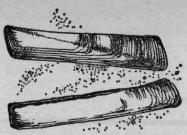

The second they are touched, razor shells burrow deeply into the sand with incredible speed. They are to be found in clean sand, beyond the normal low-tide line and alternative methods of harvesting are to sprinkle salt over their holes or to dig with a garden fork. The effort of getting razor shells is exhausting but rewarding, as the meat is rich and full of flavour. Wash the shells, discarding any that are open, and leave them in cold, fresh water for 6 hours. Steam the shells open and make a soup with the shellfish liquid and a flavouring of onion, garlic and parsley. Serve the razors in their shells with the liquid poured over.

Winkles (Littorina littorea): Although plentiful on rocky shores, these dark, spiral-shelled creatures are some of the least rich and well-flavoured shellfish. If enough are gathered, however, they can make a passable food despite the fact that each one has to be coaxed from its shell on the point of a pin.

Rinse the winkles and leave them in cold, fresh water, for about 10 hours. Cover the container to prevent them from escaping. Plunge them into boiling water and cook for 10 minutes. Cool, remove the hard film from the mouth of the shell, and winkle out the meat with a pin.

Shrimps and prawns are plentiful in many parts of the country in shallow water and rock pools. Cook them in boiling fresh or sea water until their shells turn pink – just a few minutes. Remove the shells before eating prawns; the shells can then be boiled to make the base of a good soup. Small shrimps can be eaten without shelling.

Crabs, large and small, make good eating, although it takes time to remove the meat from the shell and claws. They can often be found in rock pools when the tide is out. Cover the crabs in cold sea water and bring to the boil. When the water reaches the bubbling stage, remove the pan from the heat and leave the crabs to cool in the water. Remove the legs of crabs and prise off the back shell. Carefully extract the stomach sac (an unpleasant-looking transparent bag at the front) and remove the feathery 'dead men's fingers' from either side. The rest of the meat and the meat from the claws make good eating.

Fish

Although there are many varieties of freshwater fish, the best by far are salmon, sea-trout and trout; all should be cooked as soon as possible after they have been caught.

Clean the fish by making a slit along the stomach and removing the entrails and blood. Wash the fish in cold water and remove the scales by sliding a sharp knife towards the head.

Trout or small sea-trout can be fried. Large fish should be poached or baked until just cooked. Salmon, like game, can be hung for 7 to 10 days before eating is necessary, and all three types of fish can be preserved by smoking.

Pike and char can be found in the deep-water lakes of the country and can be baked, poached or cut into steaks and fried.

Small minnows can be deep-fried and eaten like whitebait.

Eels can be caught in most rivers on a bait of worms threaded with 6 to 8 strands of cotton. The eels get their teeth caught in the cotton and can be lifted to the side or the bank (see page 51). Eels should be skinned and gutted, cut into 5-cm long slices and fried or grilled until crisp, when they make delicious and rich eating. Eels can also be smoked in the same way as salmon.

Freshwater crayfish can be found in limestone rivers and lakes and can be caught in nets baited with high meat, or by turning over large stones at the water's edge. Cook crayfish in boiling salted water until they turn pink, remove the shells and crack the claws to extract the meat. In some parts of the world crayfish are considered a tremendous delicacy, but in Britain they are seldom bothered about.

Wild animals

Fortunately, due to the sporting nature of the British gentleman and to the nature conservation movement, game and wildlife of all kinds are still plentiful in Britain, although it is hard to tell whether much of the game in our woods and countryside is technically wild, since so much of it is now reared. In times of emergency man has eaten any animal he could catch, including rats and mice; and, with the exception of the badger (which carries a TB virus), almost anything that moves is edible to some extent.

Young squirrels (preferably the grey variety) can be roasted or stewed and have good flavour, and the nocturnal edible dormouse, the glis-glis popular on the Continent, is sometimes found in this country. All British frogs are edible – if you can catch them. All British snails are edible: feed them on lettuce only for a few days to 'clean' them, then eat only the muscular foot that projects below the shell.

Game, however, makes the best eating provided you have access to it and the means of shooting or trapping it.

Game birds

Hang for 5 to 14 days, depending on the weather, to allow their flavour to mature. Pluck the birds by pulling out the feathers towards the head, using sharp, jabbing movements. Singe off feather tips over a naked flame. Cut off the head (except in the case of snipe and woodcock), leaving as long a neck as possible. Pull back the neck skin and cut off the neck at its base. Make an incision (except in the case of woodcock) just above the parson's nose and remove the entrails, reserving the heart and liver, which usually make good eating. Truss the birds and tie or skewer the legs and wings in position to prevent the flesh from drying out while cooking. Old birds that are to be used for stewing can be skinned instead of plucked, to save time. Make a slit along the backbone with a sharp knife and peel off the skin and feathers, cutting around the legs and wings. Soak water birds in water to which some vinegar has been added to get rid of their fishy taste, or stuff them with a raw potato and a raw onion seasoned with salt. All young game can be roasted; old birds should be casseroled or stewed.

Seasons for game

Blackgame: 20 August to 10 December. Found only in Scotland. 1.4 to 1.8 kg.

Capercaillie (capercailzie, capercailye): 1 October to 31 January. Found only in Scotland. 2.7 to 5.5 kg.

Geese (pink-footed and greylag): Below high-tide mark, 1 September to 20 February; elsewhere 1 September to 31 January. 2.7 to 4.5 kg.

Grouse: 12 August to 10 December. Do not hang at the beginning of the season when the weather is warm. 0.5 to 0.7 kg.

Hares: No close season. 1.5 to 2 kg. Hare should be hung for up to 1 week and skinned as for rabbits. When removing the entrails, keep the blood if you want to jug the hare.

Mallard or wild duck: Below high-tide mark, 1 September to 20 February.

Partridge: 1 September to 1 February. 340 to 425 g. Hang young birds for 3 to 5 days; hang old, tough birds for up to three weeks to tenderize them.

Pheasant: 1 October to 1 February. 900 g to 1.6 kg. As pheasants are rather long, thin birds, they are inclined to dry out whilst cooking and need plenty of basting to keep the flesh moist.

Pigeon: No close season. 0.5 to 0.6 kg. Empty the crop as soon as the pigeon has been killed. The birds do not need to be hung and the flesh has a rich, gamy flavour. The meat on the legs of old birds is too tough to provide good eating, so the birds can be skinned and the breasts cut neatly from the bone.

Rabbits: No close season. 1 to 1.6 kg. Beware of rabbits suffering from myxomatosis. Check round the eyes and do not eat any rabbit with swollen or running eyes or with scars over the eyes. Eat rabbit fresh, not hung. To skin, cut off the feet above the knees and lay it on its back with the tail towards you. Make a cut with a sharp knife in the belly, close to the thighs and about 2.5 cm long. Pull the skin away from the thighs and towards the tail until the lower part of the body is skinned. Turn the rabbit round, with the head towards you, cut around the head and pull off the rest of the skin from the body and legs. Cut through the stomach and remove the entrails. Soak the cleaned, skinned rabbit in cold water for 2 to 3 hours before cooking. Rabbits have little natural fat and need frequent basting if they are to be roasted.

Rooks: No close season. Young rooks make a good pie. Use rooks that have got their feathers, skin and clean them and stew the birds under a pie crust.

Snipe: 12 August to 31 January. 99 to 128 g. Although small, snipe make good and rich eating. Leave the heads on and the entrails inside, and skewer the long beak through the legs.

Squirrel: No close season. 0.4 to 0.9 kg. Skin and clean in the same way as rabbit. Roast or stew.

Swan: Most swans in this country are protected and the property of the Queen. Their flesh is dark and has a fishy flavour, although the meat of the breast is similar to fillet of venison in texture.

Widgeon and teal: 1 September to 31 January. 312 g to 1.25 kg.

Woodcock: England and Wales, 1 October to 31 January; Scotland, 1 September to 31 January. 227 to 400 g. The entrails give flavour to the bird and should be left in. The head is left on the bird and the long beak skewered through the legs. The top of the head can be sliced off the cooked bird and the brains scooped out to make delicious and nourishing eating.

Venison

Roe deer: Buck, no statutory season in England; in Scotland, 1 May to 20 October. Doe, 1 November to 28 February in England and 21 October to 28 February in Scotland. Average weight 15 to 23 kg.

Fallow deer: Wild buck or park buck, 1 August to 30 April in England and Scotland. Wild doe and park doe, 1 November to 28 February in England and 1 October to 15 February in Scotland. Weight varies between 38 and 95 kg.

Red deer: Wild stag and park stag, 1 August to 30 April in England and 1 July to 20 October in Scotland. Wild hind and park hind, 1 November to 28 February in England and 1 October to 15 February in Scotland. Weight varies between 64 and 153 kg.

Deer should be bled, skinned, cleaned, and hung for 2 to 3 weeks before eating. To skin, cut the throat of the deer as soon as it has been killed and allow the blood to flow out freely. Cut a slit through the stock of the animal and remove all the entrails and organs, paying particular attention to the bowels, which can taint the flesh. Remove the feet and hang the animal from the hocks. Carefully cut a handful of skin from the flesh around the thighs, using a sharp knife. Peel off the rest of the skin by pulling with one hand and easing the skin away with the thumb of the other hand. In the case of an old animal, or one that has been allowed to get cold before skinning, the skin may have to be cut from the flesh, but the hand process is preferable whenever possible.

The heart and liver should be kept for eating. Deer are butchered in the same way as beef and the best cuts should be roasted. Tougher cuts can be marinated and stewed.

Nuts

Acorns (Quercus robur) : Acorns are extremely bitter to eat, but their fruit has been ground to make flour, or chopped, roasted and then ground to make a bitter coffee (see page 71).

Beechnuts (Fugus sylvatica) : Although small, the beechnut is remarkably high in proteins and can make a valuable food for domestic animals or for humans.

The oil from beechnuts has a distinctive but not unpleasant flavour. During the war it was so highly prized in Germany that children were given holidays from school in the autumn in order to gather them.

Beech trees fruit only once in every three or four years, and the nuts should be gathered soon after they have fallen, before they dry out. The nuts can yield as much as 17 to 20 per cent of their own volume as an oil that is extremely rich in protein, vitamins and minerals.

The raw nut has a slightly bitter flavour which goes when it is roasted, and the oil has keeping qualities superior to most vegetable oils. It should be stored in sterilized jars and tightly covered. Beechnut oil makes an excellent salad dressing and can be used for frying or other cooking.

Remove any husk, earth, leaves, etc and roast the nuts in a moderately hot oven. Grind the nuts through a mincing machine or in an electric liquidizer. Place the nut pulp in a muslin bag, place it in a strong sieve and press down with a heavy weight to extract the oil.

The nuts can also be peeled and roasted to eat with salads.

Hazel or cobnuts (Corylus avellana): Nut trees or nutalls are plentiful in the hedgerows throughout Britain and their fruit makes good eating, provided you harvest it before the squirrels or jays do. Like all nuts, hazels are rich in protein (weight for weight they contain 50 per cent more protein than an egg) and in fats. They should be picked in late September when the nuts are just turning brown and the fruit is full and firm. Store hazels in the shells, but without the husks, in a cool, dry place. Chop shelled hazel nuts to eat in muesli, salads and in place of almonds. To make a delicious protein drink, use 2 parts shelled hazel nuts to 6 parts milk and 2 parts honey. Grind the nuts until they are fine and then blend in the honey and milk.

Sweet or Spanish chestnut (Castanea sativa): Fairly plentiful through-out Britain, with the nuts conspicuous for their casings of bright green spines. The nuts are ripe to eat in late October or November, when they fall to the ground and the casing splits open. Chestnuts can be eaten raw, with the shell and slightly bitter inner skin removed, or they can be nicked with a sharp knife and roasted or boiled until soft. The fruit is rich and nourishing and the cooked fruit can be pickled in vinegar, candied in syrup or puréed and bottled as preserves. Raw chestnuts will not keep longer than a couple of months, but the raw fruit can be shelled and dried and then reconstituted by soaking in water. Chestnut purée can be used in sandwiches in place of butter.

Walnuts (Juglans nigra): Walnut oil is highly prized in France as the main ingredient of salad dressings in the walnut-growing areas. The leaves of the walnut tree and the shells of the nuts as well as the nuts themselves have been used for extracting oil. The oil was also used in gold size and paint varnishes.

For domestic purposes, the nut, which is high in protein and vitamins, is probably the most realistic source of oil.

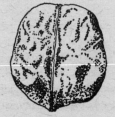

Pick ripe, damp walnuts and process them in the same way as beech nuts, but without roasting them.

Butter and cheese

Butter

Butter is made from cream, and the higher the butterfat content of your milk, the more butter it will yield. So, for example, Channel Island cattle will produce more butter per litre of milk than will, say, Friesians. However, you can make butter from any milk, cow or goat, fresh or soured.

Skim the cream from the top of the milk each day. If you leave fresh milk to stand for about an hour, the cream will settle at the top. Keep the cream cool while it is being stored and each time you add more, stir it thoroughly. Leave the cream to stand for 24 hours before you make butter and aim to make it twice a week.

Keep the cream cool while you are making butter. Its temperature should be between 11° and 19°C, cooler in warm weather; in cold weather it may be closer to the upper limit.

You do not need a churn, but if you are making a large quantity it will help. Without a churn, you can use a large mixing bowl, stirring it with a wooden spoon or with your hand (washed first, please) or you can use an electric mixer running at its slowest speed.

Paddle the cream around. After 20 to 30 minutes it will begin to turn yellow and then globules of butter will begin to form. When these are about a centimetre in diameter, stop paddling and strain off the buttermilk. What remains is butter. Now you must wash it to remove the milk that still remains.

Use a bowl of water at the same temperature as the butter. Pour the globules into the water and fold them over slowly. The water will become milky. Strain off the water and go on repeating until the water remains clear. Now you must remove the water from the butter.

Use a flat board and a flat-bladed knife or spatula. Spread the butter thinly on the board, pressing it down with the flat blade, and tilt the board so that the water runs away. Fold the butter over and then press it out again and repeat this until no more water flows from it. The more water you remove, the better the butter will keep.

The butter will also keep better if it is slightly salted. How much salt you add is a matter of personal taste and you must experiment, but to start with try about one part of salt to thirty parts of butter.

If butter does not form after you have been paddling for half an hour, it may be because the temperature is wrong, or because your equipment is not clean, or because the butterfat content of the milk is too low – in which case butter should form but will take longer.

All the equipment you use must be sterilized with boiling water, then rinsed with cold water. This will also help to prevent the butter from sticking to it.

Cream cheese and cottage cheese

Take thick cream, skimmed from the top of fresh milk. Place it in a container in cold running water to bring the temperature down to below 15°C, then keep it at that temperature for 12 hours. Make a wooden form or frame (one $46 \times 36 \times 10$ cm deep will hold the cream from 4.5 litres milk). Place a piece of fine linen across the top of the form, which should stand on a level stone or slate surface, and pour the cream into it. The cream will force the linen into the shape of the form and slab. Fold the edges of the linen loosely over the cream and place a flat wooden board on it with a 3-kg weight on top. Skim milk will drain from the sides; open the cloth once or twice in the first hour and scrape the cream from the sides to the centre to prevent the cloth from becoming clogged. After an hour add another 3-kg weight. The cheese should be ready in 3 or 4 hours. If you wish to salt the cheese, the salt must be added to the cream before you begin. Use about 6 g salt to each litre of cream. This cheese can be flavoured with wine, chopped herbs or nuts, or with practically anything.

To make cream cheese, fold thick cream into the above recipe until it forms a pat of cheese of a consistency that seems right to you.

You can make cheese from single cream, but then you must add about 1 drop of rennet (see below) for each litre of cream, and leave it to stand for 8 to 12 hours at 18°C before draining. Then the procedure is as above.

Rennet cheeses

Other hard and soft cheeses are made using rennet to curdle the milk. Its active constituent is rennin, an enzyme secreted in the fourth stomach (abomasum) of a cow. When added to milk it causes the molecules of one of the several kinds of casein in whole milk to break down. You can extract rennet by cutting up the abomasum of a calf, covering it for several days with a 10 per cent solution of brine and a preservative, such as thymol, and then removing the resulting liquid, which will have the power to curdle many times its own volume of milk.

Alternatively, you can buy extract of rennet as a liquid or as tablets, although these days it is not always easy to obtain.

If you are using Lady's Bedstraw (*Galium verum*) for dyeing (see page 121) you will need only the roots; the rest of the plant, with nettles added, can be used as a substitute for rennet.

For rennet cheeses, the milk must be ripened. Allow a quantity of fresh milk – say 4.5 litres – to stand overnight in a cool place. The next morning add an equal volume of fresh milk. The milk will be on the point of turning sour, but it should still taste sweet. If it sours too much it will be very difficult to use.

Warm the milk to about 30°C and thoroughly stir in the rennet or its equivalent. (If you are using rennet tablets, dissolve them in a little water first, then add in the proportion of half a tablet to every 9 litres of milk.) Keep the temperature absolutely constant and leave the curd to set. This will take anything from a quarter of an hour to an hour.

Cut the curd into small cubes, using a long-bladed knife, and stir the curds and whey together. Warm them gently to about 38°C after you have stirred for about 15 minutes. This heating must be very slow – let it take an hour to reach 38° and then keep it at this temperature for a further hour. The curds are now fairly firm (or they should be!). Strain off the whey by pouring curds and whey through muslin. Add salt; again, the quantity is a matter of personal taste, but try using about 30 g to 9 litres.

What happens next depends on the kind of cheese you wish to make. You must break up the curds and then squeeze them together. The looser the pieces of curd, the more crumbly will be the final cheese. To make a hard cheese, the curds are pressed together hard.

Place the curds in a piece of cheesecloth and shape them into a disc about 15 cm across. Place a second piece of cheesecloth around this. Now the cheese is ready for pressing.

If you have a genuine cheesepress, all well and good. If not, you can use an empty food can or an old saucepan. Drill holes in the bottom to allow surplus whey to drain off, and make a second cylinder or disc that fits inside the first on top of the cheese. Weight it – using bricks, perhaps – so that the weight on the cheese remains constant, even when the cheese shrinks. Make sure there are no cracks in the cheese. Allow two pressings, of about 12 hours each, turning the cheese over and doubling the pressure for the second pressing.

Place the cheese in a cool place to ripen, turning it over once a day for the first few days, then once every three or four days. When the cheese is firm and hard, it is ready to eat. This will take three to four weeks. You can now preserve it further by dipping it into a bath of paraffin wax. The cheese will taste better if you can manage to wait for two months before eating it.

Yogurt

To make yogurt, bring 1 litre of milk to the boil, cool it to 35°C, stir into it $1\frac{1}{2}$ teaspoons of plain live yogurt, and keep it at that temperature for about eight hours. A wide-necked thermos flask is a good container for this.

Breadmaking

Most of the bread eaten in this country is white bread made from imported, hard wheat; the soft wheats produced in this country have less rising and elastic properties, and less gluten. Wholemeal flour, which can be produced in this country, is undoubtedly better for you than white flour. It is only habit that has made the consumption of white bread as high as it is.

Bread is a staple part of our diet and provides much of the starch and bulk needed in our everyday diet. Risen bread is lighter to eat and far more easily digested than unleavened bread, and therefore far more palatable; it is for this reason that yeast is used in bread making in order to produce the carbon dioxide gas which makes the dough rise if it is left to stand in a temperature of between 24° and 27°C.

Yeasts

The earliest known and most universally used forms of raising agent are members of a fungi family – minute, microscopic plants made of one cell which reproduce at an incredible speed if given the right conditions. In the wild, yeasts are found in the soil, in the skins of fruit (the 'bloom') and in dust. The wild yeasts are cultivated to get baker's and brewer's yeast. Before the special baker's yeast was cultivated, the yeast in the froth from beer (today found only in out-of-the-barrel beers – Bass Red Label and Worthington Blue Label beers) was used, but this needed longer to rise and is not as good a raising agent as special baker's yeast. Baker's yeast can work only when it is alive, so it must be fresh to multiply. Yeast needs sugar, flour, water and warmth before baking. Fresh yeast will keep for 2 to 3 days in the refrigerator and can be bought from bakers or some dairies. As a substitute, dried yeast can be used to make dough rise, although it is not as strong as fresh yeast. Baking powder is used as an alternative form of raising agent.

Successful bread making

Use fresh yeast whenever possible. Have all the ingredients warmed to 26°C (tepid to the touch) and maintain this temperature throughout the mixing and rising process: too high a temperature will kill the enzymes in the yeast. Use yeast in the following proportions for a plain bread: 14 g yeast to 450 g flour; 28 g yeast to 1.35 kg flour; 42 g yeast to 2.7 kg flour.

The dough should be soft and pliable but not sticky. Knead dough with the flat of the thumbs, the palms of the hands and the knuckles for at least 10 minutes so that the yeast cells are distributed evenly through the mixture and the gluten of the flour is strengthened. Place the dough in a greased, warmed basin and cover with a cloth dusted with flour. Leave it to rise in a temperature of 26°C, until it has doubled its bulk, before baking.

Bake the bread in a very hot oven.

For making white bread a 'strong' flour should be used.

Bread recipe

450 g plain 'strong' flour or wholemeal flour, or half and half; 2 teaspoons salt; 14 g fresh yeast; 0.25 litres water.

This quantity makes two 285-g loaves. Warm two baking tins, grease lightly and dredge with flour. Warm the flour and sieve into a warmed bowl with the salt. Warm the water to blood temperature. Add 2 teaspoons of this water to the yeast and mix to a smooth cream. Stir in half the remaining water.

Make a well in the centre of the flour, pour in the yeast-and-water mixture and add the remaining water, after using it to swill out any yeast left in the bowl in which it was creamed. Mix the flour into the yeast mixture, drawing it in from the sides of the bowl and mixing with the hands in a clawing movement with the fingers separated. Beat until the dough stops sticking to the fingers.

Turn the dough on to a well floured board for 10 minutes, lifting one end and pummelling it into the other, turning the dough all the time and punching it thoroughly until it is smooth and elastic. Halve the kneaded dough, make into a roll, press the ends of each roll into the centre and drop the dough into the greased tins without touching the top. Leave the dough to rise, covered with a floured cloth, in a temperature of 26°C, for 45 minutes or until it has doubled in size. Brush with cold water for a hard crust and bake in a hot oven (230°C, 450°F, gas mark 8) for 35 minutes or until the bottom crust sounds hollow when tapped. Cool on a wire rack.

This mixture can be used to make cottage loaves, rolls or stock loaves.

Grain mills

You do not need to mill your grain in large quantities, certainly not the grain intended for human consumption. A small mill in the kitchen, rather like a coffee mill, will allow you to grind grain as it is needed, and to use it when it is fresh. The difference between freshly ground grain and grain that has been stored as flour is similar to the difference between freshly ground coffee and coffee that has been stored ready ground.

By grinding the grain yourself you can choose how coarse or fine it will be; a good mill will produce grain as fine as talc.

Just like a large mill, a small hand mill consists of two stones, one of which is fixed and one of which rotates. The lower, fixed stone is convex in shape and the upper, rotating stone is concave to fit over it, so that the grain entering at the centre moves downwards and outwards as it is ground. The grain enters the stones through a hole in the upper stone. The stones themselves must be made of the hardest rock obtainable. Commercially, flakes of emery are often embedded in hardened magnesite cement, to give a stone that wears very slowly indeed.

Your hand mill will grind not only wheat, but also barley, rye, oats (with their hulls removed), rice, buckwheat, soya beans, maize, and any other grain or bean.

The economical use of an animal carcass

Butchery is a fine art and if you wish to freeze a bullock or sheep it is advisable to have the butchering done by a professional for a fee, rather than to try to do the job yourself. The better the butcher, the less waste there will be on the carcass, so expert butchering will pay off in the long run (for the really ambitious, though, see page 40).

Anybody who plans to freeze a considerable quantity of meat should attend a course of lessons in butchering.

Nearly every bit of meat on sheep, bullocks or pigs can be utilized, although, during the past decade, we have grown so lazy that we ignore even some of the most delicious offal like brains and sweetbreads; it is almost impossible to find pig's trotters in the average butcher's shop and difficult to track down even a meaty oxtail. Cow heel and pig's trotters make good eating and produce a rich, strong gelatine that is both nourishing and excellent for making such items as brawns. Calves' and sheep's heads can make delicious meals and a stuffed ox heart will provide plenty of food for an average family for at least two meals. Excess fat on cuts of meat can be rendered down and strained through muslin for use as cooking and frying fat. With a little trouble, all left-overs can make first-rate dishes and all bones should be boiled to make stock that has a high nutritional value.

Far too little use is made of even an ordinary chicken carcass these days. The giblets, for instance, can be boiled to make a rich stock for gravy; three or four sets of giblets (which can be stockpiled in a deep freeze) make an aromatic stew. The chicken carcass itself can be boiled after it has been served as a main meal to make the base of a chicken soup to which any left-overs, chopped finely, can be added. Minced, cold chicken can be stretched by the addition of a little minced bacon and some fresh breadcrumbs to make any number of interesting dishes.

Even the cheaper cuts of beef, lamb and pork are often ignored. Belly of pork stuffed or roasted plain makes a good hot or cold meal; shin beef can be stewed or potted, and scrag end of lamb was once one of the most popular British dishes in the form of Lancashire hot pot. The marrow bones of beef were also once prized highly as a savoury dish; with the bones cut into 15-cm lengths and boiled in a light stock, not only does the marrow make a delicious meal, seasoned and spread on toast, but the resulting stock itself can be strained and used as a rich soup base. Those who keep their own sheep will find it worth while to keep an animal or two until they reach the mutton stage of growth as the meat is far more flavourful, infinitely richer, and has a more economical ratio of meat to bone.

Modern cookery books refer all too seldom to cooking with these cheaper cuts and to cooking with offal, but there are many excellent Victorian and Edwardian books, sold now in facsimile editions, which can be used as a guide to getting the best possible value out of any cut of meat, from the lights to a piece of skirt.

Edible wild plants

Many species of wild plants are threatened with extinction and all are growing more scarce. Do not pick them in any location where they are not common and plentiful. At present, the picking of some plants and the uprooting of many is not only antisocial, it is also illegal.

Horseradish (Armoracia rusticana): Found on waste ground throughout England and Wales. The roots peeled and grated can be used as an accompanying sauce for beef (combine grated horseradish with cream or yogurt) or as a spice in preparing a marinade or devil sauce.

Wild parsnip (Pastinaca sativa): Found on waste ground and grassland in south and east England. Dig up the roots after the first frosts. Peel and cube the roots, boil in water until soft and rub through a rough sieve to remove any tough fibres. To roast wild parsnips, remove the tough central core, cube the remaining flesh and roast in a little fat.

Dandelion (Taraxacum officinale): Found all over England, Scotland, Wales and Ireland. Use the young leaves as a salad ingredient or braise as a vegetable. Use the roots as a vegetable: scrub them, cut the flesh into thin slices and braise in a little stock until tender. The roots can also be made into a substitute coffee (see page 71).

White waterlily (Nymphaea alba): Found in many country ponds. Use the underwater tubers as a vegetable. Peel and chop the tubers and cook them until they are tender in boiling salted water.

Wild turnip (Brassica rapa): Found throughout the British Isles. Use the tender young leaves as a green vegetable; the roots, peeled and chopped, can be boiled or roasted.

Bitter vetch (Lathyrus montanus): Found on moor and heathland. Peel and chop the roots to use as a boiled vegetable.

Silverweed (Potentilla anserina): Grows on damp wasteland. The starchy roots can be used in place of potatoes or can be dried and ground to make substitute flour.

Herb Bennet (Geum urbanum): Found in woodland. Peel and chop the roots and use in small quantities to give flavour to soups and stews.

Large evening primrose (Oenothera erythrosepala): Grows on wasteland and roadsides. Boil the roots and young shoots to use as vegetables.

Sea holly (Eryngium maritimum): Found along the sandy sea shores. The roots can be peeled and boiled until soft and were once made into sweetmeats by boiling the softened roots in a strong sugar syrup.

Pignut (Conopodium majus): Found in woods, meadows and heathland. The peeled tubers can be eaten raw or boiled in soup to give flavour.

Spignel-meu (Meum athamanticum): Found in Scotland and on high ground. The aromatic roots can be used as a vegetable by peeling, chopping and boiling until tender.

Ox-eye daisy (Chrysanthemum leucanthemum): Found throughout the British Isles. Use the boiled, sliced roots as a salad ingredient.

Flowering rush (Butomus umbellatus): Found on the edge of ponds and rivers and in marshy ground. Use the roots as a vegetable, peeled, chopped and boiled.

Galingale (Cyperus longus): Found in the southwest of England. Dry and grind the roots to use as a seasoning for sweet or savoury dishes.

Salsify (Tragopogon porrifolius): Found mainly in south England in rough, grassy land. The long thin roots make the most delicious and sophisticated eating. Peel the roots and drop them immediately into cold water to which some lemon juice has been added. Boil the roots until tender and eat them with butter.

Common Star of Bethlehem (Ornithogalum umbellatum): Found mainly in East Anglia in rough grassland. Peel the bulbs and use as a boiled vegetable.

Early purple orchid (Orchis mascula): Found throughout the British Isles in damp places. The peeled roots can be dug after flowering and used raw or boiled as a salad ingredient or as a vegetable. The roots can also be dried and ground to make a rough flour.

Lords and ladies (Arum maculatum): Found in shady places through-out the British Isles. Peel the roots and bake in a moderate oven until absolutely tender in order to counteract any poisonous element in the plant. The baked roots can be used as a substitute for arrowroot as a thickening agent for soups, stews and sauces.

Watercress (Rorippa nasturium-aquaticum): Grows throughout the British Isles in and beside streams or rivers, but should not be picked near where sheep are grazing. Use as a salad ingredient, picking the dark, mature leaves and removing any tough stems, or as a vegetable in the same way as spinach.

White mustard (Sinapis alba): Plentiful in arable land and chalk soils. Pick the young leaves to use as a salad ingredient.

Hairy bittercress (Cardamine hirsuta): Plentiful in rocky and sand dune areas. Use like watercress as a salad ingredient.

Common wintercress (Barbarea vulgaris): Found by streams and in hedge banks. Use like watercress as a salad ingredient or a green vegetable.

Jack-by-the-hedge (Alliaria petiolata): Found on the edge of woods and in hedge banks. Use the leaves as a garlic flavouring for salads or in sauces.

Lime (Tilia europaea): Found in parks and woods. Use the leaves as a salad ingredient and the flowers as tea (see page 69).

Wood sorrel (Oxalis acetosella): Found in woods and other shady situations. Use the leaves as a salad ingredient or boil and purée them to make a delicious sauce (see page 99)

Wild strawberry (Frageria vesca): Found in heathlands, grassy fields, woods and hedgerows. Eat the fruit and use the leaves as a green vegetable.

Parsley piert (Aphanes arvensis): Found on dry, stony ground. The leaves can be used medicinally as a preventative for kidney stones and can be chopped and used as a salad herb.

Salad burnet (Sanguisorba minor): Found in grassy places on chalk soil. Use the leaves, slightly braised, as a salad ingredient, or as the base of a cool summer drink.

Brooklime (Veronica beccabunga): Found by streams and in damp meadows. Use like watercress as a salad ingredient.

Cornsalad (Valerianella locusta): Found in dry land on banks and walls. Use the leaves, whole, as a salad ingredient.

Hawthorn (Crataegus monogyna): Found throughout the British Isles. Use the young leaves as a salad ingredient or as a green vegetable.

Beech (Fagus sylvatica): Found in woods throughout the British Isles. Use the young leaves as a salad ingredient or as a green vegetable.

Chicory (Cichorium intybus): Found in grassy wasteland and chalk soil. Use the leaves as a salad ingredient. The roots can be dried and ground to make a coffee substitute (see page 71).

Nipplewort (Lapsana communis): Found by roadsides, hedgerows and banks. Use the leaves as a salad ingredient.

Cat's-ear (Hypochaeris radicata): Found in the edge of woods and on grassland. Use the leaves as a salad ingredient.

Rough hawkbit (Leontodon hispidus): Found by roadsides and in dry grassland. Use the leaves as a salad ingredient.

Wall lettuce (Mycelis muralis): Found in walls and on stony ground. Use the leaves as a salad ingredient.

Greater prickly lettuce (Lactuca virosa): Found near the sea on chalk soil. Use the leaves as a salad ingredient.

Corn sow-thistle (Sonchus arvensis): Found by the roadside and in any cultivated ground. Trim off the bristles from the edges of young leaves and use as a salad ingredient.

Garden cress (Lepidium sativum): Use the young leaves as a salad ingredient.

Common scurvy-grass (Cochlearia officinalis): As its name suggests, this plant has a high concentration of Vitamin C; the leaves can be eaten raw, dried or used in drinks. The taste is bitter but the results are satisfactory as a safeguard against scurvy.

Golden saxifrage (Chrysosplenium oppositifolium): Found in damp, shady highlands. The leaves can be used as a salad ingredient or boiled to make a green vegetable.

Wintergreen (Pyrola minor): Found in the north of England, on the moors in Scotland and in conifer woods. Use the leaves as a salad ingredient or as a substitute for tea. The berries can also be eaten and make a good pie filling.

Yarrow (Achillea millefolium): Use the leaves, first removing them from the tough stem, as a boiled vegetable.

Sea spinach (Beta vulgaris): Found in England and Wales near the sea shore. Use the leaves in the same way as spinach as a vegetable, soup base or tart filling.

Fat hen (Chenopodium album): Grows on waste land. The leaves are full of protein, vitamins and iron, and should be used in the same way as spinach.

Good King Henry (Chenopodium bonushenricus): Grows by roadsides and in cultivated ground. Use the leaves like spinach or as a salad ingredient when they are young.

Sea purslane (Halimione portulacoides): Found in salt marshes in southern England. Use the leaves as a salad ingredient only.

Chickweed (Stellaria media): Found throughout the British Isles. Use the leaves as a green vegetable, cooking them in a little boiling water.

Shepherd's purse (Capsella bursa-pastoris): Use the chopped leaves like cabbage.

Rosebay (Epilobium angustifolium): Grows on heathland and in waste places. Use the young leaves as a green vegetable.

Hogweed (Heraclium sphondylium): Found in hedgerows and grassy places. Use the leaves, picked young, as a green vegetable.

Hop (Humulus lupulus): Found in hedges and copses. Pick the young shoots and leaves as a green vegetable or use as an addition to vegetable soup.

Stinging nettle (Urtica dioica): Common throughout Britain. Use the young shoots to make a soup (see page 98) or use as a green vegetable in the same way as spinach.

Comfrey (Symphytum officinale): Found in ditches and other damp situations. Use the leaves like spinach.

Pigweed (Amaranthus retroflexus): Found in waste ground. The leaves can be used like spinach and the black seeds can be dried and ground into a flour.

Curled dock (Rumex crispus) and *Common dock (Rumex obtusifolius):* Found throughout the British Isles. Use the young leaves as a green vegetable.

Lungwort (Pulmonaria officinalis): Widely spread. Use the leaves as a green vegetable.

Oyster plant (Mertensia maritima): Found along some stretches of coastline. Use the raw leaves as a salad ingredient or cook them like spinach.

Goosegrass (Galium aparine): Common throughout the British Isles. The young leaves make an acceptable green vegetable and the seeds can be used as a coffee substitute (see page 71).

Red valerian (Centranthus ruber): Found in the southwest of England on walls and in rocky places. The very young leaves can be used as a green vegetable.

Sea kale (Crambe maritima): Found throughout the British Isles on the sea shore. Strip the leaves from the stems and boil the stems until tender.

Marsh samphire, Glasswort (Salicornia europaea): Found on salt marshes. Cook the young stems like sea kale. Very young stems can be cooked with the leaves and roots on.

Alexanders (Smyrnium olusatrum): Found in hedgerows and waste-land near the coastline. Use the leaves as a herb to give flavouring. Cook the young stems in boiling water until tender.

Rock samphire (Crithmum maritimum): Found on rocky places near the coastline in the southern part of the British Isles. Cook the young stems and leaves in boiling water or pickle in brine to preserve.

Lesser Burdock (Arctium minus): Found on the edges of woods, road-sides and waste ground. Cut young stems into 5-cm lengths, peel off the outer skin and boil until tender. The stalks of the flowers can also be used.

Marsh thistle (Cirsium palustre): Found throughout the British Isles. Prepare the stems like those of burdock and use raw in salads or boiled as a vegetable.

Rock tripe (Umblicaria pustulata): Full of nourishment. Wash and boil until tender.

Seaweeds

Carragheen moss (Chondrus crispus): A source of vegetable gelatine which can be used to make both sweet and savoury dishes. Wash the carragheen, combine it with two parts milk or water and sugar or seasoning and simmer slowly until the carragheen dissolves. Strain and leave to set firm. The carragheen can also be dried and stored, and the fresh seaweed has been used to make edible sausage skins.

Dulse (Rhodymenia palmata): Use raw in salads or fry the fronds and crumble them to make a savoury relish.

Kelp (Laminaria digitata): Use as carragheen or raw, chopped, as a salad ingredient.

Laver (Porphyra umbilicala): Use as a base for a sauce or as a bread substitute. Boil the laver to make a thick purée.

Sea lettuce (Ulva lactuca): Use as a green vegetable.

Flowers (see also page 68 for substitutes for tea)

Broom (Cytisus scoparius): Use the tight buds as salad or as a pickle.

95

Cowslip (Primula veris) and *Primrose (Primula vulgaris)*: Use as a drink base or as a flavouring.

Dog rose (Rosa canina): Use the petals in salads or to make jam.

Elder (Sambucus nigra): Use the muscat-scented flowers to make a summer drink, in fritters (see page 99) or as a champagne base.

Violet (Viola odorata): Make into candied sweets or use as a garnish.

Herbs

The following herbs have been used for culinary purposes in the British Isles. Strip off the leaves and use fresh or dried as flavouring.

Balm *(Melissa officinalis)*
Borage *(Borago officinalis)*
Common calamint *(Calamintha sylvatica)*
Corn mint *(Mentha arvensis)*
Cow parsley *(Anthriscus sylvestris)*
Fennel *(Foeniculum vulgare)*
Fenugreek *(Trigonella ornithopodioides)*
Ground ivy *(Glechoma hederacea)*
Horse-mint *(Mentha longifolia)*
Lady's bedstraw *(Galium verum)*
Lovage *(Ligusticum scoticum)*
Marjoram *(Origanum vulgare)*
Meadowsweet *(Filipendula ulmaria)*
Pennyroyal *(Mentha pulegium)*
Peppermint *(Mentha piperita)*
Ramsons *(Allium ursinum)*
Sand leek *(Allium scorodoprasum)*
Spearmint *(Mentha spicata)*
Sweet Cicely *(Myrrhis odorata)*
Sweet gale *(Myrica gale)*
Tansy *(Tanacetum vulgare)*
Water mint *(Mentha aquatica)*
Whorled mint *(Mentha verticillata)*
Wild angelica *(Angelica sylvestris)*
Wild basil *(Clinopodium vulgare)*
Wild celery *(Apium graveolens)*
Wild garlic *(Allium oleraceum)*
Wild thyme *(Thymus serpyllum)*
Woodruff *(Galium odoratum)*
Wormwood *(Artemisia absinthium)*

Spices

Use the dried seeds of the following plants to give flavour. Dry the plant and then shake out the dried seeds.

Black mustard *(Brassica nigra)*
Coriander *(Coriandrum sativum)*
Poppy *(Papaver rhoeas)*

Juniper berries can be dried, crushed and used as a flavouring for many meat dishes.

Fungi

There are over a hundred well-flavoured edible fungi in Great Britain and, contrary to general belief, there are in fact very few species which are deadly poisonous. To be on the safe side, however, a good field guide to fungi should always be consulted when collecting, and the mushrooms or toadstools should always be picked when large enough to give a positive identification. Fleshy fungi can be dried for storage and reconstituted by soaking in water. Slice the fungi, thread them on cotton and hang them in a warm, dry place. The following is a short list of the edible wild mushrooms and fungi most valuable for cooking purposes. Clean fungi well before using them and cook all varieties before eating. Except for field mushrooms, beech, conifer and other woodlands make the best hunting grounds for edible fungi.

Beefsteak fungus *(Fistulina hepatica)*
Cep *(Boletus)*: A large family of fungi with a thick, yellowish, sponge-like texture under the cap.
Chanterelle *(Cantharellus cibarius)*
Common puff ball *(Lycoperdon perlatum)*
Field mushroom *(Agaricus camperstris)*
Giant puff ball *(Lycoperdon perlatum)*: Pick while it is still white all over.
Horn of plenty *(Craterellus cornucopoides)*
Horse mushroom *(Agaricus arvensis)*: The common mushroom.
Ink cap *(Coprinus comatus)*
Morel *(Morchella esculenta)*: Distinctive because of its honeycomb-shaped cap.
Parasol mushroom *(Lepiota procera)*
Shaggy parasol *(Lepiota rhacodes)*

Fruits

Barberry *(Berberis vulgaris)*

Bilberry – also known as blueberry, whortleberry, hurts or worts *(Vaccinium myrtillus)*
Blackberry *(Rubus fruticosus)*
Blackcurrant *(Ribes nigrum)*
Cherry-plum *(Prunus cerasifera)*
Cherry, wild *(Prunus avium)*
Cloudberry *(Rubus chamaemorus)*
Crab apple *(Malus sylvestris)*
Cranberry *(Vaccinium oxycoccus)*
Dewberry *(Rubus caesius)*
Elder *(Sambucus nigra)*
Gooseberry *(Ribes uva-crispa)*
Hawthorn *(Crataegus monogyna)*
Oregon grape *(Mahonia aquifolium)*
Redcurrant *(Ribes rubrum)*
Rose hip *(Rosa canina)*
Rowanberry *(Sorbus aucuparia)*
Sloe *(Prunus spinosa)*
Snowberry *(Symphoricarpos rivularis)*
Whitebeam *(Sorbus aria)*
Wild raspberry *(Rubus idaeus)*
Wild strawberry *(Fragaria vesca)*

A meal based on wild foods

This meal for four people includes some ingredients which are usually at hand in the larder, but it aims to show how very well balanced and delicious food produced from natural, wild ingredients can be.

Nettle soup

500 g nettle tops, 1 small onion, 25 g butter, 1 litre stock, salt, pepper, pinch of ground nutmeg, 2 tablespoons cream

Remove any stalks from the nettles, wash the leaves and dry them well. Peel and finely chop the onion. Melt the butter in a saucepan, fry the onion until soft and add the nettles. Cook for 2 minutes, add the stock and mix well. Bring to the boil, cover and simmer for 20 minutes or so until the nettles are soft. Purée through a fine sieve, a food mill or in a liquidizer, and return to a clean pan. Heat, season with salt, pepper and a little nutmeg, and stir in some cream just before serving.

Rabbit with sorrel sauce

1 rabbit; milk, flour, salt and pepper; butter or oil for frying;
2 handfuls sorrel, 14 g butter, 1 tablespoon flour, 3 dl milk,
pinch of mace (optional)

Joint the rabbit and soak in milk for 30 minutes. Drain and pat dry.
Coat the joints in seasoned flour and cook in butter or oil for about
20 minutes over a medium heat until they are tender.

Wash the sorrel and remove any tough stalks. Chop the leaves
finely. Melt the butter in a saucepan; add the sorrel and cook over a
low heat for 3 minutes. Mix in the flour and gradually blend in the
milk. Stir continuously over a medium heat until the sauce comes to
the boil and is thick and smooth. Season with salt, pepper and a pinch
of mace (this is optional).

Serve the rabbit with the sorrel sauce poured over it and accompanied by roast wild parsnips and a wild green vegetable or leaf salad
with chopped nuts. Pickled broom or gorse buds also go well with
this dish.

Elderflower fritters

2 dozen elderflower clusters; 2 eggs, pinch of salt, 3 dl milk,
1 teaspoon melted butter, 100 g flour; oil for deep frying

Remove the main flower stalks, leaving the flowers intact in clusters.
Wash them gently in cold water and shake to remove excess moisture.
Beat the eggs well, mix in the salt, milk and melted butter and
gradually blend in the flour to make a smooth batter. Dip the flowers
into the batter and fry in deep oil for a few minutes until they are
golden-brown. Sprinkle them with sugar and serve as soon as possible.

A vegetarian menu

Meatless meals contain all the nutrients needed for a balanced diet,
can be made both interesting and delicious, and are cheaper than
meals incorporating meat. There are meat substitutes made from
spinning the fibres of soya beans with added flavouring, but although
these have a high protein content, they tend to have a 'false' taste and
an unattractive texture, so that a *fresh* vegetable dish is much more
acceptable.

The following menu is for four people.

Individual cheese soufflés

100 g butter, 50 g flour, 5 dl milk; 4 eggs; 100 g grated Gruyère or Cheddar cheese; salt, pepper and 1 teaspoon made English mustard

Melt the butter in a saucepan. Add the flour and mix well until the mixture forms a ball and leaves the side of the pan. Gradually stir in the milk and cook over a medium heat until the mixture is thick and smooth. Remove from the heat and leave to cool. Separate the egg yolks from the whites. Beat 3 of the yolks one by one into the mixture until each has blended in. Add the grated cheese and mix well. Season with salt, pepper and mustard. Beat the egg whites until stiff and fold them gently into the cheese mixture, using a fork. Pour into buttered ramekins, being careful not to fill each one more than half full. Bake for 20 minutes in a moderate oven (190°C, 375°F, gas mark 5). Serve immediately.

Crackerjack

225 g haricot beans, 2 carrots, 1 large onion, 4 medium potatoes, 2 mushrooms, 3 ripe tomatoes; 50 g butter; 5 dl stock, 3 tablespoons tomato purée, 1 tablespoon cider vinegar; salt and pepper; 50 g grated cheese (optional)

Soak the beans overnight in cold water and drain off excess water. Generously grease a casserole with a lid. Peel and slice the carrots lengthwise. Peel and finely chop the onion. Peel and thinly slice the potatoes, thinly slice the mushrooms and skin and slice the tomatoes.

Heat the butter in a frying pan, add the onions and cook over a medium heat until the onions are soft and transparent. Remove onions with a slotted spoon. Add the stock and tomato purée to the juices in the pan, mixing well; bring to the boil, mix in the cider vinegar and season with salt and pepper.

Arrange the soaked beans, the onions, carrots, mushrooms, and tomatoes in layers in the casserole, top with the potatoes and pour the stock over it. Sprinkle with cheese if desired, cover tightly and bake in a slow oven (140°C, 275°F, gas mark 1) for 2½ hours. Remove the cover and cook for a further 15 minutes, or until the potatoes are crisp and golden brown.

Serve with peas, French beans, cabbage, spinach or broad beans and a crisp mixed salad.

Honeyed fresh fruit salad

2.5 dl water, 1 tablespoon clear honey, 50 g sugar; juice of 1 lemon; any combination of fresh fruit, peeled and cut into small dice or thin slices as necessary

Combine the water, honey and sugar in a saucepan and heat until the sugar melts. Add lemon juice and leave to cool. Prepare the fruit (halve grapes and remove the pips, peel, core and dice apples, etc), adding the fruit to the syrup as it is prepared. Chill the fruit salad for at least 4 hours before serving with cream.

Home-made wines

Dried basic ingredients for making grape wine can be bought from chemists or shops specializing in home-made wine, but wines made from hand-picked fresh ingredients are infinitely preferable. Almost any fruit, vegetable or flower can be made into wine: carrots, for instance, produce a good flavour; redcurrant wine is delicious, and elderflower 'champagne' a first-rate summer drink. Most vegetables need the addition of brewer's yeast to set off the fermentation process, but some fruit and flowers contain their own natural yeast, which is often more than adequate to ferment the liquid.

Very little equipment is needed when making wine on a small scale, but it is important to bear in mind that metal containers, or metal of any kind, should never be used once fermentation has begun, as it will produce a tainted flavour and may even destroy the fermentation. A large polythene vessel or bucket can be used for fermentation purposes; gallon glass wine jars can often be bought cheaply from wine merchants and old wine or cordial bottles, provided they have been well cleaned, will provide adequate containers for the final brew. For many wines a fermentation lock is an essential piece of equipment; it cuts off the oxygen supply to the yeast in the liquid. This can be bought from a firm specializing in wine-making equipment or from many chemists. To be more scientific about making wine at home, a hydrometer is also required to test the alcoholic content of the wine.

Any other utensils required, such as funnels, will probably be available in the home, but it is important to stress the absolute necessity of sterilizing all the equipment used in making wine.

The yeast that is all-important to many wines can be bought from home wine-making suppliers, and the better the yeast the better the wine will be; with good yeast, a home wine-maker can hope to produce an alcohol content of 26° proof.

Grapes combined with wild fruits such as sloes make delicious wine and so do combinations of wild leaves and flowers; many traditional recipes use a combination of wild ingredients and raisins to make a more fortified wine.

Once you have embarked on home wine-making there is an infinite number of variations which make use of the most modest of ingredients to make good drinks. Flowers and plants to be used in home-made wines should be gathered after the dew has dried, but before the heat of the sun has dried them out.

Broom bud wine

Broom buds have a slightly almond flavour and make a delicious base for a home-made wine that is richly golden in colour.

4.5 litres broom flowers; 4.5 litres water; 1.35 kg sugar; juice and rind of 2 lemons and 2 oranges; 2 packets yeast

Combine the sugar, water, thinly pared lemon and orange rinds; bring to the boil and boil for 30 minutes. Cool the mixture to blood temperature. Place the broom flowers in a clean container and pour over them the lukewarm liquid. Mix the yeast with a little of the liquid and stir it into the flower mixture. Cover the container and leave to ferment for 10 days in a warm place.

Strain the fermented liquid into a scrupulously clean container, pressing out as much juice as possible from the flowers. Cover the container tightly, seal it well and leave for six months. Bottle the wine very carefully, pouring it gently so that the sediment remains in the bottom of the container and the wine is clear.

Elderflower 'champagne'

This wine requires no yeast.

6 elderflower heads; 900 g loaf sugar; 2 tablespoons white vinegar; 4.5 litres cold water; 2 large lemons

Pick elderflowers when they are fully out and shake to remove any insects. Place the elderflowers in a large, clean container. Add the lemons, cut into thin slices, the sugar, the water and the vinegar, and mix well. Cover and leave to stand for 24 hours. Strain off carefully and pour into bottles with screw tops. Leave to stand for 2 months before drinking, checking the screw tops of the bottles every few days to release any excess 'fizz' which might cause the bottles to burst.

Home-made liqueurs

Most liqueurs are made by adding fresh ingredients to alcohol, producing richly flavoured drinks with a high alcohol content.

Sloe gin, for example, is made by adding 1.8 kg sloes, pricked with a knitting needle, to 4.5 litres of gin and 1.8 kg loaf sugar. Mix well and leave to stand in a tightly covered container for 6 to 12 months. Strain off the liquid and bottle.

Rose petal liqueur

5 dl rose petals; sugar; 2.5 dl water; 5 dl brandy;
1 teaspoon glycerine

Layer the rose petals in a container with a sprinkling of sugar over each layer. Cover and leave to stand for 3 days. Bring the water to the boil, add the brandy and glycerine and pour the warm mixture over the rose petals. Cover and leave to stand for a week before straining the liquid off into bottles.

Home-made beers

The art of making home-brewed beer is a satisfying and rewarding one. Even the complete amateur can produce a beer as good as any that comes out of a publican's barrel and at considerably less cost. To make life even easier for the home brewer, many firms now specialize in complete beer kits which contain everything you need for your brewing. The best beer, however, is that brewed from natural ingredients. Hops can be picked in many hedgerows and the essential malt can be bought from a good chemist or wine supply store. You can malt your own barley if you grow it.

Equipment

You need an aluminium boiler with an 18- to 22-litre capacity, or an electric boiler or immersion heater; a muslin bag in which to tie the hops; a rubber syphoning tube; a steamer; a nylon sieve; a large polythene bucket or polythene dustbin; 4.5-litre glass jars with a fermentation lock; a hydrometer.

Hard water is essential for home brewing. If your water is soft it will need a 'water treatment', which can be bought from chemists or home brewing suppliers.

The ingredients and methods of home-made beer vary according to the type of beer you wish to produce. Recipes and instructions for brewing can be found in any of the many books now available on the subject.

Perhaps the simplest way to make beer is to take 1.8 kg malt, 1.8 kg sugar (if you have plenty of malt, then substitute malt for sugar on a one-for-one basis, by weight) and 140 g hops. Boil all but a handful of the hops in 23 litres of water for three-quarters of an hour. Five minutes before the end, throw in the last handful to add a little extra flavour. Place the malt and sugar in the bucket or dustbin and strain the water over it, mixing well. Wait for it to cool to blood temperature, then add yeast. Cover and leave to stand in a warm place. A crust will form over the liquid. Wait until this crust has disappeared, leaving only a few bubbles in the centre. Syphon the liquid off the sediment and bottle it, adding another teaspoon of sugar for every litre of liquid, to produce a slight secondary fermentation that will give the beer 'life'. It will be ready to drink in about a week. Remember that the amount of malt or sugar you use will determine the final alcohol content – the more sugar, the more alcohol – and that the hops give beer its bitter flavour, so the more hops you use the more bitter the beer will be.

Heather ale

Fill an aluminium boiler with heather flowers and cover them with water; bring to the boil and boil for 1 hour. Strain off and measure the liquid. To every 4.5 litres liquid, add 14 g ground ginger, 1 table-spoon hops and 5.5 dl sugar syrup. Return the liquid to the boiler, bring to the boil, and strain once more. Leave it to stand until the liquid has cooled to blood temperature and mix in 50 g yeast. Cover and leave for 2 to 3 days before drinking.

Textiles

Wool

There are three main types of British fleece from which the others have been bred:

A Down breed, originating from the South Downs, which has a short staple (the staple is the length of each separate fibre), is fine and non-lustrous.

A mountain breed, such as the Welsh Mountain sheep, which gives a medium staple and is woolly and half-lustrous.

A long-staple-fleeced sheep, originating from Leicester, which gives a strong, coarse, inelastic wool, which is very lustrous.

The Down breeds are:

Southdown: Very short staple, 1.25 to 10 cm, but fine, soft, elastic and well crimped ('crimp' refers to the wave in the wool). The fleece is pure white and each sheep gives 1.4 to 2 kg of wool. It is used for lightweight tweed, scarves, socks and similar fabrics.

Shropshire: Has a good average staple length, of a soft, white, dense fleece, weighing 2.7 to 8 kg. It is used for lightweight fabrics.

Oxford Down: A medium-length fleece with a 15-cm staple, coarser than the Southdown. Used for tweeds.

Dorset Horn: Similar to the Southdown but coarser. Each fleece weighs 2.3 to 6.25 kg.

Suffolk Down: Has a staple length of 7.6 to 15 cm and the fleece weighs 2.3 to 2.7 kg. There are black hairs in the fleece, which is less fine than Southdown. Used for tweeds and upholstery.

There are three breeds that are intermediate between the **Down** breeds and the mountain breeds:

Kerry Hill: The fleece is rather like the Shropshire fleece but not quite such good quality. The staple length is 12.7 to 15 cm.

Clun Forest: A black-faced, black-legged sheep with fleeces similar to Kerry, but not so white and with a shorter staple. Each fleece weighs 1.8 to 2.6 kg.

Ryeland: This is good-quality, fine wool. The staple length is 9 to 11 cm and on average the fleece weighs 3.4 kg.

The mountain breeds are:

Welsh Mountain: Gives a good quality of wool with a short staple. The average weight of the fleece is 1 kg. There is quite a lot of kemp (coarse hair). It is used for flannels, blankets and tweeds. Some Welsh Mountain sheep are black and their wool was much used for cloth in the Middle Ages.

Cheviot: A good-quality, medium wool with a 10-cm staple and a fleece weighing around 2.7 kg. It is used for tweeds.

Scottish Blackface: A coarse, wiry, non-elastic fleece weighing 2.3 to 2.7 kg with a 20- to 25-cm staple. It is excellent for carpets.

Herdwick: Has a long-stapled, very coarse wool with some grey in the fleece.

Derbyshire Gritstone: Has a dense fleece with a medium staple and fine texture.

The long-staple-fleeced breeds are:

Leicester: Strong, lustrous wool with a 15- to 25-cm staple and a 3.6-kg fleece. It is used for heavy fabrics.

Border Leicester: A very silky fleece with a 15- to 38-cm staple, which spins to a fine, hard, silky yarn.

Lincoln: Also a very strong and lustrous fleece, which is white. The staple is 38 to 46 cm, dense and wavy. The fleece weighs 5.4 to 6.4 kg. It is used for heavy fabrics.

Devon Longwool: This is a lustrous wool, coarse, with little crimp and a long staple, 30 to 46 cm. It is good for carpets.

Wensleydale: A long staple, 20 to 30 cm. It is lustrous and strong and will spin to a fine but inelastic thread. It is used for harder types of cloth.

Cotswold: A coarse, heavy fleece, weighing on average 4.5 kg with a 30- to 36-cm staple. It is used for carpets.

Among the other sheep breeds there are:

Merino: Gives a top quality wool.

Shetland: Has a double layer of fleece. The top fleece is used for tweed, the undercoat for knitwear.

Preparing the fleece for spinning

The fleece may be taken from a live sheep or a dead one. Wool taken from a dead sheep is called 'pulled wool' and is of poorer quality because lime water is used to remove it (see page 259) and this softens the roots.

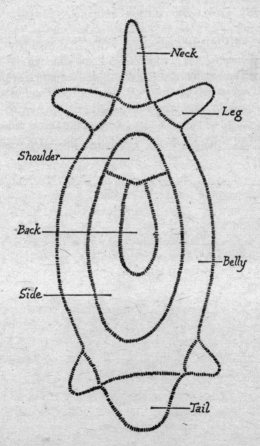

Up to half the weight of a shorn fleece may be grease and per-spiration salts, and most of the grease (lanolin) and vegetable matter remains in the fleece after shearing.

Ideally, the fleece should be removed in one piece (see page 39). It must then be sorted according to its qualities. Long-staple wool with a good crimp is the easiest to hand spin. Staple lengths can range from 3.8 to 25 cm, but the average is about 10 cm.

The quality of wool depends on the breed of the sheep and on the part of the animal from which it was removed. The best wool is found on the shoulders and back; the tail and legs have coarser wool, and the wool from the belly is fine but often felted. The coarser wool is used for making carpets; finer, softer wool is used for dress and hosiery making.

Industrially, wool is scoured before spinning. Scouring is washing in a tepid, mildly alkaline solution, such as ammonia, followed by thorough rinsing in pure, lukewarm water. The wool is well dried and oil, such as olive oil, is added to facilitate spinning. Hand-spun wool can also be scoured first (some people do not like the smell of lanolin) but in fact it is easier to spin 'in the grease' and to wash the skeins afterwards in lukewarm soapy water.

Before spinning, the wool is 'teased out'. Each tuft is pulled apart at the top, then at the bottom, to produce a thin mat of fibres ready for carding.

Carding

Cards are flat pieces of wood with handles, covered on one side with leather into which bent pins are inserted, with the hooks bending towards the handle.

The mat of fibres is laid over the bent pins of one carder, which is held in the left hand. The pins of the other carder, held in the right

wool carders

hand, are drawn across it. The bent pins work antagonistically, straightening and separating the fibres. Most of the fibres are drawn on to the right-hand carder as it pulls across the left-hand carder. The process is repeated by hooking the veil of fibres back on to the upturned left-hand carder.

When the fibres are straight enough they are unhooked from one card to the other until they can be laid easily on the back of the left-hand carder and rolled into a neat roll, or 'rolag', with the back of the right-hand carder.

Carding is well worth the effort, since it makes a considerable difference to the evenness and fineness of the yarn that can be spun.

Flax

Preparing for spinning

Linen fibre comes from the inner bark, or 'bast', of the flax plant. The plant grows to a height of 0.9 to 1.2 metres and the prepared linen fibres average 45 to 50 cm in length, made up of 5-cm fibres overlapping and joined together (see page 33 for growing flax).

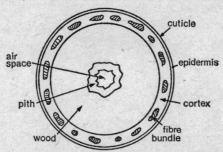

Flax must be pulled from the ground whole. Cutting shortens the fibre and reduces its quality.

The stalks are dried by stooking and then 'rippled' – drawn through iron combs to remove the seed pods, which are taken for crushing to extract linseed oil.

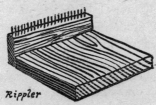

Rippler

The flax stalks are 'retted' (partly rotted) to remove the woody portion from the fibre, either by being immersed in still water in a pond or stream, or by being spread thinly on the ground ('dew retted') and left to weather. Decomposition is effected by bacteria present in the water or soil. Retting takes from two to four weeks and it is completed when the bark is loose enough to peel from the woody core. It is essential not to over-ret and spoil the fibre. The stalks are then stacked into 'wigwams' and dried thoroughly; otherwise retting will continue.

Wigwam

Then the flax is broken, or 'scutched', so as to chop up the straw and leave the fibre intact. This used to be done on an adapted heavy table with attached beater that came down into a slot in the middle of the table. An alternative is a hand beater.

Hand beater

The straw and short ends are now removed by 'hackling' or combing. Bunches of fibres are drawn through heavy combs – blocks of wood set with iron teeth. The first combing is through coarse hackles, then through progressively finer ones, until all the broken straw is removed and the long fibres, or 'line', are lying parallel and even. At this stage the flax looks like long, fair (flaxen!) hair.

Hackling

The short fibres are called 'tow' and they can be used for padding and stuffing, or else hand carded and spun into heavier yarn.

The bunch of flax is tied loosely to a distaff. The distaff is a rod which holds the flax fibres above the level of the wheel or spindle, so that the strands can be drawn out during spinning. Some wheels are fitted with a distaff arm. For spindle spinning a rod distaff is tucked under the arm, or you can devise a tall pole and tripod arrangement.

Distaff & tripod

Spinning

Spinning consists of drawing out a thin sliver of fibres, a 'roving', from the rolag, or bundles of flax, and twisting it so that the fibres, which tend to adhere to one another naturally in any case, curl round each other. With woollen fibres this can be done quite easily with the fingers. All methods of spinning are developments designed to achieve this drawing and twisting with greater speed and evenness.

Linen spins more finely if it is wet. The tensile strength of the fibre increases and the water softens the fibre and allows it to be pulled out more finely. You can apply water with your fingers during spinning, by dipping them in a bowl.

How much twist a thread is given depends on its eventual use. Up to the point of strain and break, a hard twisted thread is stronger, but not so soft. Generally, the shorter the fibres the more twist is needed to bind them.

Most yarn, including wool and flax, is given a 'Z' twist – i.e. it is spun clockwise. If thread is then plied with another thread, the opposite or anticlockwise 'S' twist is used. Plying threads gives a stronger yarn.

Spindles

In nearly all cultures it has been found that a weight attached to the end of the roving (the thin sliver drawn out from the rolag), spun and allowed to fall gently, considerably eases the process of drawing out and twisting the fibres. In some cases a stone has been used, but mostly some kind of spindle has been devised.

A spindle consists of a round wooden stick, rather like a crochet hook, but with the hooked end tapered and the other end, on which the weight or whorl rests, thicker. The whorl can be of any material of reasonable weight, but it must fit well and give an even spin. The length of the spindle stick varies, but the average one might be 23 to 30 cm.

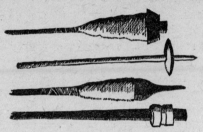

To spin wool on the spindle you must first hand twist about 60 cm of wool fibre, drawn from a prepared rolag. Try to aim for about the thickness of double-knitting wool. Tie it on to the stick above the whorl, take it under the whorl, around the stick, back up over the whorl again and round the hook in a half hitch.

Suspend the spindle and roving from the left hand, holding the roving firmly between thumb and forefinger so that no twist goes up the thread into the rolag, which is draped over the back of your left hand. Give the spindle hook a sharp twist with your right hand and then use your right hand to hold the roving, while the left thumb and forefinger travel up the roving, easing out more fibres from the rolag. Aim for an even sliver. When you have drawn out a few inches, let go with your right thumb and forefinger so that the twist runs up the thread to where the left hand is holding it. Slide your right forefinger and thumb up to hold the thread again, draw out fibres with your left hand and repeat the process in a continuous motion until the spun yarn is as long as your arms will allow. Keep the thread taut by winding it round your fingers, take the half hitch off the spindle hook and wind the thread round the stick just above the whorl. Then re-hook the thread for further spinning. You must keep the whorl turning to twist the thread and you must be careful not to let the twist run into the rolag or it will be difficult to draw out the fibres.

When one rolag has been used up it is quite easy to join it to the next one by fuzzing the fibres together.

Spinning wheels

Most fibres were spun on spindles for thousands of years until the invention of the spinning wheel. Early spinning wheels used the action of the wheel to twist the thread. The spindle was turned on its side and the whorl grooved and attached to the large wheel by a driving band. Spinning was done in two stages. A thin sliver was attached to the sharp point of the spindle and the roving drawn out and held at an angle, so that when the big wheel was turned with the hand the sliver remained caught by the end of the spindle, whose turning inserted a twist. As the spinner backed away from the wheel, at the same time drawing out fibres from the rolag, a very loose twist was inserted. To wind on to the spindle, the wheel was first reversed, which removed the twisted fibres from the tip of the spindle, and then the sliver was held at right angles to the wheel and wound on to the base of the spindle by spinning the wheel in the original direction. When the spindle was full, the loosely spun roving was removed from the spindle and the process repeated to spin a more tightly twisted yarn.

With the addition of the flyer mechanism of the modern spinning wheel, the spun thread is also wound on a bobbin in one operation. Individual spinning wheels vary slightly, but the general principle is that a treadle mechanism turns the big wheel, which is connected by a tension band or bands to the pulley of the bobbin and/or the pulley

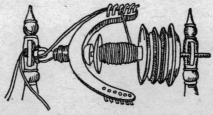

of the spindle with attached flyer. When the wheel turns the pulleys turn, but because of the different diameters of the pulleys, the bobbin turns faster than the flyer, so that it pulls the thread on to itself.

Alternatively, some wheels have a retarding mechanism, where only one band goes round the big wheel and spindle pulley, the spindle and flyer rotate, but the bobbin is braked by a cord and held still, so that the flyer winds on the thread.

The roving is drawn out by the spinner from the rolag in just the same way as for a spindle, except that it is easier for the right hand to ease out the fibres from the rolag. The roving is fed into the bobbin spindle through the inner tube of the spindle facing the spinner, emerges again from a hole in the spindle, and goes over one of the flyer hooks and on to the bobbin.

The yarn is pulled on to the bobbin fairly quickly as it is spun, although the speed of treadling can be adjusted, within limits. Gradually you will acquire the knack of treadling to the right speed and paying out the fibres. Hard and soft spins are achieved by varying the rate at which the thread is allowed to wind on to the bobbin in relation to the twist that is being imparted by the turning spindle.

To ply two or more spun threads together, the spinning wheel is set in motion in the opposite direction, so that it does not unspin the spun threads.

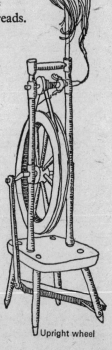

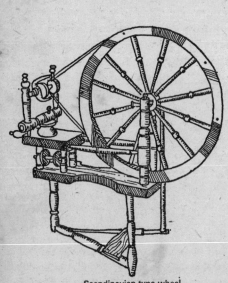

Scandinavian type wheel

Upright wheel

Flax is spun best on a small wheel that keeps the spindle spinning quickly and continuously. A larger wheel, 45 cm or more in diameter, is used for wool. The larger wheel revolves more slowly for each depression of the treadle, and so therefore does the spindle. Combination wheels, 40 to 45 cm in diameter, are suitable either for flax or for wool; the speed of spinning can be adjusted.

Dyeing

'Dyed in the wool' is an expression derived from the practice of dyeing wool fibres before they were carded or spun. The dyestuff can penetrate the loose fibres more thoroughly and so the fastness of the colour is increased. In general, the earlier the stage at which dyeing is carried out, the better the colour can penetrate. In practice, the wool is usually dyed at the yarn stage by hand spinners, after being washed. Linen is often not dyed at all, of course, but just bleached, or half-bleached. It can be dyed at yarn or cloth stage, though by the time it has been made up into fabric it is often block printed, because it is difficult to get dye to penetrate the closely woven fibres (see page 123).

Wind wool off the spindle or bobbin of the spinning wheel into skeins. These are *loosely* tied in several places to keep the yarn together, then the skeins are washed in mild, soapy water two or three times to get out all the impurities, rinsed thoroughly and hung up to dry with weights attached to pull out all the kinks. While it is still damp, the wool is mordanted – the first step in dyeing – or if it has dried it is first re-rinsed.

You must bleach or half-bleach linen before mordanting and dyeing. Strong bleaches are harmful to linen. A quick method of bleaching is to boil the linen in an alkaline liquor, then neutralize in a weakly acidic liquor, then bleach with a weak solution of hydrogen peroxide or sodium hypochlorite, chlorine, etc, and finally rinse and dry. A safer but slower method, used by the American colonists, was alternately dampening and drying in the sun until the right whiteness was achieved. During medieval times, bleaching fields in Britain copied Dutch methods of open-air bleaching. Linen was steeped in lyes (see pages 117, 265-6) for several days, then washed clean in a process called 'bucking'. The linen was then spread on the grass for several weeks ('crofting'). Bucking and crofting were repeated five or six times. Cloth or yarn was then steeped in sour milk or buttermilk for several days, washed clean, then crofted. The processes were repeated until the linen was the required white colour. Flax fibre can also be bleached.

Mordants

A mordant is a substance capable of combining chemically with the colouring matter applied to the fibre and so fixing the dye in the yarn or fibre. Most plant dyes need a mordant, the most important exception being lichens.

Yarns are treated with mordants in solution preparatory to dyeing. The mordant must be absorbed evenly to get an even colour and the actual colour of the dyed yarn as well as its fastness depends on the mordant used. Different mordants will bring up different colours, even with the same dye-bath.

Many substances have been used as mordants: acetic acid (even unpurified vinegar), ammonium hydroxide, caustic soda, common salt, lime, tannic acid, oxalic acid and, last but by no means least, urine. However, the most important mordanting agents are alum (potassium aluminium sulphate), used since antiquity, chrome (potassium or sodium dichromate), iron (ferrous sulphate, known to dyers as green vitriol or copperas), tin (stannous chloride) and cream of tartar.

Recipes for wool

Alum: 50–100 g potassium aluminium sulphate (the lesser quantity for fine wool – too much alum makes wool sticky); 25 g cream of tartar (helps to brighten colour); 450 g wool.

Dissolve alum and cream of tartar in 18 to 20 litres of soft water. (Soft water is recommended at all stages of dyeing.) Warm the water, put the wool in, bring towards the boil gradually, spreading and stirring the wool. Simmer for 45 minutes for fine wool, 60 minutes for coarse wool. Leave to cool. Lift wool out with a stick, squeeze it gently and leave for 2 to 3 days in a cool place without drying.

Tin: 14 g stannous chloride; 50 g cream of tartar (dissolved in water before the tin); 450 g wool.

Use as for alum. Tin produces very bright colours: a common use for it used to be with cochineal for scarlet; it is also used for yellows and oranges. Too much tin makes wool brittle and it should be rinsed in soapy water afterwards. It should not be used for linen, although a few crystals of tin in the alum mordant will brighten the colour – a process called 'blooming'.

Chrome: 7 to 14 g potassium dichromate; 450 g wool.

Same process as with alum, but the lid should be kept on the mordant solution because it is very sensitive to light. When it is cool enough, rinse the yarn and keep it covered until you are ready to dye it – which should be as soon as possible. This mordant makes wool soft and silky.

Iron: 14 g ferrous sulphate; 25 g cream of tartar; 450 g wool.

This is often added to the dyebath during the dyeing process instead of mordanting first. It darkens and dulls colours, in a process called 'saddening'. The wool should always be lifted out while the mordant is dissolving. As a desperate substitute, American colonial housewives used rusty iron nails and rusty kettles to make a metallic mordant. It worked, but the colours were rather drab.

Recipes for linen

Linen has to receive somewhat different treatment. An American handbook, *Dyeplants and Dyeing* gives this method: 225 g alum; 50 g sodium carbonate (washing soda); 25 g tannic acid; 450 g of dry material.

Take half the alum and half the soda and add it to 18 to 20 litres of cold, soft water. Put in the previously wetted linen and heat gradually. Boil for one hour, then leave to cool overnight. Squeeze out the moisture and put it into a bath of the tannic acid dissolved in 18 to 20 litres of water. Heat it almost to boiling point and hold it at this temperature for one hour, making sure the solution is penetrating. Let it cool and stand overnight. Then rinse the linen. Make a third bath of 100 g alum and 25 g soda. Boil for an hour and leave overnight. Squeeze out the moisture, rinse, then dye.

Alternatively, *The Use of Vegetable Dyes* (see page 306) suggests you boil the linen in water with washing soda and leave it to steep in the solution overnight. Then 'gall' the linen in a solution of tannic acid: steep it in a solution of 25 g tannic acid for each 450 g linen, bring it to the boiling point and simmer for half an hour. Let the solution cool and leave it overnight. Wash the linen, mordant (as for wool) with alum, simmer for an hour and leave to soak, then dye.

None of these mordants can be obtained easily from nature; they must be bought. However, tannic acid can be procured from gallnuts on plants, particularly oak trees. Gallnuts are abnormal growths caused by the larvae of an insect (a wasp) whose feeding causes tannic acid to be concentrated in the gall. Cream of tartar was also called 'winestone' and an ancient source of it was the sediment from grapes in wine casks. Alum can occur in nature in varying degrees of purity. It can be extracted very simply from alunite, a rock that is a basic double sulphate of aluminium and potassium; the extraction of alum from the shales in the Whitby district of Yorkshire was once a major industry there. There are conflicting accounts of how this was done. In one version, the shales were heated, and treated with sulphuric acid; alum crystallized from the solution. Another version holds that the shales were leached (soaked in water) and decomposed urine was added, which gave ammonium alum. If you were to leach alunite with water, alum crystals would form from the solution, or you could calcine (roast) the rock, and treat it with dilute sulphuric acid, which would give you a solution containing an excess of aluminium sulphate. Then you would add potassium sulphate, which would enable the aluminium salt to be converted to alum. In America, alum was obtained by treating bauxite or clay with sulphuric acid, then adding potassium sulphate to the solution. The alum crystallized on cooling.

Vegetable dyeing

Many of the most famous natural dyes were made from plants or insects not native to Britain – dyes such as logwood, indigo, cochineal, cutch, fustic chips etc. However, colour can be extracted from many British plants or parts of plants. Some colours are more abundant than others. There are many yellows, greens and browns, for example, but not so many good reds and blues.

Vegetable dyes fall into two categories: those that require a mordant to prepare the fibres, and those that do not, which are called 'substantive dyes'. Lichens are the most important providers of substantive vegetable dyes.

In general, it is best to collect dye plants when they are young and strong. Resinous bark should be collected in the spring and non-resinous bark in the autumn. However, it must be emphasized that stripping the bark from trees indiscriminately may kill them – it will certainly kill them if you take bark from all round the trunk and so ring-bark them. Indeed, some restraint is urged in all collecting of plants. Denuding an area could have serious consequences for the survival of the plants themselves, and it could cause soil erosion. At one time in the Outer Hebrides, grazing land was becoming so badly eroded by the harvesting of Lady's bedstraw roots that the practice had to be forbidden by law, on penalty of death.

Main British dye plants

Common name	Latin name	Part used	Comments
Weld, Dyers' rocket, Wild mignonette	Reseda luteola R. lutea	Whole upper plant, chopped up	Lemon-yellow with alum mordant. Very fast
Dyers' greenweed, Dyers' broom, Woad-waxen	Genista tinctoria	Flowering tops	Bright yellow with alum and cream of tartar mordant. With woad gives green. Can be dried
Onion skins	Allium cepa	Dry outer skins	With alum mordant and steeped in hot water gives yellow, going brown if boiled. Tin mordant gives orange
Dog's mercury	Mercurialis perennis	Chopped up plant	Gives yellow with alum mordant but turns bluish with longer boiling
White birch	Betula alba	Leaves, twigs, bark	With alum mordant leaves give yellow; twigs give yellow-green with alum; bark gives light brown and needs no mordant. Dried bark keeps well
Bracken	Pteris aquilina	Fronds	Yellow with alum mordant. Needs a long simmering. Curled-up ferns are best
Saffron crocus	Crocus sativis	Orange stigma of flowers	Yellow with alum mordant
Goldenrod	Solidago	Flowering heads	Alum mordant gives yellow; chrome mordant old gold

Main British dye plants *continued*

Common name	Latin name	Part used	Comments
Walnut	*Juglans nigra*	Green husks	Dark browns and blacks. No mordant needed, but a richer colour is obtained if you use one. Shells can also be used but it is harder to extract the dye. Can harden wool
Reeds	*Phragmites*	Pink flower heads	With alum mordant gives a green for linen
Dandelion	*Taraxacum officinale*	Taproot	Magenta
Crottle (lichen)	*Parmelia saxatalis*	All	Common grey species found on stones and trees. No mordant. Dyes reddish-brown. Dye with alternate layers of lichen and wool; the lichen brushes out when dry
Lichen	*Usnea comosa*	All	Filamentous lichen, found all over Britain, mainly on trees but also on rocks. Dyes reddish brown
Dog lichen	*Peltigera canina*	All	Yellow with alum mordant for linen. Grows on grassy places, common on sand dunes
Cudbear (lichen)	*Ochrolechia tartarea*	All	Red. Found on trees and rocks in upland areas. Soaked and fermented in urine

Lady's bedstraw*	Galium verum	Flowers, roots	Flowers give yellow with alum or chrome mordant; roots give red with alum mordant
Wild madder*	Rubia peregrina	Roots	Rose pink with alum mordant
Woad	Isatis tinctoria	Leaves	Dye fermented over a period of time out of crushed leaves. Mordanted with alum and heated for a long time. Blue colour is brought out by the oxygen in the air. Rare as a wild plant but it can be cultivated in Britain

Other colours: *Greens:* privet, elder leaves, ling, horsetail, nettles; *Violet:* elderberries; *Blue-purple:* blackberry, sloe, ivy berries, privet berries; *Grey:* yellow iris, young blackberry shoots; *Yellow:* broom, agrimony, dock root (which gives black or grey with a copperas mordant)

*Lady's bedstraw and wild madder are related to dyers' madder, *Rubia tinctoria*, which does not grow wild in Britain but which can be cultivated here. The roots of the madder give deep red colours mordanted with alum or chrome. In this case, hard water is preferable. With an alum-tannic acid mordant it will dye linen.

Some plants, lichens, berries, bark and roots can be dried successfully; leaves are difficult to dry. The depth of the colour obtained from plants can vary from one part of the country to another, and with the weather preceding their collection, and with soil conditions.

How to use vegetable dyes

As a very rough guide to quantities, you should use equal weights of plant material and yarn to be dyed. Individual plants can vary considerably, however. For your own future reference, it is a good idea to take samples and make detailed notes of a dye batch: what was used, when it was gathered, the mordant used, etc. You will not be able to repeat the shade exactly, so you should always aim to dye as much as you will need in one batch.

Soak the plants overnight, then boil them up for half an hour to 2 hours, depending on how much colour comes from them. Strain the liquor into the dye kettle and make it up to 18 to 20 litres of liquid for each 450 g wool. Rewarm it and put in the wool. Alternatively, the plant material may be tied in a muslin bag and simmered with the wool.

Simmer the wool in the dyebath until it has acquired the colour you wish. It is important that the wool should not be subjected to sudden changes in temperature and if anything has to be added to the dyebath, remove the wool first, add the substance, then put back the wool. The time the wool spends in the dyebath may be anything from half an hour to 3 hours. Leave it to cool in the dyebath, where it will continue to take up colour.

The dye must be able to penetrate right through the yarn, so the dye kettle must be roomy enough, but the wool should not be stirred about too much. Use soft water. When you lift out the wool with a clean stick, squeeze it gently, then rinse it until no more colour comes away, if necessary bringing down the temperature gradually with each rinse. Dry away from the light.

The general procedure for linen is the same as that for wool, but the dye is accepted less readily.

Printing on cloth

Resist printing or dyeing

Batik: The parts of the cloth that are to resist the dye are covered with wax. The cloth is dyed, then dried, and the wax removed. The undyed part may be painted by hand.

Tie-dyeing: Parts of material are tied in bunches with string. The material is immersed in dye which cannot penetrate properly where the material has been tied. After dyeing and drying, the material is untied to reveal a sunburst type of design.

Hand block printing

A wooden block with part of the design that is to be in one particular colour carved on it is inked with dyestuff and printed on to the material. Another wooden block carrying the carved design for the second colour is inked and overprinted to register with the first printing. Good linen cloth has the right texture and quality for this treatment. Needless to say it requires great skill to achieve even repeats, with clear outlines and the same depth of colour.

Weaving

Cloth may be made from one type of yarn, such as wool, or of mixed yarn – linen and wool, cotton and linen. We have dealt with the production, spinning and dyeing of linen and woollen yarns because these are the fibres that can be produced most easily in Britain. Silk can be produced, but it is highly energy-intensive because the silkworms must be kept warm. Nettles and hemp (see page 33) can also be used for making cloth. The extraction and preparation of their fibres is very similar to that of flax. Nettles have been used mainly for sailcloth or canvas. They are retted to free the bark from the core, and the bark is then boiled to loosen the fibres, which are hackled and oiled for spinning. The nettles used most commonly for their fibres are the perennial common or great nettle (*Urtica dioica*), and the annual small nettle (*Urtica urens*). Hemp is a satisfactory substitute for flax in many uses, but in Britain to grow it is illegal.

Weaving is rather like darning a huge sock that is all hole. At the other end of the scale, it is like producing a fine patterned brocade or a tapestry. And between these two extremes of aspiration and skill, for thousands of years, man has found ways to cover himself and keep warm. The information that follows relates to the production of *necessary* cloth; further developments and refinements are up to the skill and perseverance of the individual weaver.

Cloth is made by holding one set of threads taut (the 'warp' threads) while the horizontal 'weft' threads are interlaced over and under them. The original loom was probably vertical, the warp being weighted by

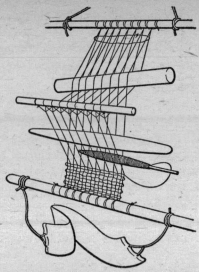

Pre-Columbian backstrap loom

many small stones attached below a stick, round which the threads were wound to hold them in position. Fine and intricate work was done on looms of this kind. The backstrap loom is another primitive design, in which the warp threads are kept taut by the weaver leaning back.

There are three basic weaves: tabby, twill and satin. All patterns are derived from developments or combinations of these.

Tabby weave

Tabby is the simplest weave and the one most like darning. In one 'pick' or row, the yarn goes under one warp thread, over the next, under the next, and so on. In the next pick the process is reversed: pick 3 is like pick 1, pick 4 like pick 2.

Weaving patterns are drawn on squared paper; the blocked-out squares indicate the action of the warp threads and the black squares show the warp lying above the weft.

As each pick is inserted, it is beaten down into position, and as the next pick follows it, gradually the cloth builds up. Many common objects, such as pocket handkerchieves, are made of simple tabby weave.

It is important to understand the principle of these squared patterns, or 'drafts', from the start, because in the more advanced textbooks instructions for different weaves are given in this form. If a

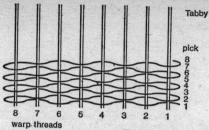

Tabby

pick
8
7
6
5
4
3
2
1

8 7 6 5 4 3 2 1
warp threads

table loom is being used, the warp threads are lifted for each black square. If a foot-power loom is used, the warp threads are usually pulled down and the weft threads pass over them. One is simply the converse of the other, of course, but the distinction should be borne in mind. With more complicated drafts, the pattern you want to produce could start appearing on the underside. The draft is read from the bottom upwards and the warp threads are numbered from right to left.

pick
8
7
6
5
4
3
2
1

Tabby

8 7 6 5 4 3 2 1 warp threads

You can make several variations on plain cloth. Different colours in the warp and weft threads combine to give stripes and checks. Different textures of yarns change the feel and appearance. A thicker material is obtained with a 'basket' weave, where two warp threads are gone over at once, and the same pick is repeated. A 'weft-faced' material is obtained by spacing the warp threads further apart and packing soft, thick threads down so that the warp is entirely covered. Many rugs are woven in this way, with the warp threads made from

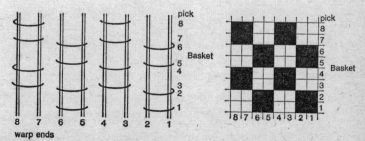

pick
8

7
6

5
4

3
2

1

Basket

8 7 6 5 4 3 2 1

warp ends

pick
8

7

6
5

4
3

2
1

Basket

8 7 6 5 4 3 2 1

thick cotton or linen. Extra strength can be given to the selvedges both by inserting double threads at the edges and by putting a double twist round the selvedge strings.

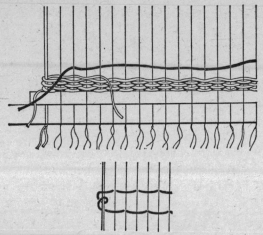

Similarly, a 'warp-faced' material can be woven by having very thick, closely set warp threads and thinner weft threads beaten together very tightly.

More complicated geometrical patterns in rugs or wall hangings can be achieved by taking the weft only part of the way across a row. The joins between the weft can be made in a variety of ways.

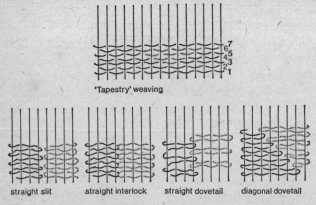

'Tapestry' weaving

straight slit   straight interlock   straight dovetail   diagonal dovetail

To make tabby cloth in the first place, you need something to keep the warp threads taut. In addition to the more primitive looms, there is the frame loom.

Frame loom: The principle of this is similar to that of the vertical loom, the warp threads being wound around a strong frame. You can make a frame loom from a picture frame, but at most it can take a warp only twice as long as its own length, and it is impractical to have it too wide.

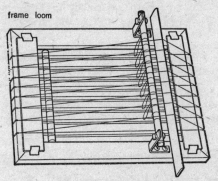

frame loom

Now you need something to give a 'shed'. This is the tunnel through which the weft thread passes after the alternate warp threads have been picked up. You can obtain one shed by turning a flat stick on its side and another shed by pulling on loops or leashes attached to a pole that picks up the warp threads in between.

The weft is carried through the shed on a shuttle. The simplest shuttle is a stick with the yarn wound round it. The weft can be beaten down with a comb.

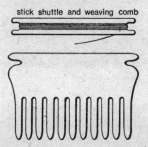

stick shuttle and weaving comb

Table loom: The table loom is an advance on this model. It will accommodate longer warp threads, because they are wound off and on to beams at the back and front. A simple model for tabby weaving has a 'rigid heddle'. The warp threads are passed through alternate slots and holes in a comb-like device. When the rigid heddle is lifted up, the warp threads that pass through the holes rise, while the others slide down the slots. This gives a rising shed for the weft. When the heddle is depressed, the warp ends in the holes are lowered, while the others slide up the slots, to give a sinking and alternate shed.

The rigid heddle loom has the added advantage that the heddle can beat down the weft more efficiently than a comb. It is restricted to weaving with only two sheds and usually it is fairly narrow, although the width and length of the material depend on the size and stoutness of the loom.

You can make a rigid heddle by binding together polished strips of wood (they must be polished so that the threads will move through and against them smoothly) with a hole drilled in each of them. The holes must all be at exactly the same height and the strips must be spaced evenly. They are held top and bottom between two pairs of 'holding strips', bound together with twine.

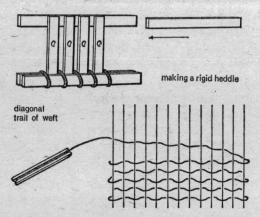

making a rigid heddle

diagonal trail of weft

The rigid heddle acts as a 'beater' and the procedure for weaving with any loom that has a beater is:

1 Open the shed.
2 Put the weft through, making a diagonal trail and leaving enough slack at the selvedge so that it will not pull in the warp when it is beaten down.
3 Beat the weft down.
4 Open the new shed.
5 Beat down the new shed to clear it.
6 Put through the next weft pick from the side.
  And so on.

Twill weaves

The next basic weave is twill. It is the weave you see on many skirts and coats. It makes a dense, hard-wearing material, and it calls for a further step forward in pattern design and equipment.

In a balanced 2/2 twill, two adjacent warp threads have been picked up, two missed out, the next two picked up, and so on. On the next pick, no 2 warp thread and no 3 are picked up, the next two left out and 6 and 7 picked up. Pick 5 repeats pick 1. The smallest repeating unit of the pattern is four warp ends in one direction and four picks in the other. This gives four permutations of warp threads to be picked up, giving four different sheds: 1 and 2; 2 and 3; 3 and 4; 4 and 5 (or 4 and 1 if the warp threads repeat in units of four).

To achieve these four permutations you will need a table loom that has four 'shafts'. It may also have ratchets for rolling the warp on and off front and back beams as it becomes cloth, and with a beater or 'reed' to press down the woven cloth. On the four shafts in the central structure of the loom, loops made of wire or string are hung – the heddles, which have a central eye through which the warp threads are

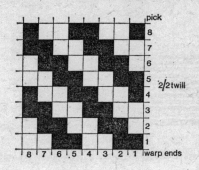

2/2 twill

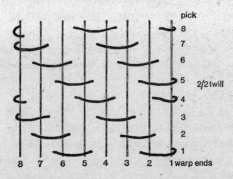

2/2 twill

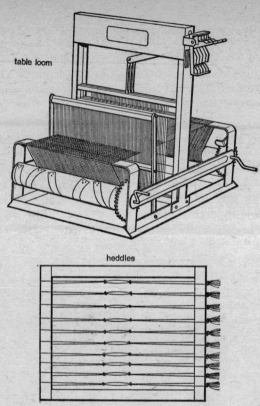

table loom

heddles

threaded through the heddles according to the threading draft, drawn on squared paper. No 1 warp thread goes through the first heddle on no 1 shaft; no 2 warp thread goes through no 1 heddle on no 2 shaft; no 3 warp thread goes through no 1 heddle on no 4 shaft. No 5 warp thread (or no 1 of the next group) goes through no 2 heddle on no 1 shaft; no 6 warp thread goes through no 2 heddle on no 2 shaft, and so on. Conventionally, the weaving draft for 2/2 twill is notated in this way.

Obviously, you can make as many variations through changes in the colour or texture of yarns in twill as in tabby. It is also possible to change the pattern by altering the order of raising. As the levers of the table loom are pressed down, the appropriate shafts are raised: depressing levers 1 and 2 raises shafts 1 and 2, and all the heddles on those shafts with them. The drafts show the order of raising, reading from bottom to top, to give each pattern. Two units of pattern are

reed

shaft
4
3
2
1

4 3 2 1 4 3 2 1

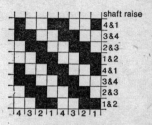

shaft raise
4&1
3&4
2&3
1&2
4&1
3&4
2&3
1&2

4 3 2 1 4 3 2 1

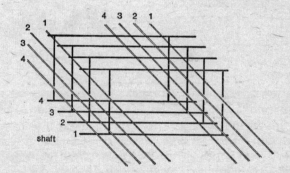

4 3 2 1

2
3
4

4
3
2
1

shaft

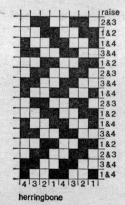

raise
2&3
1&2
1&4
3&4
1&2
2&3
3&4
1&4
2&3
1&2
1&4
3&4
1&2
2&3
3&4
1&4

4 3 2 1 4 3 2 1

herringbone

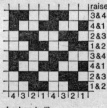

raise
3&4
4&1
2&3
1&2
3&4
4&1
2&3
1&2

4 3 2 1 4 3 2 1

broken twill

raise
2&3
3&4
4&1
3&4
2&3
1&2
2&3
3&4
4&1
3&4
2&3
1&2

4 3 2 1 4 3 2 1

waved twill

given in each case, and when these picks have been done the pattern starts again at the bottom.

Because in this threading alternate warp threads are on odd- and even-numbered shafts, by lifting 1 and 3 together, followed by 2 and 4 together, it is possible to accomplish ordinary tabby 'darning' weaving. Tabby and twill can be combined, which means you can elongate the twill pattern by repeating the picks but putting a tabby binding row in between. This is particularly useful with the 'point draft' (so called because the design comes to a point) in which the threads are entered 1,2,3,4,3,2,1, instead of 4,3,2,1,4,3,2,1.

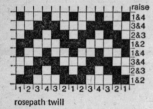

rosepath twill

rosepath reverse twill

Satin weave

This is a more decorative, less functional weave, and we need do no more than note its existence. Either many warp threads are raised at a time so that the surface ends up mainly warp (satin cloth), or single, far-apart warp threads are raised so that the surface of the cloth is mainly weft (sateen cloth). A true satin needs at least five shafts.

However, there are many more overshot designs that are both decorative and functional. By and large, the smaller pattern repeats are more useful for linen, which is a springy, inelastic material, and the longer overshots suit the soft drapiness of wool. The smaller linen designs do not usually have a tabby pick between them, while the longer overshots are generally bound between each pattern row with a tabby pick in a fine thread.

There are many beautiful pattern designs published (see page 306) but here are a few examples to illustrate the principle.

M's and O's is a linen weave that was used generally for plain towelling. No true all-over tabby is possible. but the ends are set close together and the weft is beaten close up. This is also suitable for a tea towel. The pattern of threading of the warp ends repeats every 16 threads. No 1 warp end goes through heddle no 1 on shaft no 1;

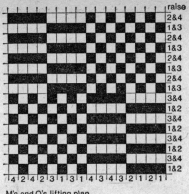

M's and O's lifting plan

M's and O's threading draft

warp end no 2 goes through heddle no 1 on shaft no 2; warp end no 3 goes through heddle no 2 on shaft no 1; warp end no 4 goes through heddle no 2 on shaft no 2; and so on, as shown in the threading draft. The lifting plan is shown, starting at the bottom with raise 1 and 2.

Goose-eye is also a linen weave, useful for household cloths. Again, no tabby binder row is needed between the picks, but a tabby weave is possible with this threading because alternate threads go in odd- and

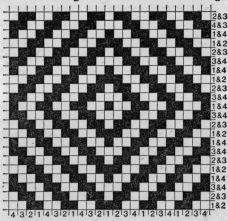

goose - eye lifting

goose-eye threading draft

even-numbered shafts. So lifting 1 and 2, then 2 and 4 gives plain tabby weave. Only one repeat of Goose-eye is given in each direction. In all, the repeating unit is 22 threads, the last entry on the left being, in fact, the start of the next repeating unit. After coming to the end of the lifting plan, start again from the bottom.

Butternut, though relatively modest in its overshots, is better suited to woollen materials. It would be a good pattern for a bed coverlet, for instance. Note that after the repeats across a row have been threaded, it is necessary to add three threads from the start of the next repeat to get the sides the same and balanced for the selvedges. A tabby binding row would be needed between pattern rows.

The best way to understand these patterns is to do them: just thread up and see how the pattern appears according to the lifting plan, otherwise the mind boggles. It's worth noting, though, that although there is nothing sacred about the lifting sequence and others can be tried, the traditional way to follow one of these patterns is to lift according to the threading sequence. For example, if the first threads are entered through heddles on nos 1 and 2 shafts, as in Butternut, then the first two pattern rows are put through a shed made by lifting 1 and 2 shafts. In this case the first four pattern rows are made by lifting 1 and 2 shafts, then there are two pattern rows of lifting 2 and 3 shafts, because threads 5 and 6 went through heddles on shafts 2 and 3. This way a squared, balanced weave is achieved. If you want to elongate the pattern, change the number of sheds for a particular number of shafts accordingly. If you don't get it at first, don't worry: try it out and suddenly it will click. From then on you can make up your own threading drafts. Remember, though, to make sure that alternate warp threads go either through heddles on no 1 shaft *or* no 3 shaft. and similarly through heddles on shafts 2 *or* 4 for the threads in between, because with long overshots a tabby binding row between the pattern rows is necessary.

It is also a good idea to thread the selvedge threads 1,2,3,4 or 4,3,2,1 before actually starting on any pattern repeats.

Finally, it's worth repeating that instructions to raise shafts are

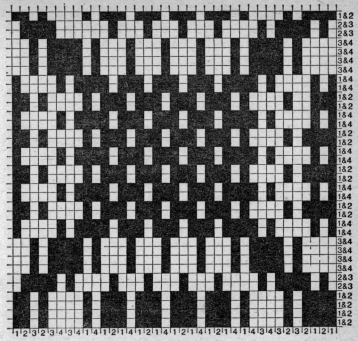

1&2
2&3
2&3
3&4
3&4
3&4
3&4
1&4
1&4
1&2
1&2
1&4
1&4
1&2
1&2
1&4
1&4
1&2
1&2
1&4
1&4
1&2
1&2
1&4
1&4
3&4
3&4
3&4
3&4
2&3
2&3
1&2
1&2
1&2
1&2

Butternut lifting plan

Butternut (36-thread repeat)

given for a table loom, which has a rising shed, so the black squares will be uncovered warp threads and the pattern given by the black squares will appear on the underside of the weaving as weft. On a footpower loom, with a sinking shed, the black squares will appear as weft on the upper side, unless you make the necessary changes in the draft. In either case you end up with the same cloth: it's up to you which way round you want it while you are weaving.

Weaving hints

Slacken the tension of the warp threads slightly between use. Both woollen and linen warps can be starched, which helps prevent fraying and breaking as the warp goes through the heddles and reed. The starch can be brushed on.

Linen is stronger when it is wet: indeed, it can be brittle if it dries out too much. The strength of the warp is increased if a damp cloth is kept lying over it at the back of the loom. A good, well-twisted double-ply thread should be used for the warps of linen and wool.

Should a warp thread break (which it will!), insert pieces using the weavers' knot. If one broken end is actually in the web, wind it round a pin in the fabric until the weaving is finished.

weaver's knot

Looms

Preparing the warp

The first step is to choose the yarns for warp and weft and, having decided on the width of the article, work out how many warp threads you will need per centimetre. For a cloth of average density, wind the threads round a ruler and count how many can be packed into the space of one centimetre. Halve this number and you have the number of ends per centimetre, or the 'sett'. Multiply this by the desired width and you know the number of threads. For example, 5 ends per centimetre and a width of 50 cm means you will need 250 threads. Add 10 per cent to this for good measure, because the weft may pull the weaving in or the finishing may shrink it, and the total is brought to 275 threads. Finally, add 6 more threads so that the 3 threads on either side can be doubled to give strong edges. You will need 281 ends. Round off this figure to fit in with any pattern repeats, in this case to 280 ends.

To work out how long the warp should be, add to the length you would like the amount of the warp that will be lost behind the heddles at the back of the loom: 50 to 60 cm should be enough. Allow 12 cm per metre for 'take up' (the loss in length caused by the bending of the warp threads in weaving). So, to produce 5 metres of cloth you will need warp threads 5 m long, plus 0.5 m loom allowance, plus 0.6 m take up, to give a total dressed length of 6.10 m. So you will need 280 threads, each 6.10 m long for your warp. From this you can calculate the amount of yarn you will need: $280 \times 6.10 = 1708$ m.

Laying the warp

Depending on the length of the warp, posts, a board or a warping mill are used. The idea is to ensure that a warp is made with the threads held at even tension and in the correct sequence, ready to be wound on to the back roller of the loom. If no better equipment is available, you can beat sticks into the ground or use chairs that are held down. There must be posts to make the cross. The yarn is wound back and forth round the posts and crossed between the posts at either end. Some people put a cross at only one end, but it is safer to have two crosses. It is a good idea to mark off the threads in convenient units: in our case, for example, 10 threads would correspond to 2 cm. A piece of yarn flipped across can be the marker.

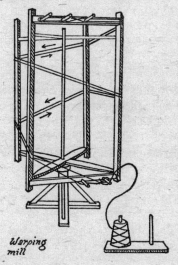

Warping
mill

When the warp is laid, yarn is tied in between the crossed threads on either side of the crosses to keep them separate. Then the warp is chained off the posts in a plait, starting with the end that was *not* marked off in units of threads so that this is the end that protrudes from the plait.

A couple of shed sticks (flat sticks with a hole at either end) are inserted on either side of the cross and tied together through their holes to secure the cross. The cross ensures that the threads lie in sequence across the width of the warp. Once the shed sticks are secured, the yarn ties can be cut and the warp spread out over the sticks.

tying cross

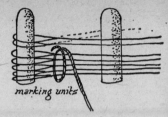

marking units

The warp is now ready to 'beam on', that is, to wind on to the back roller. It needs to be spread out as it winds on to ensure an even warp tension. The protruding end of the chain is spread over a raddle, which is like a closed rake, whose teeth may be from 2 to 5 cm apart. The warp is then slipped over the apron bar stick at the back of the loom and the warp beam is turned to wind the warp on. It takes two people to wind the warp on satisfactorily, one to turn the ratchets and one to hold the plait at tension and comb out any tangles with the fingers.

As the layers of the warp wind round the beam, insert flat sticks between them and keep moving the shed sticks forward so they don't get wound on to the apron bar. When all but about 60 cm has been wound on, the warp is ready for threading through the heddles and reed.

If you have no raddle, it is possible to thread the warp from the front, using the reed as a raddle by threading the warp out in an approximately even spreading, slipping or tying the warp on to the back apron bar as before, and winding on. However, the heddles must

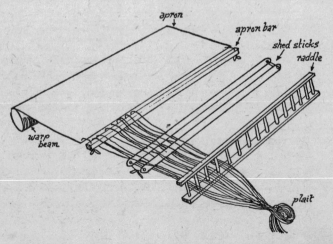

apron

apron bar

shed sticks

raddle

warp beam

plait

be out of the way and at the end of the operation the shed sticks will be at the front of the loom and the cross must be transferred by moving the sticks right up against the reed, cutting the ties holding them together, and turning the first one on its edge, which makes a shed behind the reed into which another stick can be put. The first stick is removed and the operation repeated for the second. The two new shed sticks are moved back to the warp beam and tied together. The remainder of the warp is now drawn through the reed and again the warp is ready for threading through the heddles. Note that rigid heddle looms would be threaded from the front in this way because the rigid heddle is both heddle and reed.

Threading

Heddles can be made from string. To ensure that the loops are of equal size, with the eye in the right place, you should tie the string round nails driven into a board. The string should be strong, smooth and as inelastic as possible. When you have made enough heddles, hang them on the shafts or put them on a frame, depending on the design of the loom. The heddles are threaded according to the chosen

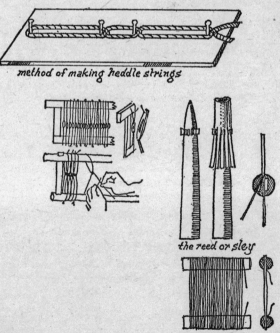

method of making heddle strings

the reed or sley

draft. Make sure that the correct number of heddles are placed on each shaft.

After they have been entered through the heddle, the threads must be 'sleyed' or put through the reed. A reed is rather essential for all but rigid heddle looms or where a comb will do. They used to be made from strong but small pieces of reed, cut and sanded. Bamboo is an ideal material which can be grown in many places, and cut with a bamboo cutter. The finished pieces are laid out between sticks which are then bound together with string. The width of the string wound between one piece of reed and the next determines the spacing of the slots in the reed. Ideally, these should coincide with, or at least be a multiple of, the spacing you want for your warp ends. The string is then covered with paper or linen.

To sley the reed, find the middle dent and mark it; find the middle threads of the warp and thread them through the reed from the centre outwards, first completely to the right, then completely to the left. It is vital to take the threads in their correct order. If you have to stop in the middle of the operation, make sure the cut ends you have threaded through heddles or reed are tied in little bunches to stop them from slipping out.

Finally, tie the front ends of the warp to the front apron bar stick, which is the twin of the one at the back. Start in the middle, making the first part of the knot, go alternately right and left outwards, tighten the warp tension and finish the knot.

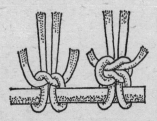

The table loom is now ready for weaving. Lift the levers, or the mechanism that drives the shafts, and if a simple and correct 4,3,2,1 threading has been done, then 1 and 3 and 2 and 4 should give a tabby weave. A few picks in a thick yarn gives a 'heading' that brings the weaving together and checks any mistake in threading.

Footpower looms

A footpower loom requires an additional set of operations to attach the shafts and their heddles to the pedals (or treadles). In principle, the tying up is done for each weave, but in practice the same tie up covers most of the basic weaves that one might need. An average footpower loom might have from 6 to 8 pedals, giving 6 to 8 combinations of shafts that might be used.

In one common tie up, shafts 1 and 2 are connected to pedal 1, shafts 2 and 3 to pedal 6, and so on as shown in the diagram. Depressing pedal 3 operates shafts 1 and 3, depressing pedal 4 operates shafts 2 and 4. So the tabby sheds are made by the middle pedals, 3 and 4.

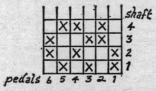

The twill sheds, 1 and 2, 2 and 3, 3 and 4, 4 and 1, can be made by alternately depressing with right and left feet from the outside pedals inwards. You will find other tie ups mentioned in other books. Choose one which suits you and stick to it while the principles sink in. The one described is convenient for most purposes.

The method used for tying the pedals to the shafts depends on the type of loom. In all tying up a particularly useful knot is the snitch knot. It is firm, but easy to adjust. A simple footpower loom might

just have the shafts tied directly to the pedals, so that when the pedal is depressed, down goes the shaft. Most looms today have 'lams', however. These are counterbalanced looms and the lams allow for a more even downward pull. A pedal on the far right may be tied to a lam which still pulls the shaft from the centre. There is a network of corresponding holes in lams and pedals, through which strong cord

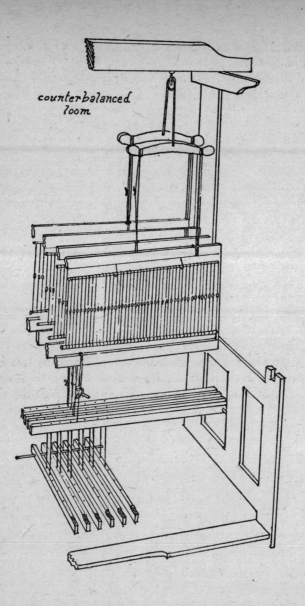

counterbalanced loom

may be threaded. The shafts may be tied at the top to horses or pulleys. When one set of shafts go down, the others go up automatically. There is not, however, a perfect shed in all combinations if an 'unbalanced' weave is desired (that is, one using one shaft at a time).

A second type of loom has a 'jack' mechanism that swivels down in the centre when the pedals and lams are depressed. This causes the shafts, attached to the jacks at the outside edges, to rise, and this loom gives a rising shed, like the table loom.

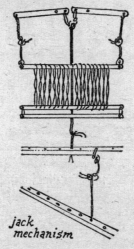

jack mechanism

The third type of loom combines both mechanisms. This is the countermarch loom, which causes one set of shafts to be depressed by the pedals while at the same time the remaining ones are raised,

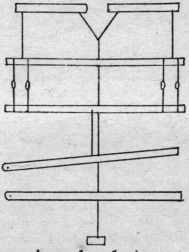

countermarch mechanism

giving a perfect shed. There are two sets of lams, the upper ones attached to the heddles and the lower ones to the jacks and both sets attached to the appropriate pedals. If you wish to depress 2 and 3, say, the upper lams pull shafts 2 and 3 down and the lower lams pull on the centre of jacks 1 and 4, so raising shafts 1 and 4.

It is possible to obtain upright looms with footpower. Only the tabby shed is available, because the loom is used for rugs and tapestries. It is much easier to knot a pile rug on a vertical warp.

Shuttles

The footpower loom increases the speed of weaving because the hands are left free to throw the shuttle from side to side.

For the wider loom a boat type of shuttle is generally used. To make a spool to fit inside the shuttle, cut out a reasonably stiff egg-shaped piece of paper. Roll it up, inserting the end of the thread, then wind the thread on, making two bumps at the two ends, then filling in the middle. A bobbin winder is a useful acquisition if you can obtain one; if not, the bobbin winder of a sewing machine will do or you can wind by putting the spool in the place where the bobbin should go on a spinning wheel: increase the tension of the wheel so that no more twist goes into the yarn and use the flyer mechanism to wind on.

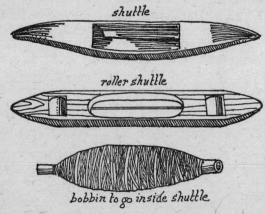

shuttle

roller shuttle

bobbin to go inside shuttle

One of the first inventions to speed up weaving was the flying shuttle. It has the added advantage that a wider cloth can be woven if the shuttle is thrown through the shed by a spring. Without this the width of the cloth is limited by the length of the weaver's arms – how far can he throw and catch the shuttle?

144

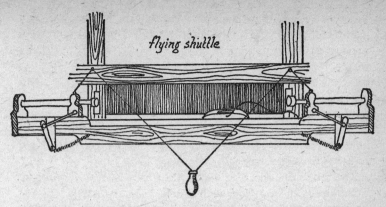

flying shuttle

The weaver uses the handle in the middle to give a sharp pull to the right-hand driver. The shuttle is thrown out of its box, through the shed in the warp, and is caught in the box on the other side. The shed is changed, the handle tugs this time at the left-hand driver, and the shuttle is shot back into the right-hand box. The modern flying shuttle is slightly different from other boat shuttles in that the thread emerges through a hole at the tip, so that it is trailed through the shed and the weft tension is kept correct. A further refinement is a lever that selects different levels of shuttle boxes, so that different colours can be combined without the weaver having to stop. With a flying shuttle a professional weaver might weave 900 cm an hour, without one about 800 cm.

Finishing cloth
Wool

The cloth can be bleached at this stage (see page 265) using hydrogen peroxide rinsed out afterwards with water. Hypochlorite bleach tends to retain active chlorine.

A more ancient method is 'stoving'. The damp woollen yarn or fabric is hung from overhead wooden poles in a closed chamber. Heaps of sulphur are ignited on the floor of the chamber and the chamber is filled with sulphur dioxide fumes, which becomes sulphuric acid on contact with the damp wool (SO_2 and H_2O to give H_2SO_4). The wool is left in the chamber overnight and the fumes whiten it. The effect is not permanent, however, and in time the wool reverts to a yellowish colour.

Woollen materials, particularly tweeds, are milled to impart a fuller, denser texture. The material is washed and squeezed in warm, soapy water, then rinsed thoroughly in pure, soft water. It should not be wrung, but the wetness should be squeezed from it. The alternate compression and relaxation felts the fibres together and shrinks the material slightly, so that it should not shrink as a made-up garment. The amount of milling required is best learned by experience. A large length of tweed can be washed blanket-fashion in the bath, with the feet. The material is laid out carefully to dry, preferably under tension and away from direct sunlight, then steam pressed.

The nap of the wool is raised to give a hairy surface to the cloth. Traditionally this was done with teasels, tied on a stick in a bunch. The normal wild teasel is *Dipsacus fullonem sylvestris*, but its bristles are not hooked. What is needed is *Dipsacus fullonem sativus*, the fuller's teasel, which has hooked bristles. Although it is not supposed to be native to Britain, in fact it grows wild all over the old cloth districts. It is quite common in East Anglia, for instance.

To obtain the opposite effect – a very smooth cloth – the hairs are raised, then singed, and the sparks are extinguished by wetting the cloth. If you are willing to risk it, having got this far, you are welcome!

Linen

Linen, too, can be bleached as cloth (see page 265).

It is also 'beetled'. Beetling of linen cloth closes up the space between the threads, flattens them and gives a smooth, lustrous look to the cloth. Both sides of the cloth in turn are subjected to rapid blows across the surface from rounded wooden hammers. The process can continue for quite some time – in some cases for up to 36 hours.

Buildings

Primitive shelters

One of the simplest shelters to make is a variant of the thatched wooden framework. Green saplings are cut to length, one end is inserted into the ground and the other lashed to a ridge pole or to another upright. The lashing can be of rope, split and soaked bark (preferably from an ash pole) or thin withies. It is important to choose a well-drained site which is reasonably level. If the ground slopes, check the direction of the watershed from higher up the slope. One safeguard against flooding is to dig a shallow trench around the outside of the shelter to carry away rainwater from the roof, and to prevent surface water from flowing into the shelter.

Such shelters have developed in two basic ways, both being adapted to the needs of their users: the tepee or tent for nomadic people, and the thatched log or stone hut for people living a settled life.

Houses

All modern dwellings have developed from primitive structures and although this is not always apparent because of new and sophisticated materials, the basic engineering principles are often similar to the methods that have been in use for hundreds of years.

The simplest permanent dwelling is a single-storey cottage, with walls of wood, stone, bricks, rammed earth (see page 150) or just earth – known in England as 'cob' – with a timbered roof covered with thatched straw, reeds, slates or tiles. In recent times building regulations have insisted that certain refinements be incorporated in any new building to improve the standard of comfort for the inhabitants and the outside appearance for passers-by.

The basic building regulations are concerned with the following:

Provision of a damp course around the walls just above ground level and beneath inside floors to prevent water from rising up from the earth below the house.

Provision of a cavity in all external walls to prevent rainwater from penetrating the walls. This cavity also acts as an insulator and in most cases it can be made more efficient by being filled with some kind of waterproof lagging, such as plastic foam.

Provision of adequate window area for the size of room and also adequate ventilation, determined by the size of windows that can be opened and that of ventilators.

Provision of adequate ceiling height in all rooms.

Limits to the height and depth of steps and stairs.

Limits to the height and pitch of roofs and the size and spacing of timber for roofs and floors.

Limits to the arrangement of rooms. A toilet must not open directly off a kitchen, for example.

Plumbing and pipe-work. Especially for sewage, plumbing and pipe-work must conform to certain standards.

Although some of these regulations are complicated and local building inspectors are often not disposed kindly toward self-builders, a basic knowledge of the regulations plus a degree of determination will generally be successful. If you can display, modestly, some knowledge of the subject and show a moderate proficiency in what you have done, most local council officials will give you advice readily and will then leave you to complete your project in peace. What they do not like is to arrive to find you building without having first submitted plans for their approval, or to find you building a magnificent eyesore. Local councils vary, but in general you do not need to have plans passed for minor alterations.

The roof

The framework of a roof is made from timbers and the roof presses outward and downward. The rafters carry the weight to a wooden wall plate that is set into the load-bearing walls at the outside of the building, and by struts from the rafters to the interior load-bearing walls. The collars hold the outward pressure together with the joists that rest on the wall plates.

The roof can be covered with a variety of materials, depending on what is available locally. Thatch is more durable and much less inflammable than you may imagine. A thatch made from rye or wheat straw will last ten years or more, especially if the straw has not been broken in threshing. A thatch made from Norfolk reed (*Phragmites communis*), which grows all over the country, in fact, makes the best thatch of all and lasts almost a lifetime – seventy years or perhaps longer. Thatch is not difficult to put on, but you need a very large amount of material. A thatch roof is light and can be fastened to round, unseasoned timber, straight from the bush.

A turf roof provides very good insulation, but it is heavy and needs plenty of timber beneath it. This can, however, be green timber. Before laying the turf, cover the timbers with strong plastic sheeting to make the roof waterproof. A turf roof looks delightful.

The roof can be covered with flexible corrugated plastic, but you are then half way to a solar roof (see page 200). Plastic sheeting looks good, lasts well and is light.

The cheapest (and ugliest) roof of all, but one of the best, can be made from old corrugated iron sheeting and fertilizer bags. Lay a layer of corrugated iron – which must have a slope. Then lay a layer of old fertilizer bags – farmers burn them by the thousand every year. Finally make a second layer of corrugated iron, to give you a roof that

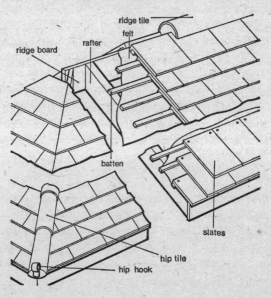

ridge tile

felt

rafter

ridge board

batten

slates

hip tile

hip hook

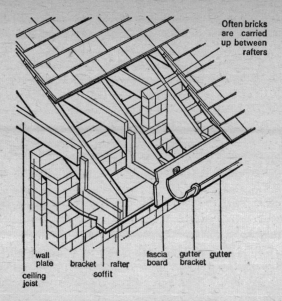

Often bricks are carried up between rafters

wall plate | bracket | rafter | fascia board | gutter bracket | gutter
ceiling joist | soffit

is weatherproof and well insulated. It does not matter how many holes there are in the corrugated iron because no water can get past the fertilizer bags: make sure they overlap when you lay them.

Walls

Walls should be made from materials that are easily available. Rammed earth should be possible in most places (see below). Mud and rock make serviceable walls, rendered with a mixture of burnt lime and sand (see page 159).

To insulate outside walls, make them at least 0.5 to 1 m thick, or, if they are to be thinner than that, in two parts with a space between. Fill the cavity with insulating material or clad the walls as they are built. Remember to fasten the inner and outer walls together with ties.

Rammed earth

Rammed earth, or *pisé de terre*, is the process of making walls by pounding subsoil. The technique is similar to the natural formation of stone, where subsoil particles are pressed tightly together, so increasing their natural cohesion. Rammed-earth walls may be made monolithically, between movable shutters, to give a solid wall made as a single unit, or from blocks made in a block moulder and used like bricks or stones.

Raw materials

The best rammed earth is made with granular, sandy soils, with an even distribution of particles of different sizes.

Dig the soil from below the topsoil level, 0.5 to 1 metre below the surface. Avoid vegetable matter and topsoil containing humus. Lay the soil out to dry, breaking up large clods. When it is dry enough, sieve it to remove stones larger than 2.5 cm diameter. Up to 45 per cent of pebbles smaller than this will increase the strength of rammed earth.

Add enough water to overcome friction between particles, but keep it to a minimum to avoid shrinkage. 8 to 12 per cent of the total weight should be water.

The addition of about 5 per cent of cement will increase weather r sistance. Sandy soils are more easily stabilized with sand than are clay soils. If you are using poor soils, increase the thickness of the walls to improve weatherproofing.

Rammed-earth walls are built on to a base of brick, stone or some other material that is highly resistant to frost attack. The base should be about 0.6 metre above ground level.

Shuttering

Shuttering is a robust wooden frame, usually between 350–600 mm in width, 70 to 90 cm high and as long as is convenient to use; usually about 3 metres. The shuttering is plumbed, locked into position, and the earth is pounded into place in 10-cm layers, using a ramming iron. The course is built up, layer by layer, until it reaches the top of the shutters; these are then moved forward. Each succeeding course is added by moving the shutters in the opposite direction to that used for the previous course.

Shuttering must be strong, up to 5 cm thick and secured with heavy

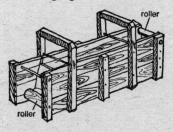

bracing. Using boards 15 × 5 cm, stiffened by wooden cleats 7.5 × 5 cm, build a frame (as shown in the illustration). At each end fit a 7.5-cm diameter roller as wide as you wish the wall to be (about 60 cm) and fixed on 4-cm axle bolts. One roller is fixed in a high position, the other low down. Inside the shutters, and free from the rollers, cut vertical and inclined grooves to accept end boards. Vertical end boards are used at the end of walls and at openings, and diagonal boards are used where rammed earth sections are to join, the boards being inclined inwards at the top. This provides a keyed sloping face and assists the bonding of the next section of earth. The cleats are fastened to the shutters by nuts and bolts. When removed, the cleats relax and permit the shuttering to be moved.

The shuttering is placed in position, plumbed and clamped. Earth is pounded in until the section is finished. Then the clamps are released and the shuttering is pushed forward until the rear, high roller is about 8 cm from the end of the completed section. The shuttering is plumbed again, clamped and the process repeated.

For corners, use a special shuttering assembly that allows both limbs of the junction to be rammed, as shown in the illustration.

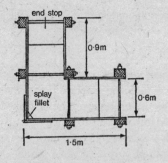

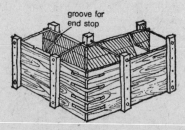

A more sophisticated method, the Cinva ram

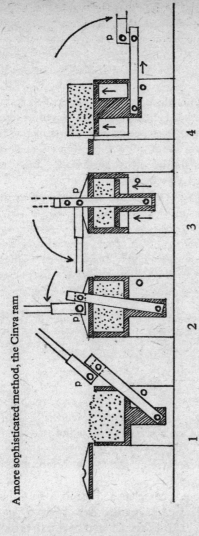

1 The lid is swung open on a horizontal pivot, the mould filled with a constant volume of soil and the lid replaced. 2 The lever pivot P is positioned in a socket on the lid. 3 The lever is depressed and maximum compression applied with lever horizontal. 4 The lid is swung open, P unsocketed and the block is extracted

Strength

A rammed-earth wall can accept loads of up to 270 kg per square metre, provided the loads are vertical. There is much less resistance to lateral pressures.

Finishing

It is usual to finish a rammed-earth wall with a rendering, but these are difficult to apply. A key helps to reinforce the rendering and can be made from chicken wire stretched over the wall surface. Rendering is made from two coats of plaster.

Alternatively, you can finish with two coats of tar. Throw sand over the second coat and then whitewash with a lime wash.

Allow the walls to dry out for as long as possible before the finish applied.

Warning

Avoid projecting walls in the design of a rammed-earth house. This causes great complications in the shuttering.

Pre-cast blocks

These have the advantage of standard size, weight and behaviour, which makes them more suitable for thinner walls and cavity walls. They are made in moulding machines which exert great pressure, but are simple to use.

Foundations

Foundations should be marked out on the levelled site according to the ground-floor plan of the house, with the aid of pegs and line and a measuring tape.

It is a good plan to remove all the topsoil before marking out, although this can be done later.

When the marking-out is complete and the lines are in place, dig the foundation trenches. Generally these are between 60 and 90 cm deep for a small house, but they should be deeper if the ground is at all soft.

When the trenches have been dug, hammer a peg into the bottom until its top is exactly level with the depth of the foundation – usually 20 cm. Then drive more pegs into the bottom of the trench and use a straight staff, about 2 m long, and a spirit level to make sure the tops of the pegs are level. Work round the trench, so that you can check

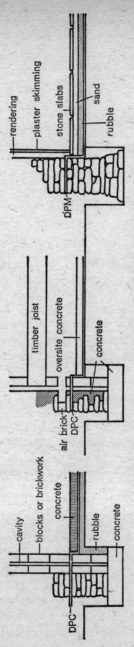

Walls: alternative methods of construction showing foundations and DPC

cavity
blocks or brickwork
concrete
rubble
concrete
DPC

timber joist
oversite concrete
concrete
air brick
DPC
concrete

rendering
plaster skimming
stone slabs
sand
rubble
DPM

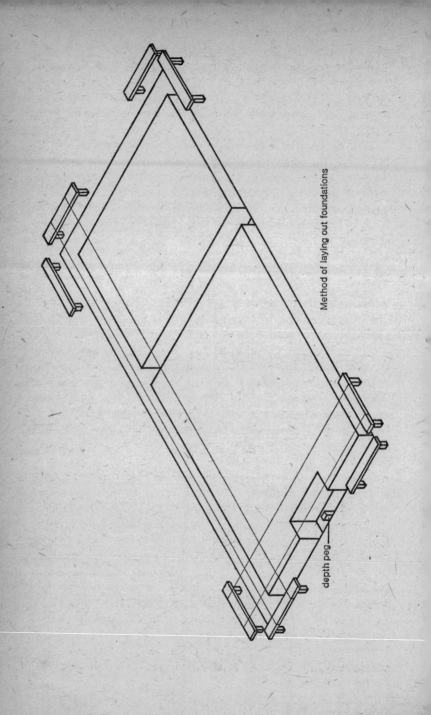

Method of laying out foundations

depth peg

your accuracy by levelling the last peg against the first.

The best material for making foundations is concrete. It should now be poured in – preferably all in one operation, which will make it stronger. If you cannot obtain concrete, you can make foundations from large flat stones, bedded in damp, stone-free subsoil well compressed.

When the foundations are complete and the concrete (if you use it) has set, you can begin the footings. For a larger, two-storey building these form a wider, solid section of wall whose width reduces gradually toward ground level. The footings spread the weight of the main walls on the foundations. For a small building, however, you should simply begin to build the walls with the same thickness below ground as above.

Walls

The main outer and inner walls and the chimney breasts are all built up at the same time, which enables them to be bonded together. Begin building the walls from the corners, making sure that they are square and upright. Then, using a line, build up the intervening sections. Build all the walls to a height of at least 10 cm above ground level and then level them off ready to receive the damp-proof course. This usually consists of a thick layer of bitumen felt, although you can use thick polythene sheet, vitreous tiles or a double layer of slates. Make sure that the two separate damp-proof courses for the inner and outer parts of the cavity wall do not meet, as otherwise cement droppings will build up and transmit moisture.

Above the damp-proof course the walls can be continued in the same manner, first building up the quoins or corners. Set the window and door frames into the walls when they reach the appropriate height.

There should be a vertical damp-proof course between the cavities around any openings, such as windows or doors, and above such openings there must be two substantial lintels to carry the weight of the wall. Usually these are made from reinforced concrete or stone. Hardwood, such as oak, can be used, but normally it will not be accepted by the council surveyor. Above the lintels the cavity must be bridged by a stepped, horizontal damp-proof course, as in the drawing of the window on page 166.

The outside walls can be finished with a variety of coating materials, such as rendering, rough-cast or pebble-dashing. If the walls are made

N

W   E

S

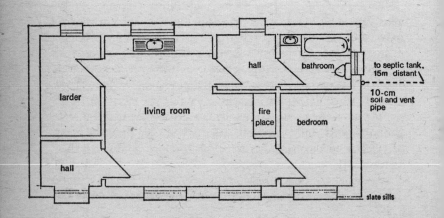

larder

living room

hall

hall

fire
place

bedroom

bathroom

to septic tank,
15m distant

10-cm
soil and vent
pipe

slate sills

Simple, single-storey dwelling of stone construction with a slate roof. Roof to be felted and insulated with 75-mm fibreglass or similar. Floors cement – on 10-cm concrete sub-floor on DP membrane. Interior walls block or brick, outer walls cavity block-work with stone outer leaf. Drainage – single stack system, 10-cm S & V pipe, 31-mm-dia. waste pipes to sink and washbasin, 38-mm dia. waste to bath, all with 75-mm deep-seal traps. 10-cm-dia. vitreous clay drains at 1–40 average fall to 600-gallon septic tank. 5-cm-dia. gutter down-pipes; 10-cm clay pipes to soakaway.

from brick or stone, they should be pointed neatly with a strong sand-cement mix (see page 161).

When the walls are above ground level, the concrete sub-floor may be put in, over a suitable damp-proof membrane such as polythene or bitumenous felt. If there is to be a suspended wooden floor on the ground floor, this sub-floor is still necessary, although it need not be quite so substantial. The damp-proof membrane should abut the damp-proof course in the walls to prevent penetration at this point. With suspended wooden floors downstairs, you should also insert air bricks for ventilation.

Mortars

Mortars are used to bond together bricks, blocks or stones, which may be of differing sizes, into a wall in which stresses are well distributed. The mortar also provides weather protection.

What is mortar?

Mud can be used in some conditions, but mortars are nearly always made with sand bonded with lime or cement or both. Until the last century they were made with sand and lime only.

Lime is made (see page 26) by burning a limestone, such as chalk, in a kiln to form quicklime, which is slaked with water. In this form it is sold under the name of hydrated lime.

Pure limes form a smooth plastic mortar which sets very slowly. Hydraulic limes, not easily obtainable in Britain, harden under water. If you can obtain them, they are ideal mortar material. The slow-setting times of pure lime mortars can be improved by adding a little cement or a pozzolanic (named after a porous variety of volcanic ash found near Pozzuoli) substance such as volcanic ash, coal or wood ash, pulverized fly ash (PFA), crushed bricks or any fired clay in a powder form.

Used alone, sand and cement form mortars much too hard for normal use. They are also very difficult to use unless their workability is increased by adding either lime or a commercial air-entraining plasticizer.

Masonry cement is a commercially available mixture of Portland cement, an air-entraining plasticizer and an inert filler.

Which mortar should you use?

In choosing a mortar you must balance cost, workability, early strength and final strength, as well as the availability of materials – which always affects their cost.

Cost: Lime is almost always cheaper than cement, certainly when measured by volume (which is how it is batched in actual use).

Early strength: This is needed if you are building quickly. In winter, frost will damage an unset mortar; under a heavy imposed load an unset mortar will ooze out. Our forefathers avoided these hazards by working slowly and not working in winter. Today, we can add cement to get an early set, but hydraulic limes and pure limes with pozzolana can set quickly enough.

Workability: If you are to work quickly and accurately, a mortar must be very plastic and retain water against the suction of dry blocks or bricks. You can achieve this by so proportioning the coarse sand and the fine particles (lime and cement) that the spaces between sand grains are completely filled. Commercial plasticizers capture small bubbles of air to lubricate the sand. Cement is much harsher than lime and should not be used on its own.

Final strength: The strength of the mortar has little effect on the strength of the wall. Except for extreme loads, one should choose a weak mortar. This is cheaper and it increases weather proofing by allowing a little deformation without breaking into wide cracks.

Recipes

If you must work in winter, use a stronger mortar. If not, choose one of these:

1 volume hydraulic lime: 2 or 3 volumes sand

1 volume cement: 2 volumes hydrated lime (putty): 9 volumes sand

1 volume cement: commercial plasticizer as instructions:
   7 to 9 volumes sand

1 volume masonry cement: 6 volumes sand
1 volume lime and pozzolana mix: 2 volumes sand (by experiment)

To produce a stronger mortar add cement or pozzolana, but retain the proportion of fine:coarse particles of 1:2 or 3.

Preparation and use

Hydraulic limes vary from source to source and you must seek the advice of the manufacturer.

If you produce the lime yourself you *must* experiment.

There is a great advantage to be gained by maturing pure lime. Mix hydrated lime with wet sand to form 'coarse stuff'. Keep it covered and wet for three weeks or more (the Romans waited for three years!). Knock up the coarse stuff and batch it with cement or pozzolana immediately before use.

Lime does not increase the volume of sand appreciably, so that for, say, a 1:2:9 mix, use one volume of cement and nine volumes of coarse stuff.

Mix with water so that the mortar just hangs from the trowel. You can mix in a small cement mixer, but muscles and a shovel will do as well.

Home-made mortar

Cement can be used to give any required properties, so builders usually prefer cement mortars. Cement requires the expenditure of much energy in its manufacture, and you cannot make it yourself. You can produce your own lime: even if you must buy it you will find it cheaper than cement. Lime mortars require much more care and sensitivity in their use.

Pointing

Pointing is the facing of joints between bricks with a mortar that is harder than the mortar used in building. Joints, especially in chimney stacks, need repointing from time to time.

Rake out the joint to a depth of at least 2.5 cm, using a special

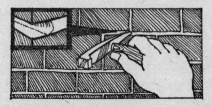

raking tool or the tang of an old file. Brush the joints with a stiff brush and wet them thoroughly.

Use freshly mixed mortar and work a small area at a time. The joint should be kept wet, and the mortar must not be too wet.

You will need a hawk, which is a board mounted at right angles to a central handle, and a pointed trowel.

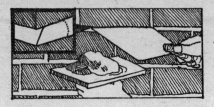

Flashings

Flashings are strips of metal, usually zinc or lead, inserted into the joints of exterior brickwork, often at the base of chimney stacks or over doors and windows not protected by the eaves. They prevent damp from entering the house.

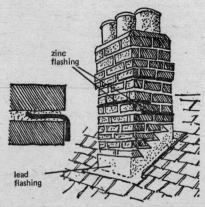

zinc flashing

lead flashing

Zinc, the most common flashing material for windows and doors, will deteriorate in time. Rake out the joint, cut new flashing to fit, and seal in with fresh, hard mortar. You will need a pair of tin snips to cut the metal to shape.

Roofs

Make the roof trusses first. Begin by making a truss of the correct dimensions from battens, and use this as a pattern. Unless the trusses are very large and heavy they can be made on the ground and then offered up. If you have no bolts or timber-connectors, the collars can be pegged with tapered wedges.

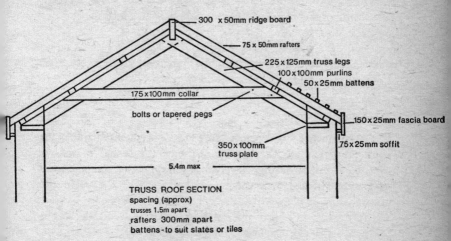

300 x 50mm ridge board

75 x 50mm rafters

225 x 125mm truss legs

100 x 100mm purlins

50 x 25mm battens

175 x 100mm collar

bolts or tapered pegs

150 x 25mm fascia board

75 x 25mm soffit

350 x 100mm truss plate

5.4m max

TRUSS ROOF SECTION
spacing (approx)
trusses 1.5m apart
rafters 300mm apart
battens - to suit slates or tiles

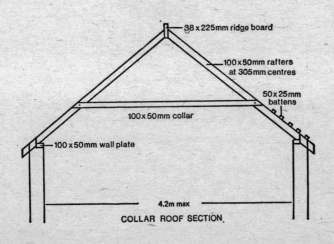

38 x 225mm ridge board

100 x 50mm rafters at 305mm centres

50 x 25mm battens

100 x 50mm collar

100 x 50mm wall plate

4.2m max

COLLAR ROOF SECTION

When the trusses are in position and aligned correctly, the purlins and rafters should be nailed on. If the roof is to be tiled or slated with slates of the same size, you must fix horizontal battens, after which the roof can be clad and the ridge-tiles cemented on. If the roof is to be slated with random-sized slates, known as 'rag slates', the rafters themselves are used as battens and so they should be of thinner section – 50 mm square – and there should be more of them. Slates should be fixed with large-headed, galvanized slate nails. Stone slabs and tiles are generally pegged.

When the roof is finished, you can fit and glaze windows, put in external window sills of slate, tile, brick or cement, hang doors, make up steps, fit down pipes and carry out any external decoration.

Roof slates

Repair cracked roof slates at once, before they begin to let in water. Use an arrowhead nail ripper, slipping the arrowhead under the damaged slate. Jerk the tool sharply downwards and it will cut through the nails holding the slate in position. Use a replacement slate of exactly the same size as the one you removed. You will not be able to nail it in place without removing many more slates. Instead, use a strip of zinc 2.5 cm wide. Make a hook at one end, slip it over the good slate, slide the new one into place and make a second hook over the lower edge of the replacement to hold it.

Inside finishing

All inside walls, other than ones made from plasterboard, are normally rendered with a fairly weak sand-cement mix and then skimmed with finishing plaster. All concealed wiring, plumbing etc, should be in place before this is carried out and all internal skirting boards, door frames, sill-boards and architraves are usually fitted before the skimming is done.

Ceilings should be timbered and clad.

Finally, the solid sub-floors should be screeded with sand and cement and if they are to be covered with tiles you can do this now. If you are having suspended wooden floors, they should be fitted before the skirting and plastering.

It is a good idea to spend a little time planning the order of inside work before you commence, depending on the type of construction and the different finishes.

Drainage

Normally there are two systems of drainage: one for rainwater from down-pipes etc, which is piped away from the house to a soakaway, and the other for foul water and sewage, which is piped to a main sewer, a cesspit (which needs emptying every time it fills) or to a septic tank, which should go on working without any maintenance for years.

A septic tank consists of two chambers, the first of which is simply a tank to contain the effluent while anaerobic bacteria begin to break it down. The second chamber is filled with coarse gravel or clinker, through which the effluent percolates downwards to permit aerobic bacteria to digest it further. At the bottom of the second chamber there is an outlet to a soakaway, as shown in the diagram on page 166.

Drainage pipes above and below ground are available in several different materials and they often have their own system of watertight jointing sold with them. The most common underground pipes are of salt-glazed earthenware (see page 257) and if all types of pipe are unobtainable these would be the easiest to make for yourself.

The most essential part of sewage or foul-water piping is to have joints that are completely watertight, particularly if you have your own water supply from a nearby well or spring which could be contaminated by leaking foul water.

Joints in salt-glazed pipes are usually made from very strong cement, applied over a caulking of coarse, tarred hemp rope.

When laying the pipes, you should allow an adequate, but not excessive, fall of about one in forty. The pipes should line up properly and should not move when the trench is back-filled, as this will cause the joints to crack.

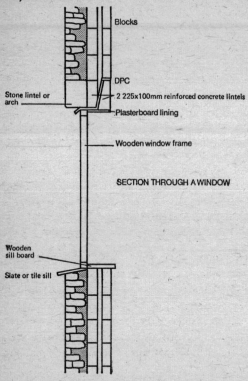

Blocks

DPC

Stone lintel or arch

2 225x100mm reinforced concrete lintels

Plasterboard lining

Wooden window frame

SECTION THROUGH A WINDOW

Wooden sill board

Slate or tile sill

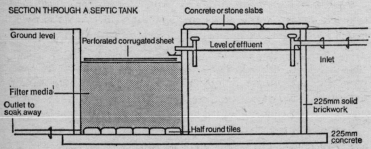

SECTION THROUGH A SEPTIC TANK

Concrete or stone slabs

Ground level

Perforated corrugated sheet

Level of effluent

Inlet

Filter media

Outlet to soak away

Half round tiles

225mm solid brickwork

225mm concrete

Plumbing

Cold-water system

If you are being connected to the water main, the local water board will supervise the tapping of the main. Thereafter any pipe work will be your responsibility, although the water board or local council surveyor may wish to inspect the work. If you have your own private supply, then you will need either a manual pump to fill the tank in the roof, or an electric pump and a float switch in the tank to keep it topped up. The float switch is a simple on/off switch activated by a lever connected to a float inside the tank, easily made from an old switch and a few odds and ends.

From the cold-water tank run the pipes that supply the bath and/or shower, washbasins, w.c. and kitchen sink. At the lowest point in the pipe work you should fit a drain cock and, if you are on mains water, a stopcock where the supply enters the house.

Where there is a ball-valve, which controls the flow of water into a water tank or w.c. cistern, you must fit an overflow pipe leading outside the house. This is seldom used, but should the ball-valve stick in the open position it will prevent flooding indoors.

Hot-water system

The simplest hot-water system is that which uses an electric immersion heater in the copper cylinder, which is fed from the cold tank. The cylinder must be situated at a lower level than the cold tank and the cold supply enters the lower part of the cylinder. The hot outlet is at the top of the cylinder, alongside the mounting for the immersion heater. An expansion pipe must also run from this top outlet, with its end positioned beneath the roof tank. This is a safety measure should the cylinder overheat.

If you plan to have a cooker or fire with a back boiler to heat the cylinder, you will need a second plumbing system, independent except for the cold-water supply from the roof tank. You will also need a different kind of cylinder, called an indirect cylinder. This second system ensures that the water which circulates through the boiler and the heating coils does not mix with the drinking and washing waters. This system, too, must have a drain cock and an extension pipe which spills into the second roof tank, known as the header tank.

Waste pipes from baths, sinks and washbasins should include a water-seal, known as a bottle trap. This seals the pipe with a layer of

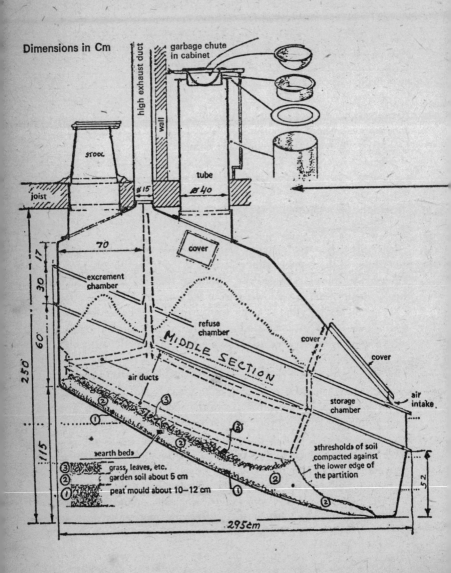

Clivus: Container consists of a bottom section and, where a greater capacity is required, also middle section(s)

Container in functioning position: height 220cm or 250cm or 280cm; length 295cm maximum; width 120cm

Dimensions in Cm

high exhaust duct

garbage chute in cabinet

wall

STOOL

joist

ø 15

tube

ø 40

70

cover

excrement chamber

refuse chamber

cover

cover

MIDDLE SECTION

air ducts

storage chamber

air intake

17
30
60
250
115
52

»earth bed»

»thresholds of soil compacted against the lower edge of the partition

③ grass, leaves, etc.
② garden soil about 5 cm
① peat mould about 10—12 cm

295cm

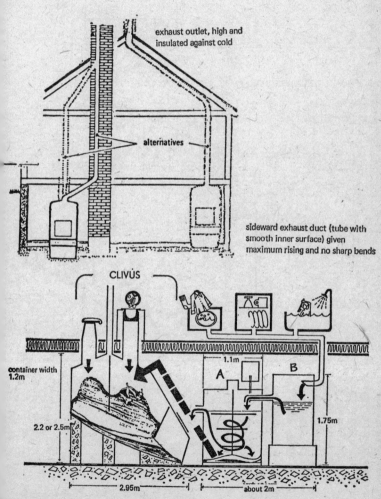

exhaust outlet, high and insulated against cold

alternatives

sideward exhaust duct (tube with smooth inner surface) given maximum rising and no sharp bends

CLIVUS

container width 1.2m

1.1m

A

B

2.2 or 2.5m

1.75m

2.95m

about 2m

Clivus combined with waste water system

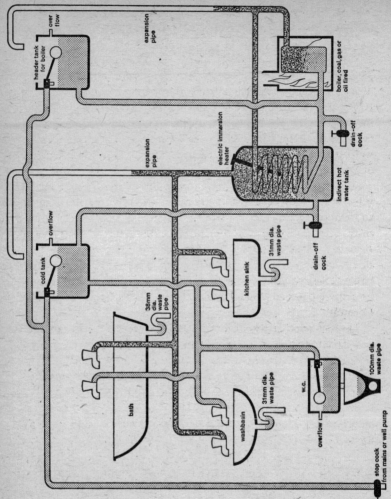

Basic plumbing for hot and cold services: most pipework is 15-mm copper-joined with compression or soldered connectors. Supply to kitchen sink, bath and indirect side of hot tank usually of 22-mm copper pipe. Waste and overflow usually of plastic pipe. All overflow pipes taken outside building.

header tank for boiler

over flow

expansion pipe

boiler, coal, gas or oil fired

drain-off cock

expansion pipe

electric immersion heater

indirect hot water tank

drain-off cock

cold tank

overflow

31mm dia. waste pipe

kitchen sink

38mm dia. waste pipe

bath

31mm dia. waste pipe

washbasin

w.c.

overflow

100mm dia. waste pipe

stop cock from mains or well pump

water and prevents foul air from entering the house from sewers. Outside gullies that are connected to the sewers should also have this.

Dry toilets

The flushing away of human sewage is a shameful waste both of the high-grade organic fertilizer in human sewage and of the 55,000 to 60,000 litres of drinking water used per WC per year. Earth closets, the time-honoured way of disposing of human excrement the world over, are not popular with health authorities, in spite of the fact that well maintained, they are safe. Chemical toilets are just plain dangerous to the biosphere.

So in the end we have to fall back on the Swedes, who have developed the Multrum Clivus, a dry toilet which composts excrement and kitchen wastes with no input of external energy whatever. No smells arise from its use, since it is designed so that a constant flow of air passes across the sewage from the inside of the house to the outside. Unfortunately, it is expensive, costing about £700; it is also bulky. These two factors have prevented anyone – so far as I know – from buying one in Britain, except for one that is being installed in Cornwall.

There is another Swedish toilet that accelerates the evaporation and decomposition of excrement to which kitchen wastes can be added, by electrical heating. The machine is kept smell-free by forced ventilation, using a fan which passes the air over the excrement from inside the house to outside. This toilet, the 'Mullbank' (see page 307), costs around £150, uses about 1,200 kw-h of electricity a year and is sufficient for a family of four. The compost tray needs emptying once a year.

Self-sufficiency in water

As with energy, so it is with water. Most of the technology developed during this century has increased our consumption. A single WC uses 55,000 to 60,000 litres of water a year. If you really wish to be self-sufficient, then cut down on your use of water, retaining only those uses that are essential and irreducible. Use a shower in place of a bath, thus saving about 90 litres per bath – 27,000 litres a year as well as over 1,000 kw-h of heat. Use hand sprinklers in the washbasins in place of fast-running taps. Your water use will now be reduced to about 23 litres per person per day for drinking, cooking, washing and showers. Even in the drier parts of eastern England and Scotland, where the rainfall is only some 50 cm a year, there is a precipitation of 491 litres per square metre per year. The roof area of the house in Kingston which we insulated (see page 183) receives an annual precipitation of 40,460 litres. Since water use is reduced to 23 litres per person per day, the family of four uses 33,580 litres a year. So wetter western areas provide a large surplus of water and, with great care, the eastern dweller also has a surplus.

The key to economical water use is storage. Periods of drought occur regularly. If your home is connected to the main supply then all you need do is economize on your use, while you plan a water cistern that will hold at least 12 months' supply for emergencies. If you are not connected to a mains supply, there is a more urgent need. If you are lucky enough to own a swimming pool you are well away; if not, a DIY self-installed pool using heavy PVC lining will give you the cheapest cistern you could have. Keep the water absolutely covered and in the dark. Always boil water you intend to drink and filter it for good measure. If you have ever lived in the tropics you will be familiar with the commonsense procedures that go with the careful use of precious water.

You can recycle your own 'grey' water using a treatment system that works in conjunction with the Clivus dry toilet. Waste water is received in one tank and then fed into a second tank where chemicals – usually aluminium sulphate – are stirred in mechanically. Wastes flocculate and are precipitated. The water is discharged and the sludge, containing almost all the nutrient salts (including phosphates if you use commercial detergents, which are a valuable fertilizer) can be transferred to the Multrum Clivus.

The house at Eithin

Members of BRAD (see page 276) count the building of their own house as one of their most important achievements. Work began on 1 April 1973 and by November the building was structurally complete and proof against the Welsh winter.

Three storeys high, with a capacity of 750 cubic metres, it accommodates eight adults and three children. The house stands as a vindication of the amateur. Built almost entirely without professional help, it has demystified such basic skills as carpentry, joinery, plumbing, bricklaying, stonemasonry, electrical wiring and glazing. With a combined previous experience ranging from nil to negligible, BRAD did it. Whilst much of what the eco-freaks call Alternative Technology is what other folk call plain labouring, given the freedom and the motivation anyone can build his or her own house. In this case the motivation was provided by the approaching Welsh winter when the existing accommodation consisted of tents, caravans and barns!

The house is really an extension to the existing farm cottage, forming a compromise between the cottage and the steep hillside. It is built almost entirely of wood, for reasons of cost (then!) and ease of amateur construction. Insulation is by 7.5-cm polystyrene blocks in walls and roof voids. Windows, home-built, are double-glazed and there is an airlock front door. Most heating is by wood stoves which consume about ten tons of wood a year – well within the productive capacity of the 11-acre hazel coppice – and the rest is by electric fan heaters and a heat pump. Most lighting is fluorescent, to save energy. Mains energy is used to pump water from a spring to the house supply, but the Savonious rotor windmill (see page 199) will take over when its pump is working properly. Hot water is provided by the solar roof (see page 200) which gives free hot water for six to eight months of the year and pre-heating for the electric immersion heater and the timber stove's back boiler in the winter. The aluminium sheeting covering the whole 60 square metres of solar roof went on in just four hours.

The house was built with no government or industrial grants. BRAD did not even receive an improvement grant for the old stone cottage, because the extension was not deemed to be a 'conventional dwelling house'.

The original farm cost £10,000 in the spring of 1972. The extension, its excavation, the architect's fee and the basic stocking of the farm cost just over that amount again. For a community of a dozen people, including, say, four children, the enterprise has cost about £1,750 per head.

Energy

What is energy?

Energy, we learnt at school, is the capacity of a system to do work. Conversely, a system without energy can do no work. The most telling characteristic of western industrial society has been, and indeed still is, its phenomenal capacity to do work, its energy. Or is it 'its' energy?

You do not need repeated the various analyses of the energy crisis that have been documented so well elsewhere. This book is intended for individuals who want to 'do something about it' themselves. To that end I may as well begin by analysing the terminology of the energy industry, because we really are in an Orwellian situation with the words used by it; a double-speak situation pivoting around the word 'production'. The energy industries talk about 'production' of oil, coal, gas and nuclear energy as if they actually were producing the stuff. Of course, they are not. They are *extracting* and *destroying* energy sources put there over hundreds of millions of years by nature. Coal, oil, gas and wood all started in living tissues, which act as solar collectors through the miraculous process of photosynthesis. Our own living today depends on these great solar collectors, our fields, forests and seas, being kept as clean and complex as nature made them; for to talk about using 'natural energy systems', without being aware that what we inhabit is already a great natural energy system, is to miss the whole point.

Photosynthesis is the process, and the sun the source, of all energy production (excepting nuclear). When we burn oil, gas, coal and wood we are, in fact, utilizing solar energy no less than if we were drawing off water from a solar collector or power from a local dam. Thus, excepting nuclear power once again, 99.8 per cent of our energy derives from the sun. Even wind and water power would not be there if the sun were not there. Thus we can and should look on the world as a giant repository of solar energy flux, only a tiny part of which is trapped into store through photosynthesis.

If we can clear our minds once again, we can see, therefore, that when we burn carbonaceous materials such as fossil fuels or wood, we are biting into energy *stock*, but when we tap directly into energy flux we are utilizing energy *income*. Energy flux, of course, is the radiant energy of the sun, the wind, the energy of the streams and sea currents, tides and waves. Energy flux over the earth as a whole is immense but almost constant. This is because the incoming energy of the sun over a wide range of radiations is matched by the equal loss of energy in direct reflection and long-wave radiation, both back into black and empty space. A small percentage of the incoming radiant energy is trapped into the life cycle, and a minute fraction of that is put into the energy bank which eventually will become a high-quality fossil fuel. That the system is in balance is of great importance to us; otherwise we would quickly frizzle or freeze to death. The only remaining energy income is the minute (by comparison) portion given by the tides.

How much solar energy is there?

At the outer edge of the Earth's atmosphere the energy flux is 1.395 kilowatts per square metre. This is called the 'solar constant' since, given minute variations, it is, in fact, constant. The total solar radiation intercepted by the Earth's diametric plane of 1.275×10^{14} (10^{14} is 10 followed by thirteen noughts) square metres is, therefore, 1.73×10^{17} watts. By comparison, the energy utilized daily (in 1975) by man is of the order of 6.5×10^{12} watts, or about one 26,000th of the total solar flux at the edge of the Earth. This would seem to indicate to the simple minded that we have not got an energy problem!

Energy and entropy

The concept of entropy is a mystery to most laymen. It ought not to be. The confusion arises because it seems to operate in reverse. It is generally a measurement of disorder in matter, and the greater the disorder, the greater the entropy. This is startling until you get used to it. Imagine, for example, particles of clay in the soil, lying at random all over the place. The second law of thermodynamics states that energy must always flow in such a direction that entropy increases. It is natural, then, for these clay particles to be distributed in a random fashion. If I do some work and make a little heap of them, then in time the rain and the wind will destroy my pile and redistribute the particles again. If I do even more work and gather clay, pack it and bake it into bricks and then assemble the bricks to make a house, I have done a great deal of work and expended much energy. In doing so I have created what in thermodynamic terms is called an unusual state of matter. I have made it much more organized, so that it forms regular patterns. I have increased its order and *decreased* its entropy. Eventually, I suppose, the house will collapse, the piles of rubble will weather away, and eventually the particles from which it is composed will be redistributed randomly. You may think something has been lost. So it has – order has been lost, but entropy has *increased*. That this law *appears* to be disobeyed in nature (it is not actually disobeyed) by the action of photosynthesis is useful to us – without it we would not exist – but it is irrelevant. When eventually the sun dies, the solar system will collapse and the famous second law will have reasserted itself.

Fossil fuel represents the most utilizable source of energy we have. Contained in a kilogram of high-grade fuel oil are 13.2 kilowatt-hours of energy. A kilowatt-hour is a 'unit' of electricity and represents the amount of power (or energy) needed to keep one bar of an electric fire hot for one hour. Because this is a unit of energy that is relatively well understood and measurable to the layman (while the joule is not) it is the unit to which I refer throughout.

The point about entropy is that once you have burnt fuel oil (with low entropy) and have turned it into gases, water and heat (with high entropy – distributed randomly) you have effectively lost it forever. The gases and water will, through photosynthesis, join to form carbonaceous fuel, but the heat will have radiated into space. You cannot recycle energy.

To get an idea of the 'quality' of various energy packages, have a look at the table comparing familiar and everyday objects. Their energy loads are related to each other in kilowatts (power units) or kilowatt-hours (energy units).

	Energy
Man sitting	0.080 kw
Olympic athlete sprinting	0.75 kw
Mini travelling at 30 mph: useful	6 kw
(50 mpg assumed) wasted	23 kw
total	29 kw
Rolls Royce travelling at 50 mph: useful	25 kw
(12 mpg assumed) wasted	96 kw
total	121 kw
Candle flame	0.1 kw
Needed to boil 1-litre kettle	0.15 kw
Flat plate collector, bright June, in midday sun, low water temperature	1 kw/m^2
Ditto, but high water temperature	0.2 kw/m^2
Flat plate collector, dull summer day, low water temperature	0.4 kw/m^2
Energy in wind at 20 mph	0.4 kw/m^2
Av. utilizable energy in London area (av. 10 mph wind) 33 per cent COP (Coefficient of Performance)	0.015 kw/m^2
Av. utilizable energy in western Britain (15 mph wind) 33 per cent COP	0.045 kw/m^2
Average three-bedroom house, wind blowing: outside temp. 7.2°C, inside temp. 20°C, insulated badly	15 kw
River 3 m wide, 0.6 m deep flowing at 30 cm/sec. over weir 1.8 m high: total available	10 kw
total usable (COP 80 per cent)	8 kw
1 kg fuel oil	12 kw-h
1 kg anthracite	8 kw-h
1 cu. metre North Sea gas (methane)	10 kw-h
1 kg wood	4.4 kw-h

An understanding achieved by a study of this table and some calculations on one's own energy-using activities will help when trying to design a way of living which either utilizes less energy or uses it more efficiently.

The way we live now

Profligately and uncomfortably! There are 55 million people in these islands. By no means are our homes, workplaces and shops comfortable, but we spend 40 per cent of our country's energy consumption on heating and servicing them. This amounts to 80 million tons of oil equivalent per year, of which 75 per cent or 60 million tons, goes to heat our 18 million houses. This amounts to well over 3 tons of oil equivalent (40,000 kw-h) per house, which is spread unevenly between the rich and the poor.

The fact that so much energy is poured into heating homes certainly does not mean that homes are heated adequately or ventilated. The reverse is true. Although central heating is a standard feature of many new homes, or older homes of the burgeoning middle classes, most homes are still heated very badly. Probably 75 per cent of homes are still below Parker Morris standards (which govern space, heating and lighting standards in Local Authority new housing). By no stretch of the imagination does this mean that insufficient energy is being expended – it simply means that most homes are badly insulated and draughty and that wildly inefficient heating systems are used. There has also been an unfortunate tendency towards increasing window area in recent years. Besides being an expensive material for walling, glass has also one of the lowest insulation values of any building material known. Were a proper programme of insulation to be embarked upon, the energy savings to the individual and to Britain would be felt in improved comfort, as well as in reduced fuel bills.

	UK stock of uninsulated houses, September 1973 (millions)	Potential savings per annum from 75 mm roof insulation	
		Cash (£m)	Energy (kw-h)
Centrally heated houses	2.4	48.6	11,520 m
Not centrally heated	7.9	59.2	14,270 m
Total	10.3	107.8	25,790 m

Table courtesy of Eurisol-UK.

The table does not show what wastage is occurring in the four million or so flats, nor what additional energy might be saved by insulating walls and ceilings against draughts. But we can hypothesize that were these done properly, we might be improving our balance of payments in this sector alone by some £250 million per year – or the equivalent of $5\frac{1}{2}$ million tons of oil per year.

In fact, this figure is only the beginning of what can be achieved by careful design, which anybody can carry out.

	Inside temperatures	
	Living areas	Elsewhere
Parker Morris	18.5°C	13°C
IHVE	21°C	16°C
My recommendation	16°C	12°C

Design for comfortable low-energy living

Over and above the need to insulate is the need to set the right internal temperature for comfort. The adoption of Institute of Heating and Ventilating Engineers (IHVE) standards shown above would, spread through the houses and bungalows of the United Kingdom, cause a loss over and above the Parker Morris standards of some $15,000 \times 10^6$ kw-h per annum. To put it another way, the adoption of Parker Morris standards rather than IHVE standards could make annual heating bills 100 per cent lower in a mild winter and 50 per cent lower in a more severe winter.

My own experience is that ambient temperatures in a house may be lower again even than Parker Morris, without any discomfort at all. Temperatures any lower than those shown are not recommended because warmth in a house controls the level of damp in walls. Control of damp is critical not only to the health and comfort of the occupants, but also to the structural welfare of the home.

A pernicious fallacy has arisen in recent years, thanks mainly to extensive advertising and propaganda by the energy agencies, that there is a sort of fundamental right of people to be unclothed in the home all winter. I enjoy nudity as much as anyone, but the energy bill for this is inconceivable. Be warmly and adequately dressed. It is the best and cheapest form of central heating and it places no imposition whatever on gracious and adequate living.

What is comfort?

The human body needs to avoid having a high net loss of radiation. If you stand near a cold window or wall you will notice that those parts of your body nearest the cold surface feel chilled. This phenomenon is called 'cold radiation'. It is desirable that so far as possible radiation from the body should be reflected back, allowing a high level of comfort at cool air temperatures.

Not all people can live by the standard I recommend. Some older

U values of common materials

	W/m²°C	50-mm insulation W/m²°C	75-mm insulation W/m²°C
Brick wall 114 mm unplastered	3.6	2.2	2.0–1.5
Brick wall 228 mm plastered	2.7	1.3	0.4–0.8
Brick wall 278 mm cavity, plastered	1.7	0.7–0.5	0.2–0.5
Concrete wall 100 mm	4.0	3.0	2.3
Concrete wall 150 mm	3.6	2.6	1.9
Single glazing	5.7	not applicable	
Double glazing	2.8	not applicable	
Concrete roof 150 mm with asphalt	3.6	2.4	0.36
Pitched roof, tiles on battens, roofing felt and plasterboard ceilings	1.5	0.48	0.36
Solid floor, contact with earth	0.6	not applicable	
Suspended floor	0.59	not applicable	

Note: the insulation is assumed to be polystyrene foam for external use and glassfibre for internal use.

people, confined to wheelchairs or to bed, need IHVE standards to avoid death from hypothermia. Younger people who are more active should keep room temperatures down and dress warmly. Keep a small but accurate thermometer in most rooms and use it. You will lower your energy consumption and give a new lease of life to the Earth's dwindling energy reserves. You will influence the price and availability of fuel and warmth for your old age and that of your children.

Calculating heat losses

Basically, there are two ways by which heat can be lost from a house. Neither is difficult to understand or to calculate. Anyone able to tot up a milk bill at the end of the week can do his own sums. Heat is lost by conduction and radiation, and by the exchange of air.

Conduction and radiation losses: Radiation losses occur because the inside wall of a house is warmer than the outside. Heat is conducted through the wall and then radiated out or lost through convection. The formula for calculating this type of heat loss, which occurs mainly through walls and ceilings, is: heat loss/hour$=$U$\times$area$\times$temperature difference. U, a constant, is called the coefficient of heat loss and is measured in watts per hour (W) per square metre per degree C.

Calculate the external skin of your house by measurement. Treat the loft as an external skin if you do not intend to heat it. Treat any rooms you do not intend to heat as though they were the outside. Having determined your internal and external design temperatures, you can do a preliminary calculation on radiant heat loss. Use a map of Great Britain and the following average temperatures in assessing

Average mid-winter temperatures °C

Kirkwall	3.8	Birmingham	3.9
Wick	3.4	Cambridge	3.4
Skye	4.4	Aberystwyth	4.5
Greenock	4.2	Milford Haven	5.2
Edinburgh	3.3	Cardiff	4.4
Newcastle-upon-Tyne	4.0	London (Kew)	4.2
Blackpool	3.9	Brighton	4.5
Leeds	2.8	Falmouth	6.8
Hull	3.7	Belfast	3.8
Liverpool	4.5		

the external temperature for which you should allow. Use the average figures because they will give you an optimum solution. When the weather is really cold, you need to readjust your life in the time-honoured fashion and limit your living area.

Rate at which temperature falls with height

Elevation (metres)	Average drop °C
100	0.5
300	1.5
500	2.5

Air change losses: The air in your room is at a different temperature from the air outside, but air changes are necessary. In a kitchen, toilet and bathroom you need about two changes per hour, and in all other rooms 1 to $1\frac{1}{2}$. Each cubic metre of air requires about 0.34 watts of heat to warm it through one degree C. Carry out a volumetric calculation of your house, room by room, and calculate the heat loss based on the *desirable* air changes. In an old house with unsealed windows and doors, it is likely that the air changes in windy weather amount to several times those desired, but we can cure that later.

Sample calculation for a house in Kingston, Surrey

Assumptions: The mid-winter average temperature is 4.2°C. Let us call it 4°C. The whole house will be kept warm. Certain areas used only occasionally will need temperature boosting for short periods from time to time. No heavy investment is required to give these rooms reasonable average comfort. No heat flow occurs through the party wall. The heating season lasts for 180 days.

Improved	Unimproved
Loss from ceiling	
Area 80.6 m²	Area 80.6m²
Temp. drop 8°C. U=0.36	Temp. drop 8°C. U=1.5
Heat loss $=80.6 \times 8 \times 0.36$	Heat loss $=80.6 \times 8 \times 1.5$
$=232$ watts	$=970$ watts
Loss from walls	
Area 238m²	Area 238 m²
Temp. drop 9°C. U=0.4	Temp. drop 9°C. U=2.5
(i.e. $\frac{8+8+12}{3}$)	
Heat loss $=238 \times 9 \times 0.4$	Heat loss $=238 \times 9 \times 2.5$
$=857$ watts	$=5{,}355$ watts

continued

Improved	Unimproved
Loss from windows	
Area, first and second floors, 12.3m²	Area 12.3 m²
Temp. drop 8°C. U (double glazing) =2.8	Temp. drop 8°C. U (single glazing) =5.7
Heat loss =12.3×8×2.8 =276 watts	Heat loss =12.3×8×5.7 =561 watts
Window and door area on the ground floor, 13.6 m²	Area 13.6 m²
Temp. drop 12°C. U (double glazing) =2.8	Temp. drop 12°C. U (single glazing) =5.6
Heat loss =13.6×12×2.8 =457 watts	Heat loss =13.6×12×5.6 =914 watts
Loss through ground floor	
Area 80.6	
U=0.5	
Temp. drop 12°C	
Heat loss =80.6×12×0.5 =484 watts	The same
Loss through air changes	
Volume of house 616 m³	Volume 616 m³
Average air changes/hour × 1.5	Average air changes/hour =6
Average internal air temp. 14°C (i.e. $\frac{16+12+12}{3}$)	Average internal air temp. 14°C
Heat loss =616×1.5×0.34×10 =3,142 watts	Heat loss =616×6×0.34×10 =12,566 watts

Note: 0.34 watts/hour raise 1m³ of air through 1°C/hour

Summary

	Improved	Unimproved
Ceilings	235 watts	970 watts
Walls	857	5,355
Windows	277	550
	455	910
Ground floor	482	482
Air changes	3,140	12,600
	5,446	20,867

Because, in fact, the average outside winter temperature is often much more than 4°C, the average heat load can often be much less than that shown.

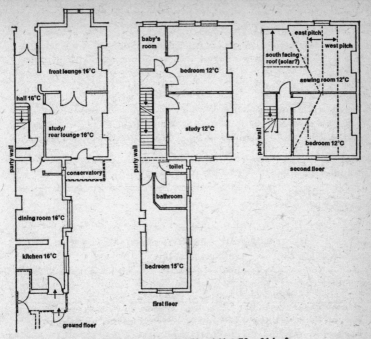

The floor area of the house $= 80.6 \times 2 + 53 = 161 + 53 = 214\text{m}^2$

Heating load, improved house $= 26$ watts/m^2

Heating load, unimproved house $= 100$ watts/m^2

Reducing heat losses

Radiation – insulation

Roof space: Seal off the roof space with 10-cm thick fibreglass roll. This should cost you approximately 74p per square metre to lay yourself and it is about the best value for money you can spend on self-sufficiency. Each square metre will save you between 50p and £1 in an average six-month heating season.

Be sure to avoid laying under the water tanks, and lag all your pipework as your roof becomes, to all intents and purposes, the outside. The little bit of warmth radiated through your ceiling to the tank should be enough to keep ice from forming. As an additional measure, wrap the tank with fibreglass or with slabs of polystyrene.

Walls: It is unwise to insulate a stone or brick house internally. In every exterior wall there is a 'dewpoint', where moisture absorbed by

185

the brickwork becomes vapourized. In a cavity wall house this dew-point is in the external skin. In a 23-cm solid brick or stone house it is mid-way between the outer and inner faces. If the inner face is insulated effectively, the dewpoint will move to the interface between the insulation and the brickwork. Moisture will collect there, form channels down toward the floor plates, and encourage moisture-associated rots and fungi in the floors. For this reason, solid walls should be insulated externally and cavity walls should have their cavities filled competently. Fears raised by the incompetence of some cavity-wall contractors are well justified. Make sure you get a money-back guarantee if inspection shows any voids left by the contractor. External insulation may be from timber weatherboarding or external slating or tiling, fastened to battens.

Windbreaks: If you wet your hand and hold it up to the wind, you will feel a chill on the damp parts. Similarly, a rain-sodden wall in a wind may experience a super-chilling effect of up to 0.3 kw/m². Therefore the drier you keep your wall the better. Welsh and Cornish walls faced with hung slates achieve this. Try also to erect a fence or hedge shelter belt on the south, west and south-west faces of the house to break up the prevailing wind and reduce the super-cooling effect. The U value (relating to tendency to retain cold) of a wall reduces noticeably when it is sheltered and dry.

Floors: In any warm room there is a heat gradient between the ceiling and the floor. The floor is generally a degree or so cooler than the ceiling. A large damp stone or concrete floor will lose heat, as will a thin wooden floor. Cover them with fabric. Don't skimp on the underfelt. If you can't afford underfelt, use old newspapers.

Windows: Glass is a disastrous building material from the point of view of energy conservation. It is also very expensive. In a room heated 8°C above the external temperature, one square metre of glass will lose about 170 kw-h per year. Double glazing will halve this loss. In cost-effective terms, however, you would find yourself paying a commercial contractor about £25 per square metre to save £0.85 a year. Do-it-yourself systems exist, using plastic glazing bars which enable you to do the job for well under £10 per square metre. Inquire at your local glaziers. Double glazing is well worth while from the comfort point of view, since the internal pane, insulated by the layer of air between the panes, is warmer than the outside pane. If you have been standing next to a single-glazed window on a cold day you will have noticed how you suffer from cold radiation (see page 180); on a warm day the reverse is, of course, true. By reducing radiant losses, double glazing improves the perceived comfort greatly and, after all, it is the comfort we perceive that is really important.

If you go out on a cold day you wrap up in a good, thick coat. You try to keep dry. Treat your house the same way. If you live in certain parts of the house more than others, then wrap up those rooms. Hang drapes on the walls. Cover the floors. Don't ignore the losses through the ceilings. Having done all this you can reduce the losses that occur as a result of excessive air changes.

Reducing losses caused by air changes

Each cubic metre of dry air requires 0.34×10^{-3} kw-h to heat it through $1°C$. This doesn't sound much. If your room is $5 \times 3 \times 2.5$ m and you wish to raise the temperature $8°C$ above that outside, with six air changes an hour, you need a total of 0.6 kw-h. So it makes a lot of sense to cut down air changes as much as possible. In order of cost effectiveness, you should first put draught sealers around the doors and any old window frames; do-it-yourself double glazing will help this. Next, plug any cracks in the walls and, again, keep the floor covered as extensively as possible. Make sure the loft hatch is well sealed. Finally, install a simple porch on all external doors. Any good hardware shop will have a wide range of patent sealers available at modest prices. If you don't think they are necessary, then calculate what a 1.5-mm gap all around your front door represents in real area (to save you the trouble, it represents at least 90 cm^2 of air gap. If your letter-box were open and gaping, you would be doing better than you would with an unsealed front door!) Much the same applies to the need to close and seal warm areas of the house from colder, less used areas. The doors of the bathroom, kitchen and toilet should receive special attention. Aim for one air change an hour in most rooms, but in smelly rooms you may need between two and six.

In practice, it is possible to regulate changes very precisely and your common sense will tell you how many changes you need. Beware

Diameter of fan (mm)	Three-speed			Single-speed
	Low	Normal	Boost	
152	198	284	340	225
191	284	425	510	300

of extractor fans: they are surprisingly powerful. The table on page 187 will give you an idea of how much air they can shift, in cubic metres per hour.

Make sure, then, that your extractor fans are only working when they are wanted. If you can afford a little extra money, then buy one of those ventilators that warm the incoming air, using the warm, moist extracted air. Several are available and more come on to the market every winter.

The table below gives you an idea of the kind of savings you can achieve if you go beyond the recommendations of the IHVE, the Government and other official bodies. There is nothing sacred, or exact, about the figures. They are meant only as a rough indication.

Improvement	Cost 1974	Annual saving kw-h	Projected annual saving at 2p per kw-h	Pay back at 2p per kw-h
Door sealing	£1.50/door	100–400/door	£2–£8	few weeks
Roof insulation	£0.75/m²	105/m²	£2.10	1 year
Window sealing	£3/window	100–300	£2–£6	1 year
Wall insulation	£1.50/m²	50/m²	£1/m²	2 years
DIY double glazing	£20/m²	100	£2	10 years
Porches	£60/door	100–500/door	£1–£10	6–60 years
Heavy curtains	£20/window	difficult to estimate		

Home energy production

Having reduced our demands for environmental comfort from the relatively high (normal) figure of 150 watts per square metre of home to 15 to 20 watts, we are now in a position to provide much of the energy we need from the Earth's income: if you pitch your demand at the right level, then all environmental comfort can be provided naturally. First, though, let us see how much energy there is in nature.

Carbonaceous (stored) fuel

Oil, coal and gas have taken millions of years to form. They are no less natural than the wind, sun and rain, but they cannot be replaced at anything like the rate at which they are being extracted. They must, therefore, be treated as capital. We would not dream of burning our savings to keep warm, so we must devise ways of living without burning these priceless assets.

Peat is a material that occurs widely and it is self-renewing over a timescale of thousands, not millions, of years. But it is a poor fuel, having less than a quarter of the calorific value of petrochemicals, and if you travel across the midlands of Ireland, which is more sparsely inhabited than almost any other western nation, you will be impressed by the ecological havoc wrought by peat digging, past and present.

Britain used to be covered mainly with mixed forest. Now, with less than 20 per cent of the land area under trees, it is one of the least wooded countries in Europe. A hectare of ground will renew timber at the rate of 2.5 tons per year. This represents about 7,500 kw-h of calorific value. With less than half a hectare of cultivable land per person in this country, it is clearly out of the question that in the long run wood should supply any more fuel than is produced by natural wastage at present. Much 'natural wastage' is actually wasted by foresters' fires which, in a fuel-hungry country like this, ought not to be allowed.

For the fortunate few who live where wood can be cut and gathered there are still small wood stoves available. The Norwegians make the handsome Jøtal. The Spaniards and Portuguese still make some models, while second-hand French stoves are obtainable on scrap heaps in France for the artistically inclined. There can be few more delightful experiences than a wood fire working with 90 per cent inefficiency in the Victorian grate!

One solution to the wastepaper glut is to make logs from compressed paper. Newsprint has the same calorific value as wood; if an elegant solution can be found to the pressing, here is an almost unlimited source of fuel when the big companies are not buying it for the more worthy cause of recycling. The fuel value of wastepaper, when compared with oil at £60 a ton, is £15 a ton.

Direct use of solar radiation

Simply because a very large energy flux falls on Britain through the year, it is wrongly assumed by many that the life to which they have become accustomed can be supported with solar energy. Even with the reduced level of energy use we managed to achieve with proper insulation, the average level of radiation occurring during the two months when we need warmth most – December and January – is down to an average over the period of 15 watts per square metre. This is vanishingly small. To make any use of such small radiation requires that correspondingly very large areas be set aside to low-temperature collection, which will be redundant during the summer months when

189

average radiation, over the month of June for example, is 225 watts per square metre. Thus, unless you can set aside at least 40 square metres of cheap solar collecting surface, facing due south at an angle of around 70° to the horizontal, it is best to forget energy self-sufficiency from the sun alone.

It is not so silly, however, to use the sun when it does shine hot to provide between 50 and 90 per cent of your hot water, usually during the months of April to September when it is warm enough. Four square metres of collecting surface plumbed into the hot-water system of

The average hours of sunshine per year.

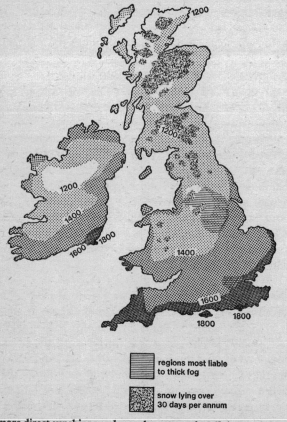

regions most liable
to thick fog

snow lying over
30 days per annum

The more direct sunshine you have, the greater the efficiency of solar collection. Maximum collector possibilities in the UK for low temperature only are in the range 600–850kw-h per square metre per year.

your house can provide up to 600 kw-h/m² per year. At 1p per kw-h this could be worth £24 a year, and at 2p per kw-h, which is the price we are likely to be paying soon, it would be worth £48 a year.

For anyone wishing to embark on this course it should be remembered that while solar collectors are very efficient in the lower temperature ranges up to around 10° to 17°C, this 'efficiency' falls off very quickly when the temperature of the heat transfer fluid inside the collector rises above 35° to 40°C. In tests carried out on an unglazed solar collector we found that we could achieve an average of about 50 per cent efficiency at 40°C. By placing a clear plastic glazing on top we increased the average efficiency from about 50 to 60 per cent in the higher temperature ranges. It is really not worth spending a great deal on glazing, since the extra energy you collect will take years to pay back the additional cost of the framing and glazing, in terms of hot water.

I doubt whether it is worth spending money on making your own solar collector (but see page 200). The cheapest do-it-yourself collector is a scrap steel radiator stripped down and painted black. Insulation and aluminium foil underneath stop radiation and conduction losses. So far as possible, collectors should face south. The cheapest place to site them is on the south wall of a house, or on the path in front of the south wall of the house. The most expensive place is on the south roof, since you will need the services, or skills, of a roofer and carpenter, in addition to those of a plumber and electrician, unless you have these skills yourself. For commercial suppliers of solar collectors, see page 308.

Photo-electric devices

Until the cost of photo-electrical generation can be reduced from the present £10 to £15 per *watt* to no more than £1 per watt, it will be hard to justify any hopes of major energy production from this source.

Direct use of wind energy

The myths woven around the 'limitless' power available from the wind are like those around solar energy. If the area is A square metres and the wind velocity (V) is measured in metres per second, then the maximum energy passing through the swept area of a windmill blade is $0.0006 \, AV^3$ kw. However, the maximum extractable energy is about 59 per cent of this figure. In practice you will do well to extract 43 per cent of the total energy available in the wind. This gives a usable energy density of only 0.25 kw/m^2 when the wind is blowing at 8.9 metres per second, because the energy in the wind is a function of V^3, so that the usable energy at 4.45 metres per second is only 0.3 kw/m^2. This is really very modest. Add to it the need to raise the operating part of your mill above all obstructions and make the structure holding it strong enough to prevent it from being blown down in gale-force winds, and you can see that there are problems. It is really not worth the trouble, let alone the danger, of trying to build your own windmill. If you have designed blades that are aerodynamically efficient but not strong enough, then they will break up at speeds which could, typically, be over 320 km per hour. If you have designed blades that are strong enough to withstand gale-force winds, but which are not aerodynamically efficient, then you will be lucky to start them turning in winds less than 20 km per hour and achieve an overall coefficient of performance better than 16 per cent.

If, after all that, you feel that the wind is not a worthwhile source of energy to tap, then think again. When compared with direct use of solar radiation, wind has several major advantages. It blows in the middle of the night, it blows when heat is needed most, it can be turned into electricity, work and/or heat equally easily. Like the solar collector, once an installation has been made it should cost very little to run. An energy system having both solar and wind inputs will be far more flexible than a plain solar system. In Britain, the average wind speed in January is, very suitably, 10 to 20 per cent higher than it is in June, thus partly offsetting the fact that average radiation is 15 times less.

Windspeed/power output per installed rated kw

Av. wind speed per month (mph)	Av. power per rated kw produced per month (kw-h)
10	350
12	575
14	935
16	1440
18	2010
20	2660
22	3250

Most machines are rated in about 22-mph winds. If the rated figure is very different, then the power produced will be different.

Probably the easiest way to use energy from the wind is to turn it into electricity. This is what all the major windmill manufacturers do. The most cost-effective use of the electric power so derived is, un-

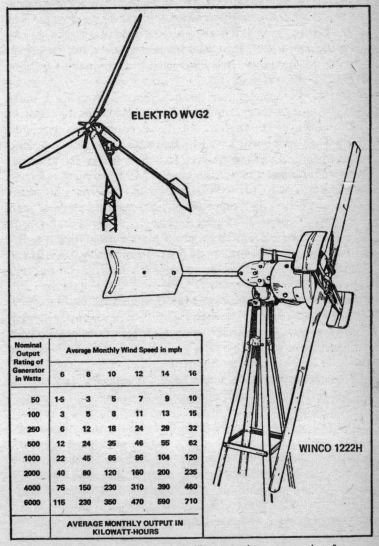

ELEKTRO WVG2

WINCO 1222H

Nominal Output Rating of Generator in Watts	Average Monthly Wind Speed in mph					
	6	8	10	12	14	16
50	1·5	3	5	7	9	10
100	3	5	8	11	13	15
250	6	12	18	24	29	32
500	12	24	35	46	55	62
1000	22	45	65	86	104	120
2000	40	80	120	160	200	235
4000	75	150	230	310	390	460
6000	115	230	350	470	590	710

AVERAGE MONTHLY OUTPUT IN
KILOWATT-HOURS

The Elektro and Winco makes of windmill cover various power ratings from 50 to 10,000 watts, and are useful for home lighting, fence electrification and general battery charging.

doubtedly, for resistance heating. The attraction of such heating is enhanced by feeding the power into storage radiators.

There is a wide range of isovents – which join together points of equal average wind speed – over the British Isles. The power you will derive from the wind in a year depends on its average speed in your area. Don't be put off by this, because there could be sharp differences in your favour locally. Erect an anemometer on the site you would choose for the mill and correlate your results with the nearest weather station, month by month.

It is less cost-effective than resistance heating, but you can store power in storage batteries to provide a buffer between the requirements of household equipment and the intermittent blowing of the wind. The power stored is discharged as a constant-voltage DC current which, to be usable by your household equipment, must be inverted to 50-cycle, 240V AC current. This costs money: a storage capacity of 1 kw-h will cost at least £1.50 and inversion is not going to cost much less than £160 per kw of installed capacity if the system is to run deep freezes and similar machines.

Perhaps the most rational use of wind power is to turn it directly into mechanical work, like the old farm wind pump. A man in Huddersfield owns a small workshop where grinders, lathes, drills and other machines are turned by a slow-speed windmill with a high starting torque, but low power output. He uses the machines only when the wind blows. Probably any handy, engineer-trained general craftsman could do the same, but if you are not a craftsman it is best to buy commercially: either parts or kits (see page 308). Never underestimate wind forces on a blade: make the structure strong. Design for the strongest wind in your area and, if in doubt, ask a civil or structural engineer to help with the basic figures.

Some time in the future, wind devices will be made that produce heat directly from the work done by the blades. A friction brake on a revolving shaft can do that, but as the blade and brake performances operate to different parameters this is ineffective as a solution. The possibility of a conjunction between a dynamometer and a windmill blade is being researched, and when the cost of the dynamometer falls below that of the alternator this will be the cheapest way to produce heat from the wind. It is doubtful, however, whether any system will be economical with a blade much smaller than 12 metres in diameter for large-scale direct heat production. We should consider the planning and architectural implications of the proliferation of such machines realistically and now.

Heat pumps

A heat pump is a mechanical device, generally driven by electricity, that extracts 'heat' from your refrigerator and 'pumps' such heat into the kitchen. If you think of entropy as a kind of energy gravity, then the compressor, which is the working part of the heat pump, is pumping energy from a low position on the entropy slope to a higher one. Heat pumps are also used in cold stores, air conditioners, heating, cryogenics and many other places and technologies.

Compressing a gas makes it hot; expanding it cools it. If you can liquefy the gas as well as compressing it, then the temperature gradient obtained is even more noticeable. If, when the gas is chilled, you supply it with heat, then the heat added becomes the net heat gain of the heat pump system.

The critical factor is not the machine used (I would recommend only a second-hand system) but the refrigerant. R22 evaporates and condenses in the right range (30°–45°C), works under reasonable pressures, and is just about ideal.

Unfortunately there is only a small amount of literature available on the use of heat pumps for domestic applications so if you cannot find the appropriate book you must rely on a local refrigeration engineer to procure the right equipment and set it up. It may not be cheap and there will be little room to make any mistakes.

The suggestions that follow are my ideas of the best 'energy value for money'. The size of the equipment will depend on the calculations you have made already.

Air-source heat pump

This is the worst way to use a heat pump. Air is drawn by high-speed fans over the refrigerated heat exchanger and the heat transferred as in the water-source heat pump. Since most people require warmth when the external air is coldest, it will operate at its lowest efficiency when heat is most needed. A round average COP in winter of between 2 and 2.5 would be as much as you could expect. Various commercial packages are available and I would recommend a second-hand hotel air-conditioning unit designed to work both ways.

Solar-collector heat pump system

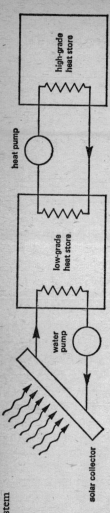

Water-source heat pump system

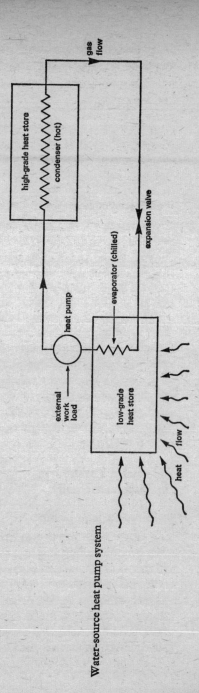

Solar collector heat pump

The solar collector always works at maximum efficiency since the water circulating through it is cool. The likely COP (Coefficient of Performance) of the heat pump will depend on the fluid used and the temperature for which it is designed. It is reasonable to expect 40°C in the high-grade heat store, and for this a COP of 35 is likely, which means 3.5 units of heat will be derived for every unit of electricity expended. The low-grade heat store might be a swimming pool, perhaps.

Water-source heat pump

If you have access to a stream or a large enough spring you can use this 'heat source' to raise the temperature of the water to 40°C. The hot end can be expressed as warm air, obtained by circulating the warm water through a car radiator and blowing it into a room, or more usefully it can be circulated directly through the radiator system and be expressed as a direct radiator. The best and worst COPs obtainable are 5 and 2.5 respectively.

Ground-source heat pump

A pipe buried a metre below ground can pick up some 30 watts per metre without causing any noticeable change in the ground structure. If you use water as the heat-transfer liquid you should allow one parallel circuit for each 1-kw exchanger, so you will need 30 metres of heat exchanger for each kw of intended output. The COP could be 3 to 4 and the capital cost will be high.

A cautionary summary

Heat pumps are machines. They will require skilled maintenance and eventually they will wear out. They depend for their production on high, production-line technology. There is uncertainty over what long-term effects the escape of refrigerants like R22 are having on the ozone layer in the upper atmosphere. The only satisfactory motor for the specialized characteristics of the average heat pump will be electrical with a capacity to withstand the high initial starting load.

Accepting all these bad things, however, heat pumps are the only way we know to make useful heat out of otherwise useless heat, and given the current realities of energy scarcity, they must be regarded as the most hopeful mechanism we have for keeping ourselves warm in the future without squandering reserves. For the dedicated survivalist able to grapple with the not too complex equipment needed to make it function, the heat pump must be one of the best tools he has. Heat pumps are nearly all built sturdily and should last twenty years or so. If you have a choice, opt for the piston rather than a rotary machine.

Direct use of water power

Once upon a time there were tens of thousands of waterwheels working in Great Britain. In the aggregate it is doubtful whether they ever contributed more than a million kw to Britain's power requirements. Now, with nearly all the 'economic' sites occupied by giant dams and huge turbines, the figure is still only 1.83 million kw, a modest 33 watts per head. So hydro-power can never be anything but a highly local energy supply.

In the North of England, Wales, Scotland, however, in fact anywhere where there are streams with a high fall and steady flow, there is a good chance of developing power from a Pelton Wheel. These can be bought in America (see page 309) to generate electricity or to do work directly. Since water flow is generally more controllable than the wind, the control mechanism for this type of installation is easier to install than that for a wind machine. Beware, though, of overestimating potential. If you have a stream with a 30.5-metre head and you aim to get 1 kw, you will need a flow of 3.4 litres per second. That is a very strong flow. In practice, you will find you need up to 30 per cent more water to overcome inefficiencies in the machinery.

Less interesting financially is the restoration of former well sites by the use of low head water turbines. You will find yourself dismayed by the Water Resources Act of 1963, which allows the water authority to tax you on the water you extract from the river and put back into it. It seems to be their general intention (which is discretionary) to discourage potential small hydro-power users.

If you use water power, each phase of the development will need approval by the local River Authority, and you will need to own both banks of the river and have riparian rights. If you are not too dismayed by all this, then contact the organizations on page 308, which may be able to help.

The restoration of old millwheels is of almost no use in terms of energy cost effectiveness. These charming anachronisms should be restored primarily because of their beauty, not their capacity to produce power. If net power is available after a wheel has been restored, then that is a bonus.

The Savonious Rotor

The Savonious Rotor was developed in 1973 by BRAD and the Intermediate Technology Development Group, from original work done in the 1920s by a Finnish engineer.

It comprises two 200-litre oil drums, three 1.14-m-diameter discs of 1.25-cm marine-quality plywood, and 3.6 m or so of 3-cm-diameter steel driveshaft. Their ends removed, the drums are cut in half lengthwise. Each semi-circular rim is cut every 2.5 cm and bent back on itself to make a small flange for bolting the half drums to the plywood discs.

A wooden frame, held by guy-wires tensioned by turnbuckles, is made from two 10×10-cm vertical members about 4.5 m long, to allow 45 cm to be concreted into the ground. The brake handle, cross members and supports are made from 10×5-cm wood, three lengths being bolted together to make a 10×20-cm cross member, which carries the weight of the rotor via the main bearing. For smoother rotation, the two rotors have a quarter-turn difference in alignment.

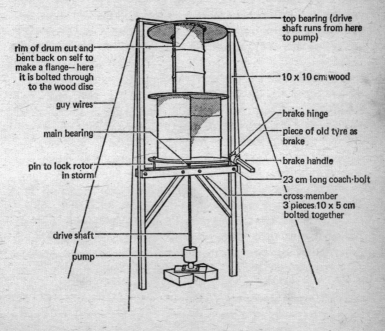

top bearing (drive shaft runs from here to pump)

rim of drum cut and bent back on self to make a flange— here it is bolted through to the wood disc

10 x 10 cm wood

guy wires

brake hinge

main bearing

piece of old tyre as brake

pin to lock rotor in storm

brake handle

23 cm long coach-bolt

cross member 3 pieces 10 x 5 cm bolted together

drive shaft

pump

It is probably only half as efficient as a multi-bladed windmill sweeping the same 160 square decimetres of Welsh air, but the Savonious has several advantages. Unlike a bladed windmill, it always spins on the same vertical axis and does not need to be turned into the wind. This makes it easier to take power directly from its rotating shaft. Its relatively low rotational speeds make precise balancing less important, and it is very simple and cheap to build.

It begins to turn in the slightest wind, but its location is constrained: no pump can raise water more than about 6 metres vertically. At present it has an Archimedes screw pump, but a reciprocating pump might be better. There is no reason why it should not generate electricity.

BRAD's solar roof

While performing all the usual functions of a highly insulated roof, BRAD's solar-roof method of providing domestic hot water is quicker, simpler and (at £8.23 per square metre, 1973–74 prices) cheaper to build than slate or tiles. The heater is the entire new rear roof of the extension to the old stone cottage (see page 173), but its principles apply equally to re-roofing a building or to letting solar panels into an existing roof. It supplies about ten people with hot water for more than half the year at a running cost of about 1p per day. In winter it acts as a pre-heater to a normal domestic immersion heater and a back boiler.

Both theory and practice are very simple. Even our notorious climate offers an average 1,400 hours of sunshine annually, delivering 990 kw-h to each square metre of Wales and England. A dark surface – in this case a corrugated anodized aluminium roof – will absorb much of this energy and turn it into heat. A layer of glass or glass-reinforced plastic (GRP) glazing, secured on glazing bars, then prevents the heat escaping skywards. Corrugations run down the aluminium roof's slope, each 'valley' being fed a trickle of water from a perforated ridge pipe running along the ridge of the roof. The water is warmed in its passage down the aluminium, collects in a plastic gutter and is fed indoors by gravity. It flows through a copper spiral within the hot water cylinder of the domestic plumbing system, where it yields up its heat, and then it is recycled back to the ridge by means of a small pump. A top-up tank in the system allows filtration and also makes good any occasional losses.

The best orientation is south, but wide variation seems possible. BRAD's roof faces 33° west of south. A slope of 30° to 35° is optimal for the six months of summer sun which comprise nearly four-fifths of Britain's annual solar energy harvest. Elsewhere, if you live overseas, make the slope about 20° less than your degree of latitude for summer use: in Florida, for example, at a latitude of about 25°, the slope should be about 5° from the horizontal. More important than the orientation is to build big. The BRAD roof is 60 square metres and on a sunny July day the lunchtime yield was 21.5 kw – about seven domestic immersion heaters – and the kitchen tap temperature was 52°C and far too hot to touch.

The snags so far have proved few and fairly unimportant. The roof makes a pleasant, friendly clicking sound as it cools but, more alarmingly, winter gales can rattle the flexible GRP sheets. 3-mm glass might be better – it is both cheaper and more transparent than GRP – but it is heavy and difficult to handle on top of a windy roof. The filtration, by a kitchen sieve above the top-up tank, must be careful and continuous, or elm seeds and other aliens will intrude and could block the ridge pipe: cleaning that out with a bottle brush is not easy.

If the pump is switched on all the time it could be wasteful. As the sun disappeared and outside temperatures fell, the roof could go into reverse, transferring heat from the hot water tank to the roof and thence to the sky. The answer is a 'black box' which electronically compares the temperature of the roof with that of the hot-water tank, and switches on the pump only when the roof is warmer. The box costs only a few pounds to make.

Minimal construction skills are required and they are learned quickly enough on the job. Materials are easy, for all the components BRAD used are readily available, except for the GRP sheets which are always made to size. Even a head for heights can be acquired in time by most folk! The total cost (in 1973–74) was £494.

Methane gas from muck

I get angry every time I am asked about supplying methane digesters for a family of four. I get angry not at the people who ask, but at the information purveyors who have represented 'methane from muck' as some sort of panacea for all our energy problems. If you want to use muck as fuel, then the most heat you will derive from it will come from burning it directly. Fuel from wood and vegetable matter is best obtained by pyrolysis.

The anaerobic digestion process that produces methane gas will only ever be a net producer of energy, in these northern climes, when there is a large quantity of sewage with which to work. This is because the sewage temperature for optimum operation must be around 33°C, a long way above the ambient. In a digester for 1,000 pigs, about one third of the gas produced is used to heat the digester. A thousand-pig (or a hundred-cow) unit would produce about 10 kw of gas or 3 kw of electricity. It becomes a commercially economic unit only with highly automated pig farms of 5,000 animals or more, and even then the capital cost for such a system is likely to be £20,000.

A well-fed family is unlikely to produce more than about 0.09 cubic metres of gas a day, which is equivalent to 0.5 kw-h – just enough to boil one kettle after the necessary heat has been extracted to keep the digester warm!

For the smallholder, a small home-made digester could produce usable quantities of gas for cooking from five cows. He would need to wander laboriously after his animals to ensure that all droppings were channelled off to the digester, but he would be rewarded by having at the end something far more valuable than gas – the high nitrogen fertilizer produced by the anaerobic process.

Even so, I am not convinced that anaerobic processes are suitable in these latitudes and I would put them very low in my list of priorities for achieving self-sufficiency in the UK.

Storing heat

A ton of water heated above the ambient temperature of 10°C has stored within it 1.18 kw-h of heat for each 1°C. Yet water is about the best material there is for storing heat. Thus, if you want to store a lot of heat you need a very large store and a high temperature. Even an economically run house, well fitted out, will use between 30 and 100 kw-h a day, so a week's store would need to be at least 200 to 700 kw-h. Ten tons of water at 40°C contain a store of 354 kw-h. Heat storage is an economical proposition, then, only if you have a large cellar that can be retroactively waterproofed and insulated – and remember that a cubic metre of water weighs a ton. The only technique for *using* a large quantity of such stored heat (apart from enjoying gorgeously profligate baths!) is with a heat pump. A swimming pool of very ample dimensions could provide a large reservoir of low-grade heat.

Cooking

The best way to save energy is not to use it! So eat raw food as much as possible. Don't worry about the energy lost in cooking, though. Cooking is unlikely to consume more than 2,500 kw-h a year, which is a very small amount.

You can economize on energy spent cooking stews and soups by using a hay box (see page 63). You can buy one for between £8 and £15, or use a large wooden or cardboard box, lined with 10 to 15 cm of hay, styrene foam, urethane foam or straw.

Lighting

A normal incandescent bulb provides only some 8 to 14 lumens per watt, compared with 20 to 60 for the far more efficient neon and fluorescent lamps. There are objections, mostly irrational, to neon lighting, but if you want economical electric light, then a well studied system employing fluorescent fittings is a must and if you have only a limited supply of electricity it is imperative. Moves are being made to improve both the quality and efficiency of all forms of lighting.

The most inefficient way to obtain light is the candle; the average light intensity is about 1 candela. The average candle burns at the rate of 80 watts or so to give about 4 lumens, so its lighting efficiency is one hundredth of even the incandescent light. However, the human eye can adapt to lighting levels between 0.01 and 30,000 lux (=lumens per square metre) so the low level of light in a candle-lit room is adequate for everything except reading and detailed work. A candle gives a delightful light and in sufficient quantities candles help to keep a room warm, so performing a dual function.

Unfortunately, today's candles are made from paraffin, which is derived from petroleum. Before the discovery of petroleum, candles were made from whale oil, tallow fat and beeswax (see page 267). I would not encourage the first, but the second and third seem sensible.

Oil lamps of one sort or another have been around almost as long as man. They can be objects of great beauty. A wick set floating on a bath of oil itself floating on water can make a beautiful light with the same power and heat as a candle.

Crafts

Timber

Alder: A tree found in low-lying land and on the sides of rivers. It withstands water, is good for turnery, and was once used for making clogs. Because it also withstands steam, it was used to make hat blocks. Traditionally, it has been used for butter-boards. It provides the best fuel for making charcoal for gunpowder.

Ash: A tough, springy wood which will not splinter easily. It was used by wheelwrights for the felloes (or rims) of wheels, for cart shafts and bodies. Boatbuilders use it for steamed or cold-bent ribs and other parts requiring strength and flexibility. It is used for all tool handles, hoops, rails, trugs, crates, hurdles and ladders. As a coppice timber, ash grows relatively fast, and often on poor, steep land. It can be 'stooled' (cut for poles and the stumps left to grow again). Ash is supreme as a firewood. It will burn wet or dry.

Beech: A white or pinkish wood which works well, even when 'green' (unseasoned). It is a magnificent tree when mature. It is not really durable when used outside, but it makes excellent furniture. The chair 'bodgers' of the Chilterns used to work in the beech woods, turning parts for chairs from green beech on primitive pole lathes. Beech is also used for wooden planes and other tools, for dairy utensils, shelves, table tops, clog bottoms, the teeth of mill gear wheels, and other machinery parts. It is also used for turned bowls, butter stamps, tent pegs, brush and broom heads (see page 235), butchers' blocks, saddle trees and the interior frames of pianos.

Birch: A tree found in poor upland areas. It is used for making brush and broom heads (see page 235) and its twigs are used for making besoms. In Scotland, birch wood imparts an aromatic quality to whisky distilling and herring smoking.

Boxwood: This is seldom found in large trees. It is a hard, smooth, stable wood used for tool handles, small, delicate turnery, rulers and other mathematical instruments, as well as wood engraving.

Chestnut: It is usually grown as coppice timber in this country and as such is excellent for fence poles and gates. Somewhat neglected in its use as sawn timber, it is used extensively in France for all kinds of building and joinery work. It matures quickly.

Elm: This is a useful hardwood but its twisting grain makes it difficult to plane. It saws and turns well and is excellent for underwater work, such as lock gates, piling, or sawn frames for boatbuilding. It makes hubs for wooden wheels, and bobbins for anything that is subject to heavy wear. From Roman times it has been used for water piping. It makes weatherboarding on buildings, coffins, keels, chocks, wedges, dough and feed troughs, turned bowls and platters, and sometimes flooring and table tops.

Hazel: A coppice wood that grows quickly from stooled stumps. It is used for wattle hurdles, baskets, trugs and fish traps.

Holly: A clean, white, dense wood used for small objects, especially those that are carved. It is similar to lime.

Larch: The tree was introduced into this country in the sixteenth century. It is used for estate work, fencing, gates, building and boatbuilding (it is excellent for planking). It is planted extensively today because it matures quickly.

Lime: This is a smooth, even-grained timber that has been sought by woodcarvers from Grinling Gibbons onward.

Oak: There are two kinds, Pedunculata and Sessiflora. With Pedunculata the leaves have no stalk and the acorns swing; with Sessiflora the leaves do have stalks. Sessiflora, which resembles chestnut somewhat, is considered slightly inferior. Both vary greatly depending on the soil in which they grow. As an all-round timber, oak is without equal. It is highly resistant to weathering, immersion in fresh or salt water, and, under reasonable conditions, it hardens with age. It is used for all kinds of building work, for furniture, boatbuilding, carriage, cart and wagon building (especially for the spokes of cartwheels), for gates and gateposts, in fact for any work that requires strength and durability. Much early work with oak was cloven rather than sawn, which increases its strength. Boatbuilders still use curved oak branches for making frames and knees (see page 222). Oak shavings and sawdust are the best fuel for curing bacon and hams (see page 67).

Scots pine: This is used for pit props, telephone poles, railway sleepers, masts and spars, ladder poles and all kinds of carpentry. It is also used for paper pulp. The Forestry Commission plant it by the million.

Spruce: A clean-grained wood which is easy to work. It is used for masts and spars, venetian blinds, roofing shingles, and toys, and it is excellent for making musical instruments (see Toys, page 231 and Musical Instruments, page 234).

Sycamore: This is a rather soft wood, very white, which is often used for domestic turnery and for draining boards. It scrubs well. It has no great structural strength, but it burns well!

Walnut: This is, or was, *the* cabinetmakers' wood. It was used extensively in the eighteenth century and there is not much of it left today. It is used solid or in veneer form for all kinds of furniture, for gunstocks (see Crossbow, page 217), and is also grown for its fruits. It grows very slowly. You plant walnut for your grandsons.

Willow: Some varieties of this springy wood are essential for the making of cricket bats. Because it is waterproof, it is used to make boat paddles and the slats of waterwheels. Blocks of willow were used to line the brake shoes of farm and railway wagons. Willow withstands heat fairly well. This wood splits readily, providing slats for making trugs, clothes pegs and 'chips' or 'punnets'. The osier is a close relative of the willow. Any swampy ground can serve as an osier bed; the wood will provide endless material for weaving baskets and fish traps (see pages 59 and 242).

Yew: Although it is classed as a softwood, this is one of the hardest and slowest-growing of woods. Traditionally it was used to make longbows (see page 215) and it is suitable for any small job requiring strength and resilience. It has a beautiful grain with a reddish tinge. It is scarce today and it is not liked by farmers because its foliage is very poisonous to animals.

Seasoning

Many timbers can be worked green, but for any quality work wood should be seasoned:

Saw the wood into planks, then stack the planks with spacers and leave it for as long as possible – anything from eighteen months to five years. If you plan to use wood over a long period, lay down a certain amount every year to ensure a steady supply.

Normally, outside work (such as gates, fences and sheds) does not require seasoned timber, although fence posts will be much easier to hammer into the ground if they have been dried out for a few months; they will also accept a coat of preservative more easily.

Carpentry

Basic tools

Many simple jobs can be done using only a very few tools, but with a more extensive range of tools work is much easier and you can achieve far greater precision. Many of our basic tools have evolved slowly over hundreds of years and so are completely suited to their purpose. No matter how elaborate your set of tools, they will be quite useless unless they are kept sharp. If you have ever changed from a blunt saw or chisel to a sharp one you will appreciate this. Your first need, then, is for some method of sharpening cutting edges.

You will need an oil stone; a combination one that is coarse on one side and fine on the other is particularly useful. When sharpening chisels and plane irons, it is important to keep the angle between the edge and the stone constant. Use long, even strokes on the oil stone: this also prevents a hollow from forming as the stone wears.

You will need saw files for sharpening saws. Use a file that is the right size and angle for the saw. Place the saw between pieces of soft wood in a vice, with the teeth protruding upwards. File with steady strokes at the angle the teeth already have.

When the teeth have been sharpened, they will need to be set (i.e. bent outwards a little so that the cut of the saw will be a little wider than the thickness of the blade). If the cut was no wider than the blade, the saw would jam in the wood and you would not be able to move it. Setting is done with a special saw set, rather like a pair of pliers. If you do not have a saw set, then you can improvise using a flat steel block with a bevel on one edge. Lay the saw on the block and use a hammer and flat-headed punch to tap alternate teeth downwards. Then turn the saw over and repeat the process so that alternate teeth lean away from each other, all at the same angle.

You will need a grindstone or grinding wheel. This is a circular sharpening stone that rotates, so it must be powered by hand or by a motor. Use this for sharpening drills. When sharpening centre bits, be careful not to damage the centre point or screw, and do not damage the outer cutters when you are sharpening the blade.

Keep all your tools clean and from time to time wipe them over with an oily cloth.

If you intend to do any serious woodwork, a good, stout bench is essential. You can make one quite easily from pine or, better still, beech, but you can also adapt an old kitchen table to make a very serviceable bench, if you stiffen the table at the top and front.

You will need a vice. It is best to buy one, although you can improvise using one or two large bolts, preferably with wing nuts, to clamp a strong hardwood plank to the front of the bench.

For large work you will find a pair of trestles, sash cramps and a long straight edge and square are very useful.

From standing tree to finished article: the tools you will need

Felling axe	Mallet
Hand axe	Jack plane
Bow saw	Smoothing plane
Sledgehammer	Rebate plane
Wedges	Claw hammer
One cross-cut handsaw	Tack hammer
One rip saw	Pincers
One tenon saw	Pin punch
One keyhole saw	Pliers
One coping saw	Vice
Grindstone	Spokeshave
Rasp	Square
Files	Rule
Saw file	Scriber
Countersink bit	Oil stone
Hand drill and twist bits	Bradawl
Brace and range of centre bits	Mortice chisels

Range of firmer chisels, from 6 to 25 mm in width
One medium and one small screwdriver

Making a chair

Cutting list:
Legs: 2 pieces 3.8 × 3.8 × 45.7 cm
2 pieces 3.8 × 3.8 × 91.4 cm
Top frame: 4 pieces 2.5 × 5 × 45.7 cm
Lower rails: 4 pieces 2.5 × 1.9 × 45.7 cm
Backs rails: 2 pieces 1.9 × 5 × 45.7 cm
Brackets: 4 pieces 2.5 × 2.5 × 15.2 cm
Seat: 1 piece 40.6 × 40.6 × 1.3 cm

Most traditional chairs require the use of a lathe to make the legs and rails rounded; if you have access to one, so much the better. However, these instructions are for making a basic chair without a lathe, using squared timber.

Make sure all the pieces are planed up square, then mark out the mortices in the front and back legs, not forgetting the longer mortices for the back rails. Chisel out all the mortices carefully to a depth of

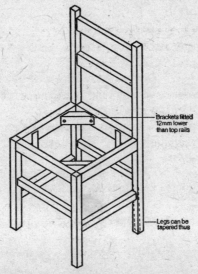

Brackets fitted
12mm lower
than top rails

Legs can be
tapered thus

not more than two-thirds the thickness of the wood, then mark out, saw and chisel the tenons. Note that it is not necessary for the lower and back rail tenons to have shoulders. Make sure all joints fit snugly before glueing and assembling the chair. Clean up with sandpaper and polish. Mitre the ends of the brackets (45°), drill the ends, then

209

glue and screw in place. Lay the seat over the top frame and run a pencil round under the frame to mark the exact shape. Cut out the seat and fit it. You can leave the seat plain, or cover it with fabric or leather above a layer of padding made from sponge rubber, kapok or horsehair. Alternatively, you can bottom the chair with rush or cord, lacing it over and under the frame, in two layers, starting with the top right-hand corner. If you need to join on a new piece of rush or cord, do so after a back turn so that the join comes underneath. You will end with a double thickness of cord or rush and you can pad between.

Making a table

Cutting list:
Legs: 4 pieces 7.6 × 7.6 × 71.1 cm
Underframe: 2 pieces 12.7 × 3.2 × 71.1 cm
2 pieces 12.7 × 3.2 × 132 cm
Top: 4 pieces 20.3 × 3.2 cm × 150 cm
4 pieces 7.6 × 2.5 × 61 cm
1 piece 3.2 × 2.5 × 30.5 cm
Screws: 16.5-cm 12-gauge

First make the legs. These must be planed square and true and the mortices marked out and cut with a mortice chisel and mallet. To do this more easily, place the work on a firm bench and either cramp it or sit on it. If you have a really solid vice use that, but place a stout piece of wood under the work. After the joints have been cut, taper the legs if you wish; mark the taper and plane down with a jack plane or smoothing plane. Mark out the underframe, saw the shoulders of the tenons with a tenon saw, holding the work in a vice or against a bench hook, and split away the waste wood with a mallet and a wide firmer chisel. When you get near to the scribed line, dispense with the mallet and pare down carefully, holding the chisel in one hand and steadying the blade with the other. Pare down the mitre on the ends of the tenons. Glue up, cramp together, drill and peg the joints. Start the top by 'shooting' the edges of the 20.3 × 3.2 cm planks: i.e. plane up the edges with a jack plane until they are straight and square. Join the planks by rebating with a plough plane, dowelling at intervals, or simply by butt-glueing them together. Whichever method you choose, the top is then glued up and cramped, and the 7.6 × 2.5-cm straps are glued and screwed to the underside. When the glue has set, the top can be fitted and secured with the turnbuttons, then the whole job can be cleaned up with a smoothing plane (set very fine) and glasspaper. Finally, the finished table should be given a coat of clear varnish thinned half and half with turpentine to seal the wood. When this is dry, glasspaper it with fine glasspaper and polish with a 50/50 mixture of beeswax and turpentine rubbed on with a soft cloth.

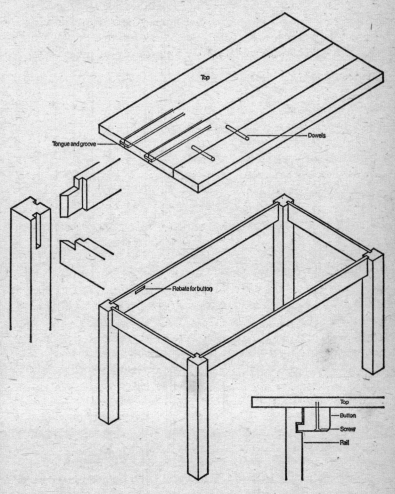

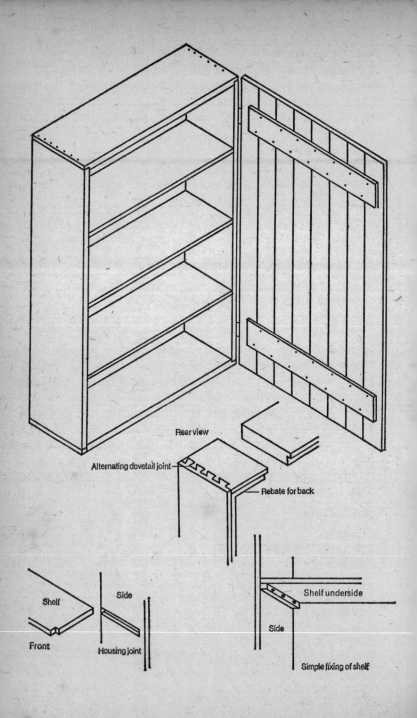

Rear view

Alternating dovetail joint

Rebate for back

Shelf

Side

Front

Housing joint

Shelf underside

Side

Simple fixing of shelf

Making a cupboard

Cutting list:

Top, bottom and shelves: 5 pieces 22.9 × 2.5 × 81.3 cm
Sides: 2 pieces 22.9 × 2.5 × 106.7 cm
Back: 8 pieces 10.2 × 1.3 × 106.7 cm, or 81.3 × 106.7 × 6 mm plywood
Simple door: 8 pieces 10.2 × 1.6 × 106.7 cm and
  2 pieces 10.2 × 1.6 × 81.3 cm
Panelled door: 3 pieces 6.4 × 2.5 × 106.7 cm, 2 pieces
  6.4 × 2.5 × 81.3 cm and 2 pieces 30.5 × 1.3 × 91.4 cm

Make up the carcass as shown. If you choose the dovetailed version, it would be advisable first to practise cutting dovetails on some scrap wood. In both versions the doors are surface hung, which avoids the need to make the door exactly the size of the front opening in the carcass. If you wish to make the door fit flush, as a refinement, make it about 2 mm larger all round and plane it down carefully until it fits snugly into the opening. When making the panelled door, construct the frame first, making sure all the mortice and tenon joints fit well. Then rebate the inside edges of the frame with a plough plane (if you use a rebate plane, work from the back of the door and secure the panels with thin beading about 6.4 × 6.4 mm). Now make up the panels, allowing about 3 mm between the edge of the panel and the bottom of the rebate on each long side. Glue up the door, making sure no glue is used on the panels and rebates. This, and the 3-mm gap, is to allow for solid-wood panels to expand and contract; it is not necessary if you use plywood for the panels. This method of making a panelled door can be used for making the ends and back of a larger cupboard, perhaps with a top similar to the table, for use as a kitchen unit.

Making a bed

Cutting list:

2 pieces 12.7 × 5 cm × 2 m
2 pieces 12.7 × 5 × 91.4 cm
2 pieces 6.4 × 6.4 × 35.6 cm
2 pieces 6.4 × 6.4 × 76.2 cm
5 pieces 10.2 × 3.2 × 91.4 cm

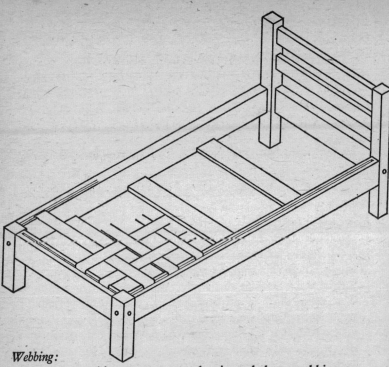

Webbing:

18 m × 6.4-cm-wide strong cotton or hessian upholstery webbing, or
13 m × 5-cm-wide laminated rubber webbing

First mark out and cut the mortices in the 6.4-cm-square legs. If you
want to taper the lower parts of the legs you can do this now, but it is
not really necessary. Now mark out and cut the tenons on the 12.7 ×
5-cm sides and ends. Cut and tenon two of the 10.2 × 3.2-cm pieces
to make the headrest. The other three pieces of 10.2 × 3.2-cm must be
tenoned into shallow mortices in the long sides: they act as spacers
and prevent the sides from being pulled inwards by the tension of the
webbing. Make sure all the joints individually are a good fit and then
work a 3.8-cm × 6.4-mm-deep rebate around the top edges of the sides
and ends. Clean up all parts and assemble with glue. The large end
joints should also be pegged, as shown. The bed can now be polished
and the webbing put on. If you use rubber webbing, be careful not to
overstretch it. For a mattress you can use horsehair, feathers, kapok
or sponge rubber. Cover the mattress with a strong cotton fabric and
button it at intervals all over to prevent the stuffing from moving
around and forming lumps.

Longbow and arrows

Materials

The traditional wood for the English longbow is yew (*Taxus baccata*) but today this is difficult to obtain. You can use North American or Australian osage orange (*Maclura aurantiaca*) or degame (*Calycophyllum candidissimum*) from the West Indies and Central and South America. A poorer, but commoner, hedgerow substitute is the common ash.

Arrows are made from white birch, Scots fir, Port Orford cedar or ramin.

All woods must be clean and free from knots or shakes (cracks or splits).

Making the longbow

Cut out the bow stave and begin to shape it with plane, spokeshave, rasp and glasspaper. Shape up the handgrip from a contrasting piece of hardwood. Glue it into position and rasp to shape when the glue has set.

Make up the tiller from any stout piece of wood. String the bow and fit it into the tiller. With the bow at different stages of draw, shape it carefully until it curves evenly and without twisting.

Wrap the handgrip with a leather or cord binding.

Try the bow a few times before finally smoothing it down and polishing with shellac or varnish.

The string

You can make bow strings from synthetic fibres such as Fortisan or Dacron 'B', from linen thread no. 40 or Cobbler's Flax no. 12 thread.

The fibres are twisted together with beeswax; loops or knots are formed at each end, and the string is served (or whipped) in the middle where the arrow is nocked (or fitted).

Arrows

The arrow stave should be about 1 cm square and planed down to a circular section in the planing board.

Smooth the stave with a sanding block or by putting it into the chuck of an electric drill or lathe.

Test the stave for straightness by rolling it on a flat surface.

Make up the nock from a scrap of hard plastic, bone or horn.

Points, or arrow heads, may be forged or may be filed up cold from a piece of suitable steel.

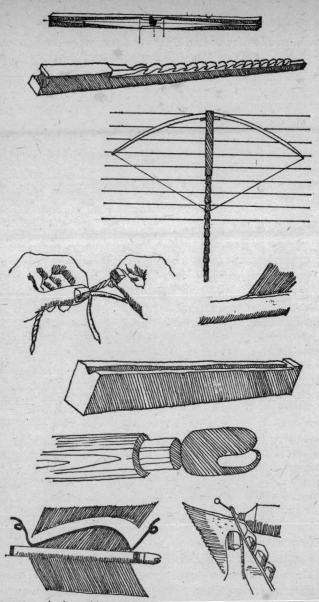

Various stages in the making and finishing of a longbow and arrows. From top to bottom: handgrip, tiller, bow fitted into tiller, twisting the string fibres, feather vane rib on arrow, sanding block, nock, trimming and glueing the vanes.

Fletching

Use the pinion feathers from a turkey, if you can get them, or otherwise any large pinion feathers from a goose or chicken. Use only one vane from each feather, and the three feathers you need for each arrow should all come from the same wing.

Split the rib lengthways and cut out three pieces of equal length.

Shape the underside of the rib to fit the shaft of the arrow, which can be marked at 120° intervals near the nock to receive the vanes.

Glue the vanes into position, using pins or a light thread binding to hold them in place.

When the glue has set, trim the feathers with a hot wire (see illustration).

Crossbow

Materials

	Length cm	Width cm	Thickness cm	Material
1 stock	91.4	20.3	3.5	walnut
1 locking-wedge	3.8	3.5	0.5	rubber
1 latch cover	8.3	3.5	1.9	walnut
2 flight paths	55.8	1.8	0.2	walnut
2×3.8-cm $\times$ no 8 and 1×1.9-cm $\times$ no 6 countersunk screws				brass
2 pivot plates	5.0	4.8	0.3	brass
2 prod side plates	14.6	5.0	0.3	brass
1 rear sight	10.8	1.9	0.2	brass
1 fore sight	12.0	1.0	0.2	brass
1 locking plate	9.9	3.5	0.3	brass
1 trigger	6.7	2.5	1.3	mild steel
1 trigger pivot	1.3	2.5	1.3	mild steeel
1 trigger guard	15.2	1.3	0.5	brass
1 bow prod	91.4	3.8	0.8	Noral alloy

Making the crossbow

Begin by making a full-size drawing of the stock on a 2.5-cm squared grid. It is a good idea to make a thin plywood template of the stock, both to draw around and to check that the stock is the correct size you want.

When you have the shape right, cut out the profile of the stock, plane up the flight path and mortice out the trigger housing.

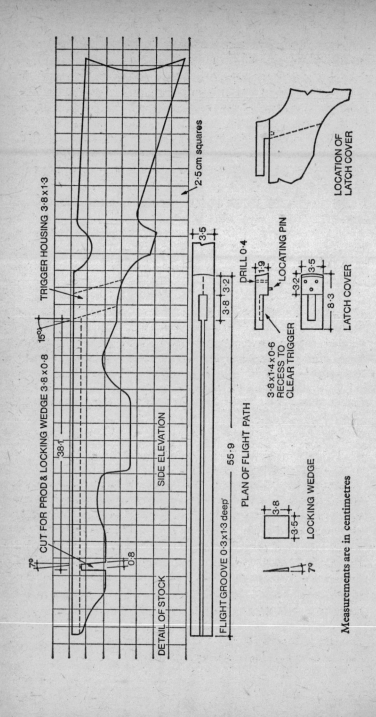

CUT FOR PROD & LOCKING WEDGE 3·8 × 0·8

TRIGGER HOUSING 3·8 × 1·3

15°

38·1

7°

0·8

DETAIL OF STOCK

SIDE ELEVATION

2·5 cm squares

FLIGHT GROOVE 0·3 × 1·3 deep

3·5

3·8   3·2

PLAN OF FLIGHT PATH

55·9

DRILL 0·4

1·9

LOCATING PIN

3·8 × 1·4 × 0·6
RECESS TO
CLEAR TRIGGER

3·2

3·5

8·3

LATCH COVER

LOCATION OF
LATCH COVER

3·8

3·5

LOCKING WEDGE

7°

Measurements are in centimetres

Cut the flight groove with great accuracy, using a plough-plane or scratch-stock.

Cut the slot for the bow prod and the locking-wedge; round the stock to its finished shape and polish it. To reduce wear on the bow-string you should face the top surface of the flight path with a laminated plastic.

Make the locking-wedge from hard rubber, such as a piece of old shoe-heel rubber.

Make up the latch cover from a piece of the same wood as the stock. Cut a recess in the latch cover to give clearance for the head of the trigger components. Before the final shaping of the rounded end, the latch cover must be fitted into place.

Fit the locating pin, drill and countersink two holes for the 3.8-cm no 8 brass screws. The locating pin is made from a 1.9-cm no 6 brass screw, screwed into the latch cover before the head of the screw is removed.

The bow prod is made from 0.8-cm Noral 42-tonne tensile alloy, and the one described is for a 45-kg prod, which should give a range of about 330 metres. If Noral alloy is unobtainable, a somewhat less effective, though serviceable, prod can be fashioned from an old car spring. Draw the shape of the prod on the metal, cut it out with a hacksaw, file it smooth and finish with emery paper. Bend it into shape by placing it in a very firm vice and pulling: this is a two-man job. Make sure each side is bent to the same extent. Then file the ends to take the bowstring.

Make the prod side plates and fit them, together with the fore sight, and give the bow prod a trial fitting. If the alignment is correct, screw the locking plate into position.

Make up the trigger assembly from 1.3-cm mild steel, and case-harden the area indicated in the drawing by heating to red heat and then cooling immediately by quenching in cold water or oil. Drill the pivot holes and the hole for the return spring before hardening.

Make the pivot plates from 0.3-cm brass plate. On one plate drill two 0.5-cm holes to correspond with those in the trigger assembly. Silver-solder two 1-cm × 0.6-cm lengths of brass rod to the other pivot and drill and tap them to 1 cm BSF. These rods must align with the holes in the trigger assembly and the other pivot plate.

Carefully recess the pivot plates into the stock, and hold the whole assembly together with two 4.4-cm × 1-cm steel bolts.

Remember to fit the trigger return spring.

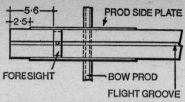

Fore sight recessed into stock showing position of prod side plate

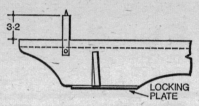

Locking plate in position showing locking wedge and prod in place

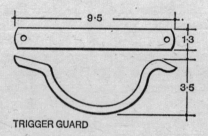

Make up the rear sight from 0.2-cm × 1.9-cm brass strip and screw it into position on top of the latch cover.

Make up and fit the trigger guard.

Finish all metal parts with fine emery paper and the exposed parts with metal polish. The trigger mechanism should have a coating of light machine oil.

The bowstring and bolts can be purchased ready-made. If you prefer to make them yourself, the string is made in the same way as that for a longbow, only much thicker. Crossbow bolts should be 25 to 30 cm long.

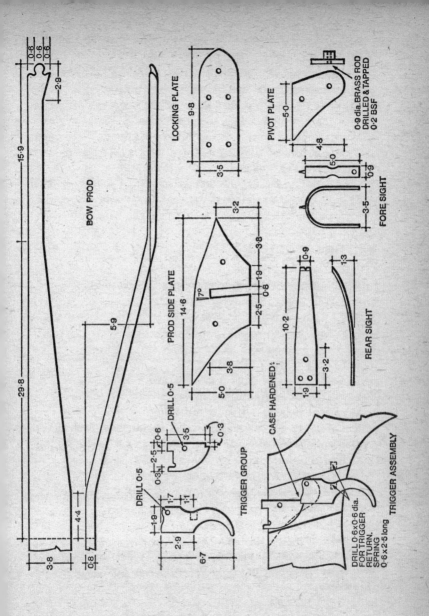

BOW PROD

LOCKING PLATE

PIVOT PLATE

0·9 dia. BRASS ROD
DRILLED & TAPPED
0·2 BSF

FORE SIGHT

PROD SIDE PLATE

REAR SIGHT

DRILL 0·5

DRILL 0·5

TRIGGER GROUP

CASE HARDENED

DRILL 0·6×0·6 dia.
FOR TRIGGER
RETURN.
SPRING
0·6×2·5 long

TRIGGER ASSEMBLY

Boats

Clinker-built boats, of overlapping boards, are difficult to make. This design is based on the flat-bottomed dory, similar to those used by the old-time fishermen of the Grand Banks off the east coast of America. Launched from a mother ship, usually a schooner, these little boats were used for long-lining for cod anything up to a hundred miles from land – and in winter! They have proved their seaworthiness. Since then they have been built and used all over the world.

Dories are suitable for fishing and other activities both in sheltered waters and at sea. If you intend to work only in sheltered waters, such as rivers and small lakes, then you may omit the mast, sail, centre-board and rudder.

Materials

Timber:

Bottom and sides: 9-mm marine plywood or 16-mm planking
Hog and keel: 100- × 25-mm oak, ash or pine
Chines: 31- × 31-mm oak, ash or pine
Sheer batten: 31- × 50-mm oak, ash or pine
Gunwale: 25- × 50-mm oak, ash or pine
Stem: 63- × 38-mm oak, ash or pine
Stem capping: 31- × 31-mm oak or mahogany
Skeg: 75- × 38-mm oak or mahogany
Rudder stock: 50- × 38-mm oak or mahogany
Rudder blade: 12-mm marine plywood or 19-mm thick planking
Centreboard case: 12-mm marine plywood or 16-mm planks
Centreboard: 12-mm marine plywood or 19-mm planks
Thwarts: 31- × 225-mm oak or mahogany
Knees: 38-mm thick oak or mahogany
Mast: 63-mm-square spruce, 3 m long
Gaff: 44-mm-square spruce, 2.5 m long
Boom: 44-mm-square spruce, 2.3 m long
Transom: 9-mm marine plywood with 25- × 50-mm oak, ash or pine framing around edges, or 19-mm oak or mahogany, in one piece if possible
Tiller: 31- × 31-mm ash, 0.85 m long
Oars: 50-mm-square spruce, 2 m long (maximum)
Oar blades: 75- × 19-mm spruce, 0.45 m long

Sailcloth:

No 4 weight Egyptian or American cotton

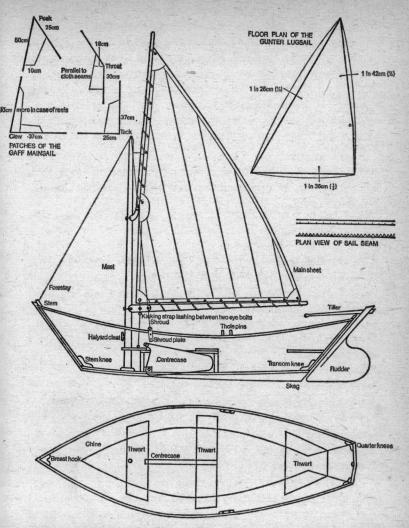

PATCHES OF THE GAFF MAINSAIL

Peak
25cm
50cm
10cm
Parallel to cloth seams
40cm more in case of reefs
Clew   37cm

18cm
Throat
30cm
37cm
25cm   Tack

FLOOR PLAN OF THE GUNTER LUGSAIL

1 in 42cm (½)
1 in 26cm (½)
1 in 36cm (⅓)

PLAN VIEW OF SAIL SEAM

Mast
Forestay
Stem
Halyard cleat
Stem knee
Centrecase
Shroud
Shroud plate
Kicking strap lashing between two eye bolts
Thole pins
Main sheet
Tiller
Transom knee
Rudder
Skeg

Chine
Breast hook
Thwart
Centrecase
Thwart
Thwart
Quarter knees

Ropes etc:

19-mm-circumference hemp rope
38-mm-diameter soft cotton rope
25-mm-circumference rope
Eyelets
Rowlocks
Thole-pins

By far the easiest material to use for the bottom and sides is 9-mm marine or exterior grade plywood. If this is unobtainable, however, the boat can be planked with any good-quality larch, pine, oak, elm or mahogany. If the boat is to be planked, some extra framing, in place of the temporary building frames, will be required, and thin battens, either bedded in a paint-putty mix or glued, should be fastened lengthwise over the seams inside the boat. These avoid the need to caulk the joints from the outside – a rather difficult job, especially for a boat this size.

The stem, hog, chines and keel can be made from oak, ash, larch or pine, bearing in mind that the more hardwood is used, the stronger – but the heavier – the boat will be. This could be an important factor if the boat has to be manhandled or transported any distance. Using marine ply and a good-quality softwood like pine, the boat will have the best strength: weight ratio.

As with other designs in this book, the dimensions, types of material and so forth can be varied within reason, to suit cost, availability and suitability for your purposes. For example, if the only plywood available were 6-mm, you could use it, perhaps with a little more framing inside; but you might find the boat limited to sheltered waters only. Survival is based on the ability to adapt, and that, in turn, is based on imagination!

Method

Scarfe-joint together enough plywood to make the bottom of the boat. Draw on the centreline, with the stations at right angles; mark the outline and cut out.

Turn it over and glue (using marine or good waterproof glue) and screw on the keel and skeg.

Throughout the boat all fastenings should be of non-ferrous metal, or should be heavily galvanized to prevent corrosion.

Set up the bottom, with the required curve, on trestles as shown. Use a spirit level and brace it well so that it cannot move.

Screw and glue the hog on to the bottom, making sure none of the screws are in the way of the centreboard slot.

Saw out the centreboard slot by drilling a 25-mm hole at each end and sawing out the middle with a padsaw (keyhole saw). Bevel the two chines and glue them in place.

Build up the centrecase, making sure it is well screwed and glued together and that it fits the curve of the hog. Bed it in soft putty or mastic and screw it into place on the hog, over the slot.

The stem can now be roughly bevelled and fixed, as can the transom and the two knees. Both the stem and the transom will need to be well braced with temporary struts to their top edges.

Using a taut line from the centre of the transom to the stem, set up the four building frames on their stations, temporarily screwing them to the bottom.

Fix the sheer battens firmly to the stem and transom, and lightly to the frames.

Check the chine bevels with a straight piece of wood and shape the bevels on the stem and transom accurately.

Scarfe together enough plywood for the sides and offer it up to the boat, holding it in place with G cramps. The top edge should be straight, and should fit the sheer batten without shaping, but the bottom edge at the chine can be marked from underneath, as also can the stem and transom.

Remove the sides and cut them to shape, but slightly oversize. Then screw and glue them into place, making sure there is a good fit at the stem.

When the sides are firmly in place, fit the gunwale, breast hook quarter-knees and tholepin blocks, and plane smooth the top edge of the gunwale and sheer batten.

Fit the thwart battens and thwarts, fixing them firmly to the sides and centrecase where applicable.

Make up the mast step block from a piece of scrap timber and fix it to the hog.

When the thwarts are in place, remove the building frames, clean up the inside of the boat and give it a coat of paint or varnish.

Free the boat from the remaining supports and turn it over.

Plane the chines smooth and slightly rounded. Stop in any gaps and screw heads with marine stopping or a mixture of putty and red lead.

Make up and fit the false stem.

When the stopping is dry, rub down the outside of the boat with glasspaper and paint it.

Make up the centreboard and hang it in the centrecase, using a brass bolt as a pivot. Stiffen the centrecase at this point with a 150-mm-square piece of 9-mm plywood on each side. The bolt must have rubber as well as metal washers to make the bolthole watertight.

Construct the rudder assembly. The tiller, which is made of ash, is

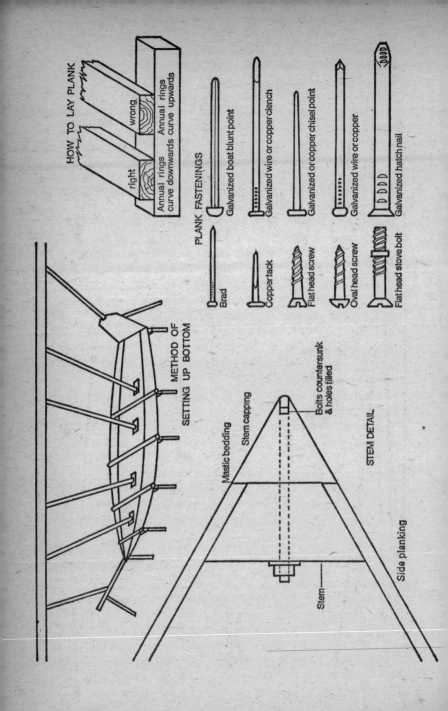

HOW TO LAY PLANK

wrong
Annual rings curve upwards

right
Annual rings curve downwards

PLANK FASTENINGS

Brad

Galvanized boat blunt point

Coppertack

Galvanized wire or copper clench

Flat head screw

Galvanized or copper chisel point

Oval head screw

Galvanized wire or copper

Flat head stove bolt

Galvanized hatch nail

METHOD OF SETTING UP BOTTOM

Mastic bedding

Stem capping

Bolts countersunk & holes filled

STEM DETAIL

Side planking

Stem

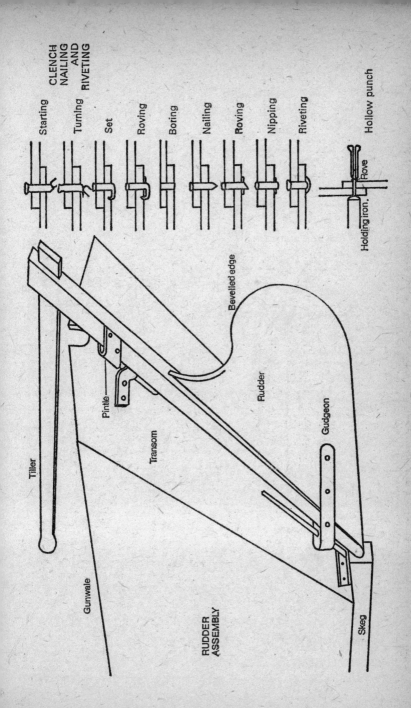

CLENCH NAILING AND RIVETING

Starting

Turning

Set

Roving

Boring

Nailing

Roving

Nipping

Riveting

Hollow punch

Rove

Holding iron.

RUDDER ASSEMBLY

Tiller

Gunwale

Transom

Pintle

Bevelled edge

Rudder

Gudgeon

Skeg

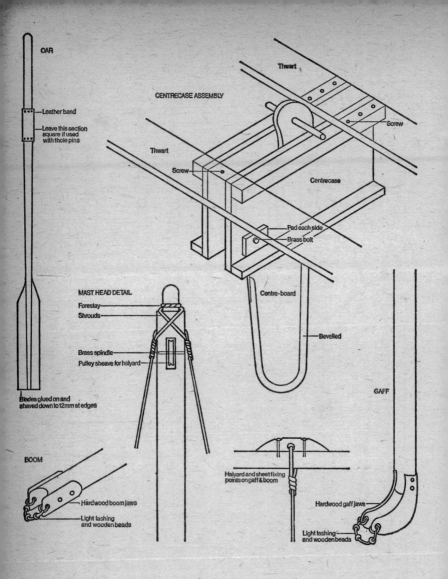

OAR

Leather band

Leave this section square if used with thole pins

CENTRECASE ASSEMBLY

Thwart

Screw

Thwart

Screw

Centrecase

Pad each side

Brass bolt

Centre-board

Bevelled

MAST HEAD DETAIL

Forestay

Shrouds

Brass spindle

Pulley sheave for halyard

Blades glued on and shaved down to 12mm at edges

GAFF

BOOM

Halyard and sheet fixing points on gaff & boom

Hardwood boom jaws

Light lashing and wooden beads

Hardwood gaff jaws

Light lashing and wooden beads

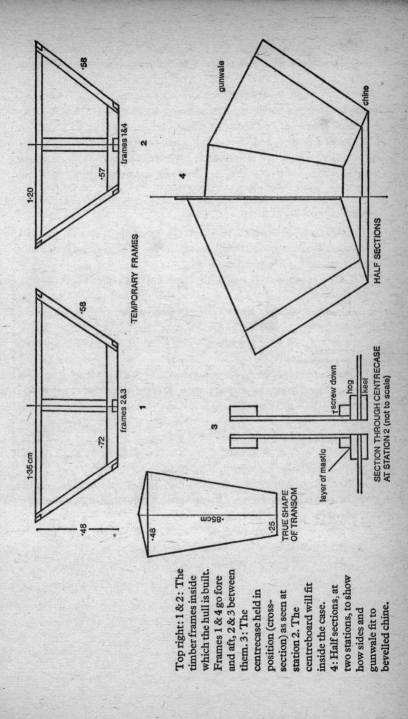

TEMPORARY FRAMES

frames 1 & 4

·58

1·20

·57

frames 1 & 4

2

gunwale

chine

4

HALF SECTIONS

frames 2 & 3

·58

1·35 cm

·72

·48

1

TEMPORARY FRAMES

·48

·85 cm

·25

TRUE SHAPE
OF TRANSOM

3

screw down

hog

keel

layer of mastic

SECTION THROUGH CENTRECASE
AT STATION 2 (not to scale)

Top right: 1 & 2: The
timber frames inside
which the hull is built.
Frames 1 & 4 go fore
and aft, 2 & 3 between
them. 3: The
centrecase held in
position (cross–
section) as seen at
station 2. The
centreboard will fit
inside the case.
4: Half sections, at
two stations, to show
how sides and
gunwale fit to
bevelled chine.

morticed into the head of the rudder stock. The mortice should be tapered and the tiller wedged in. The rudder can be hung on bought fittings, or they can be made up from mild steel and galvanized. It should be possible to lift the rudder off its hangings, but it may be necessary to fit a retaining nut for rough-water use.

Another modification for rough-water use is to box in the space under the thwart, and to put in a small foredeck and box in under that, too, making two watertight compartments. These will be useful for keeping gear dry at sea, and if you do not overfill them they will act as buoyancy chambers.

Mast, spars and sail

The mast, gaff and boom, which should be of clean spruce, must be rounded up from squared timber with a plane. The gaff and boom jaws are made up from hardwood and fitted.

Make a mortice at the top of the mast and fit a pulley sheave to take the halyard.

It is not absolutely necessary to fit standing rigging, provided the mast is held firmly on the hog and through the forward thwart. If you plan to do much sailing in strong winds or rough conditions, however, it should be fitted.

The sail can be purchased ready-made, or it can be sewn from no 4 weight Egyptian or American cotton. It should be false-seamed vertically at 300-mm intervals. Cut out the outline as shown and seam the edges. For extra strength, you can sew a 19-mm-circumference hemp rope on to the luff and foot of the sail.

Provide eyelets at 200-mm intervals for lashing to the gaff and boom. This lashing can be of light cord.

Fix a soft cotton rope of about 38-mm diameter to the boom for the sheet, and a longer piece of hemp rope, of about 25-mm circumference, to the gaff for the halyard.

Make up the oars from some 50-mm-square spruce, which can be mounted in bought rowlocks and thole-pins, as shown.

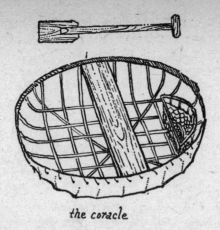

the coracle

The coracle

Coracles are small boats made from willow lath covered with tarred canvas. They are very simple to make and very serviceable in sheltered water.

Toys

Toys made from wood are most effective and develop creativity when the designs are kept simple. Traditional wooden toys have always followed the natural limitations of the material, which has given them a true economy and beauty. From the earliest times men have whittled branchwood into dolls, balls, miniature animals, tools and weapons. Traditional toys have almost always miniaturized the adult world, helping children to understand and prepare for their entry into this world. When children make toys themselves they often show an unsuspected inventiveness, while at the same time they learn practical skills that are useful in later life.

These toy designs and ideas are suitable for both adults and children to make. Often making them will give as much enjoyment as playing with them.

Branchwood toys

You can produce all manner of animals, people, carts and wagons with little more equipment than a saw and a sharp knife. The drawings are self-explanatory. Green wood is easier to work with, but do not place the finished article too near a source of heat, or the wood will

dry out too quickly and split. You can achieve a decorative effect by leaving on some of the bark. Toys can be left plain or given a coat of clear varnish.

Toys from sawn wood

About the simplest toy for children of all ages, and always a favourite, is a set of building blocks. The most durable ones are made from beech, but you can make them satisfactorily from pine. You can add interesting variations with pieces cut from triangular section timber to make roofs for houses and with arches for bridges. A few thin, wide pieces of plank can be used as ramps, platforms or roofs. Flat planks about 25 mm thick can be used to cut out many animal shapes, using a coping saw or fret saw. You can make sets of animals for a zoo, farm or Noah's ark, drawing on the features and painting them in gay colours.

Make sure that all paints used on toys (or on anything else children are likely to put into their mouths) are guaranteed by the makers to be free from lead.

You can use sawn wood to make more complicated toys, such as farms, forts, doll's houses and furniture, model boats, cars, trains and aeroplanes.

Dolls and puppets

You can make very simple dolls from round pieces of wood (or round clothes pegs), shaping the head and painting it, and clothing the body. Improved versions may have jointed arms and legs.

Glove puppets are simply a carved head and two hands, with a cloth body.

Marionettes are rather more complicated, but both marionettes and glove puppets give tremendous scope for combining art and craft techniques in a very creative way. A marionette show allows individual expression in the making of the puppets themselves, the scenery and proscenium, and it provides a good basis for a group activity for adults or children or both. Knees, hips, shoulders, neck and wrists of each marionette are joined with hooks and eyes; the elbows are joined by a piece of leather which acts like a hinge.

Musical instruments
Wind

Pan pipes: These are a good introduction to more sophisticated wind instruments.

Cut a hollow piece of bamboo or elder to the approximate length. Shape a cork to fit one end, but before glueing it into place cut a segment away to make it flat on one side, to form a narrow hole through which the instrument will be blown.

When the glue has set, shape the mouthpiece.

Carefully, cut a square hole in the top of the pipe, far enough forward of the mouthpiece to be clear of the cork and your lips, and bevel the edge furthest from the mouthpiece. Keep blowing the pipe while you are cutting and bevelling, to make sure the sound is right.

Make up as many of these pipes as you will need and tune them by cutting them to different lengths.

Glue the pipes together in a row.

Recorder: As soon as you have become proficient at making a simple whistle, as for pan pipes, you can attempt a recorder.

Make the basic pipe and determine the key note by cutting it to length.

Mark out the approximate positions of the other holes. Begin with the next note up the scale from the key note. Drill a hole. Make it small at first and tune it by enlarging it with a round file.

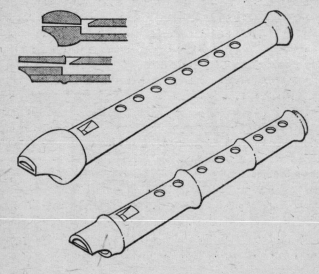

The holes need not be in a straight line; they can be arranged around the pipe to suit the positions of the fingers.

Ocarina: The clay flute makes an interesting variation. It is not really a flute, but it has the same kind of mouthpiece as a recorder. It must be fired in a kiln (see page 254).

Percussion

A drum is basically a hollow tube or sound-box of quite large diameter covered with a stretched skin. Sound-boxes can be made from wood, clay or metal. You can buy a proper drumskin or make your own from any well-cured (see page 257) thin but strong animal skin. Damp the skin and tension it either with strong cord and wedges, or with a metal ring held down with adjustable clamps.

Cymbals and gongs can be hammered from discs of steel or brass. Do not soften the metal with heat while you are hammering it as this will make it hard and resonant.

West Indian steel band instruments are made from oil drums and several notes can be obtained from a single drum by dividing the top into areas and giving each area a different tension by hammering it carefully.

Brushmaking

Brushmaking is a craft that calls for great skill; it takes years to master the more dextrous hand techniques used by the craftsman brushmaker. However, you can make serviceable basic brushes and once you have learned the skills involved in making them you can experiment and develop your craft further.

There are two types of brush: those for decorating, and domestic or industrial brushes. Both can be made by a fairly simple binding process.

Start by making a besom or birch broom. The materials are readily available and it is a useful tool when finished. Twiggy, resilient branches from the birch make the best filling, but local variations, such as heather, can be used. It is best to cut the filling in spring, when the sap is rising. The true besom maker ties his bundle with split willow or cane, but wire, stout string or even large jubilee clips can be used. The sticks or handles that you use need not be straight and you can use timber that is unsuitable for other purposes. The handle is pointed and then driven centrally into the bound filling. After you

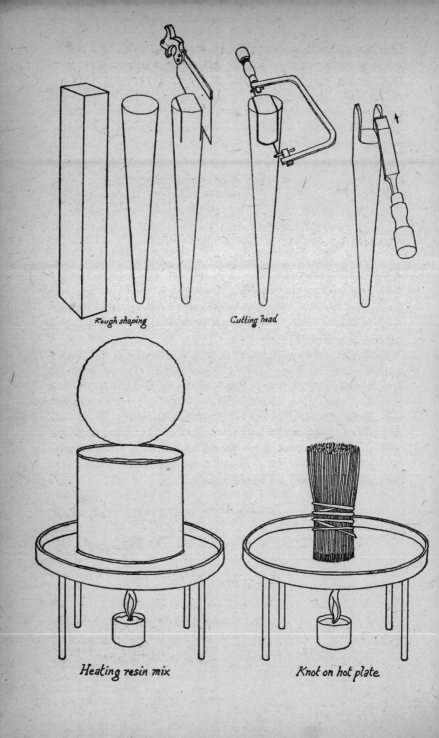

Rough shaping

Cutting head

Heating resin mix

Knot on hot plate

have tapped it home it can be secured with a peg driven in sideways.

Tying shorter, smaller bunches without a handle produces useful hand brushes and for these such softer materials as grass or rushes can be used. These small brushes used to be called swales. For more advanced besom making, see page 310. Pig bristle is usually used for hair brushes, being straight and stiff. Horse hair can be used for painting brushes and vegetable fibres for coarser brushes.

Besom

'Swale' hand brush

Painting brushes

Once you have mastered binding large brushes, the next stage is to tackle small brushes. Formerly, all painting brushes or sash tools were made in this way and it is only in the last fifty years that flat painting brushes have replaced them.

Form a handle by whittling or turning a short stick or a section of branch and shape the top to take a knot of bristle or hair. First tie the knot securely enough to hold it together round the middle (this is a temporary binding which will be removed when the brush is finished) and dip the root or 'butt' end of the bristle into a warm can of resin and linseed. Then stand it butt end down on a hot plate to allow the resin to penetrate upwards within the knot. Keep the temperature below the smoking point of the oil. When it is cool, the permeated resin mix helps to lock the bundle together.

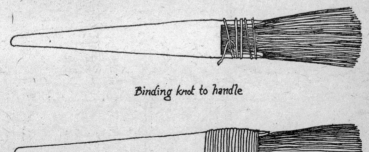

Binding knot to handle

Place the knot at the top of the sash handle, which is secured up-right in a vice, and bind it on with stout twine. You can varnish the finished binding to make it more durable.

It is best to practise 'dry' tying first, using no resin mix on the knot, until you have acquired two skills – that of selecting the right size of knot for the handle and that of securing the knot to the handle tightly.

You can make brushes of any size between 1 and 5 cm in diameter by this method, but one of about 2.5 cm will be the most acceptable.

Drawn work

This is a fairly straightforward way to make brushes which can be mastered quite easily.

Drill holes right through the stock, making the final exit hole about one third the size of the knot hole. Do this by drilling right through the stock with a fine drill, then changing the bit for a larger one and drilling about two-thirds of the way through.

Hold the stock in a vice. Thread a length of fine string or wire through the first hole and tie a slip knot in the lower end. Place a knot of material through the slip knot, so that it is held in its centre, and pull the knot tightly into the hole. Thread the string or wire through the second hole and back again through the same hole, leaving a loop into which you insert the second knot of material. This is pulled into the stock in the same way.

Thread the string or wire through the third hole, and so on until the holes are all filled. Then secure the end of the string or wire.

Glue and screw a veneer backing over the brush to protect the binding.

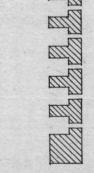

Slip knot ready for first knot

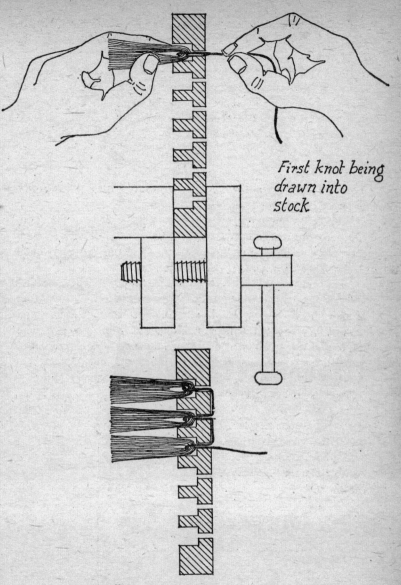

*First knot being
drawn into
stock*

*Progression of
brush-filling using
continuous cord*

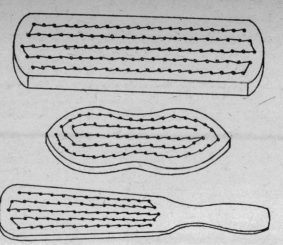

Typical pattern for wire-drawn brushes

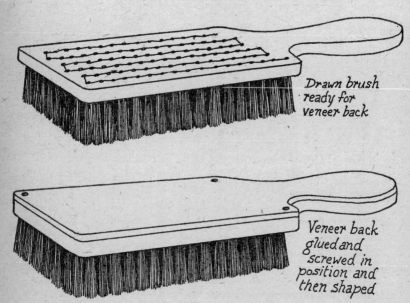

Drawn brush
ready for
veneer back

Veneer back
glued and
screwed in
position and
then shaped

Miscellaneous brushes

There are some simple, primitive brushes that require no skill at all to make and which are used to this day in various parts of the world. You can make them from off-cuts of old rope or any similar material.

To make a hand brush, fold a length of rope in half and bind it for most of its length. Unravel the tip and comb it out to provide the working end. As the brush wears down, simply cut back the binding to expose more rope.

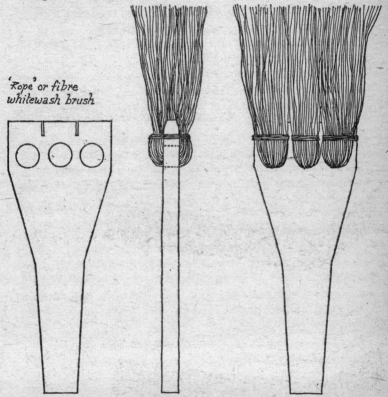

'Rope' or fibre whitewash brush

To make a cheap brush for whitewashing or similar kinds of decoration, form a simple triangular handle from a piece of old timber and drill holes in the top that are large enough to take the rope or other filling material. Loop the rope through the holes and bind it securely to the handle end with wire or string. Unravel the ends of the rope and comb them out, using a home-made comb made from nails, a fine rake, or the kind of steel comb that is used for grooming animals.

241

Basket weaving

Baskets can be made from a large variety of materials, but in the British Isles the traditional material is willow, or osier as it is otherwise called (see page 59). It is possible to use wild willow, but experiment first with different varieties from your own locality.

The wands or withies may be cut at any time of year if they are to be used green, and if they are to be split this should be done as soon as they are cut (whether they are to be used green or not). Make two cuts with a sharp knife at right angles to one another on the butt, then slide a cleaver of egg-split down the length of the rod.

Sort the rods into the various lengths you will need, soak them well in water, and you are ready to begin.

Traditional willow craftsmen will frown upon you, but you can make very serviceable baskets from a wooden base, setting the upright stakes in holes round the edge. Weave a few rows below the base to secure it to the rods, then turn it the other way up and weave the sides between the upright stakes, using one, two or even three rods at once. To join on a new length, leave the short end on the outside, place the new rod to its right, and the pressure of the weaving will hold the two together. Trim the ends flush with the sides of the basket when the work is finished. To finish the top edge, bend the stakes at right angles and weave them down with the horizontal rods.

You can make a basket without a wooden base by binding a number of stakes together to form a cross, then bending them out to form a star. Commence weaving at the centre and work outwards. When the base is wide enough, bend the stakes up to form the sides. You may need to insert additional stakes around the edge of the base. Sharpen them and push them into the weaving, then bend them up, like the others.

The main techniques, and the terms that describe them, are:

Randing: a single rod woven in and out of the upright stakes.

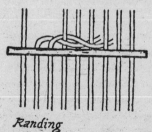

Randing

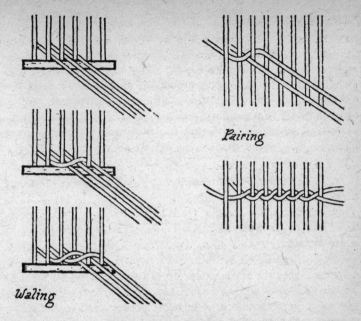

Pairing

Waling

Slewing: two or more rods worked together in and out of the stakes.

Fitching: the rods worked alternately over and under each other, trapping a stake as they do so. This is useful for open-work in baskets for livestock, lobster pots and fish traps.

Pairing: two rods worked alternately over and under each other, the reverse of fitching.

Waling: three or more rods worked alternately one by one in front of two, three or more stakes and behind one. This is a very strong weave and is used at intervals up the side of a basket to give stiffness.

Upsett: two, three or more rods worked alternately on the stakes at the base of the basket to 'set up' the shape.

Spale baskets

Spale baskets are woven from thin slats of coppice-grown oak. They are extremely durable, and because of the closeness of the weave they can be used for carrying powdery substances, seed-corn, animal feed and so on. The rim of the basket is made from hazel, though ash or oak can be used. The rim is called the 'bool'. It is made first by steaming the wood, bending it into a circle or oval, and fastening the bevelled edges with a nail. Take poles of coppice-grown oak about 15 cm in diameter and 120 to 180 cm long, and split them lengthwise with a mallet and a kind of wedge with a handle called a 'froe'. Smooth and shape the split pieces using a draw knife, holding them in a foot vice. Slot the staves into the bool after soaking and steaming them, and bend them to the centre or right round to the opposite side of the bool. Soak thinner strips, with or without their bark, and weave them round, starting at the bool and working in to the middle of the basket. Spelks, or spale baskets, are extremely strong and serviceable and used with the minimum of care they will last a very long time.

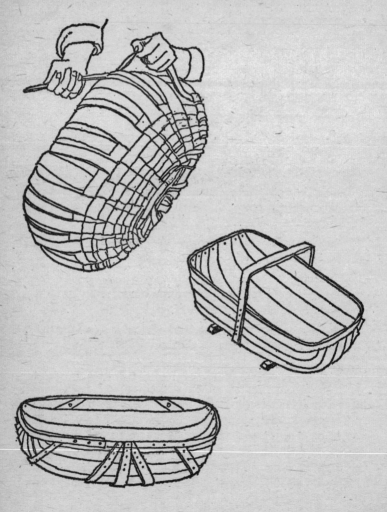

Coiled grass baskets

This is a traditional American Indian craft. Use long-bladed grass, which is cut in mid-summer and laid out carefully in a shady, well-ventilated place until it is thoroughly dry. Immerse it in water before

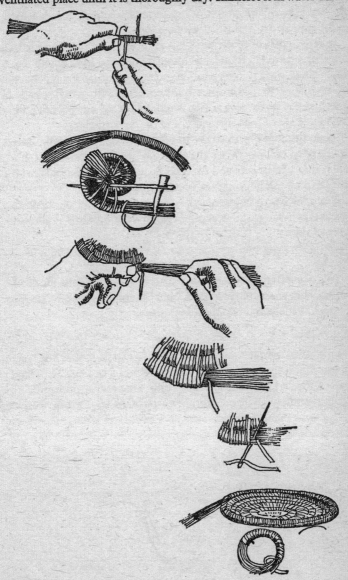

you use it and soak it until it is pliable, then lay it between wet cloths, from which you should take it as it is needed. Raffia – which this is – can be bought and used in the same way. If it should become dry while you are working, dip your hand in water and moisten the grass by running your hand over it. When you finish work for the day, hang up the grass to dry or it will grow mouldy.

Take a bunch of grass and bind it together by wrapping it in a single strand wound round and round. When you have bound 3 to 5 cm, begin to work it into an arc. As soon as you have bound enough, twist it into a tight coil and sew it into position with a single strand of grass and a large darning needle, pulling it as tight as possible. Bind some more grass, coil some more, and continue stitching.

When the core begins to get thin, shove a few more stalks into it and carry on binding. When the grass you are sewing with gets short, pull it through the core and cut it off flush. Thread the needle with a new strand, push it through the core and carry on.

When the base is large enough – the work may stop here to make a pad or mat if you wish – you can begin to slope upwards as you work to make sides.

To finish, taper off the core so that it makes a neat, smooth join to the edge.

To make a ring for a handle, or to act as a flange on the inside of a basket below the rim to hold a lid, bind the core into a circle, pushing the grasses at one end into those at the other.

Straw rope

Long stalks of wheat straw are the best and easiest to use. Soak them in water until they are pliable. You can adapt a carpenter's brace to make a throw hook, but it is not really necessary: you can do the twisting entirely by hand, using two bunches of straw or working from a large pile of straightened stalks held down with a heavy piece of wood. Twist the straws together tightly and leave them in a coil.

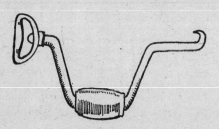

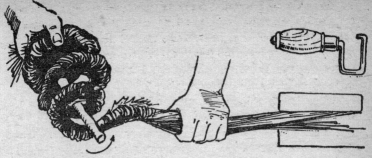

Bind them together with blackberry or willow, using barked or split stalks soaked beforehand, or with raffia or string.

Horn

You can obtain horn from most slaughterhouses, although it is less common than it used to be now that most animals are de-horned when young. Work the horn with a hacksaw and files to make a variety of useful objects such as spoons, buttons, combs and drinking vessels. You can shape some horn by heating it in boiling water or with a gentle flame. This is useful when shaping the handle of a spoon or pressing the base of a beaker tightly into position. If you saw off the solid tip of a horn and drill a hole through it you have an excellent toggle. Horn can be smoothed with wet carborundum paper and polished either by hand or with a revolving calico wheel coated with a wax-based silicon polish.

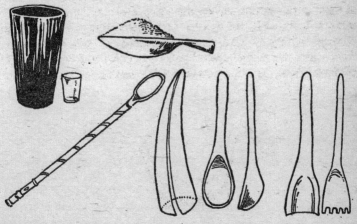

Wooden spoons

These can be made from a variety of woods, but the best to use are beech, lime or sycamore. Turn the basic shape on a lathe or cut it from a flat plank with a coping saw. Carve out the inside of the bowl with gouges, then shape the outside of the spoon and sand it smooth. Traditionally, wooden spoons receive no finish and through long use they acquire a dense, non-absorbent surface. They are essential for making porridge, jam and wine – metal must never come into contact with a fermenting liquor.

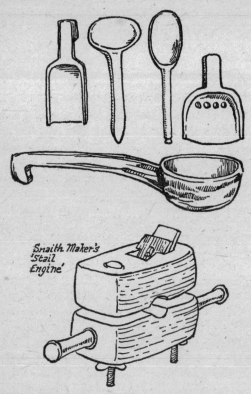

Snaith Maker's 'Stail Engine'

Coppice crafts

You can make rakes and handles for forks, spades, scythes, axes and other tools and implements. The best wood for tool handles is ash, although for axe and hammer handles imported hickory is better at withstanding the repeated vibrations during use. Handles can be rounded on a lathe, but traditional handle makers – in some places they were called 'snaith makers' – used a special plane called a 'stail engine'. This was fitted on to the shaft and turned by hand, gradually screwing the two halves of the stail engine closer together until the wood was perfectly round and smooth. The secret of snaith makers lay in the very precise balance of the tools they made, a secret based on skills acquired over centuries and handed on from craftsman to craftsman. The tradition has all but died out and the only way we can emulate their work is to study examples of it that still exist in museums, to handle the tools and to come to appreciate their true economy – no material wasted in their making and no effort wasted in their use.

Pottery

There are three basic types of clay used for making pottery:

Stoneware, which fires at about 1200°C. This temperature is difficult to achieve in a simple kiln.

Earthenware, which is found naturally in many localities. It contains quantities of iron oxide which acts as a flux and lowers the firing temperature to between 900°C and 1000°C. It is the most widely used pottery clay; it fires to a reddish-brown colour.

Fireclay, which is usually found near coal seams. It is grey when raw and fires to yellow. It is coarse in texture and because it can withstand rapid heating and cooling it is added to other clays to open the texture and to counteract warping and cracking. It is also used for firebricks in the construction of kilns.

Clay is found in many areas but not all local clays are suitable for making pottery. Look for clay along river banks, where water has eroded the topsoil, or in any places that have been excavated. Take a sample from at least 1.5 metres below the level of the surrounding ground and make a roll as thick as your finger and about 12 or 13 centimetres long. You may need to wet the clay and knead it in your hands before you can do this. Now bend it into a ring and stand it on its edge on a flat surface. Leave it to dry, preferably away from direct heat and in the shade. If it dries without cracking and without signs of undue shrinkage, there is a good chance you will be able to make pottery from it. If you can test-fire it in a kiln, you can be absolutely certain of its properties before you try to make useful articles from it.

Preparing the clay

Once you have found a suitable clay you can dig it in large quantities and prepare it.

The clay must be weathered in the open for as long as possible. If it is attacked by frost, so much the better.

Mix the clay with water until it has the consistency of cream, then sieve it to remove small stones and other impurities.

Leave the 'slip' to settle and pour off the excess water.

When the clay has dried sufficiently, place it on clean boards and allow it to dry still more until you can knead it. At this stage its plasticity will be increased if you can keep it covered with damp sacks in a cool cellar, or if you can keep it moist in an old dustbin.

The final stage in its preparation is called 'wedging'. Just before the clay is to be used, place a lump of prepared clay, weighing between 2 and 4.5 kg, on a firm bench, and cut it in half with a cheese wire. Lift up one half and smash it down hard on to the other half. Repeat this several times. It will remove air bubbles and make the clay homogeneous.

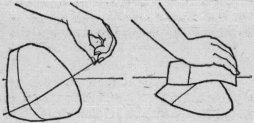

Gather the clay together in a roll, knead it by pressing it against the bench with the palms of your hands, and cut it with the wire into lumps that are of a convenient size for working.

Pinch, coil and slab pots

With a little perseverance you can make simple, functional pottery to a very high standard without a wheel and with little or no special equipment.

Pinch pots are easiest of all, and in making them you will learn much about the working properties of clay. You should do this before you attempt throwing.

Take a ball of soft clay of a size that will fit comfortably into your palm. Press the thumb of your other hand about two-thirds of the way through the ball. Then, with the same thumb on the inside and

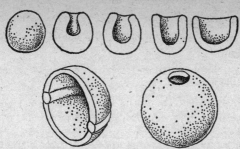

your forefinger on the outside, gently pinch once. Rotate the ball and pinch again. Try to build up a rhythm – pinch, rotate, pinch, rotate – each time making the walls a little thinner and taller until you have a pot.

To make coil pots, take several pieces of clay and roll them with your palms on a dry wooden bench to make long rolls about 1.5 cm in diameter. Using a piece of scrap wood as a base, make a spiral of clay, working from the centre outwards, to form the bottom of the pot. When you have reached a large enough diameter, start placing the coils one on top of the other to build up the walls of the pot. As each layer is added, work round the circumference rhythmically, pressing it into the layer below. Your thumb marks can remain as a decorative

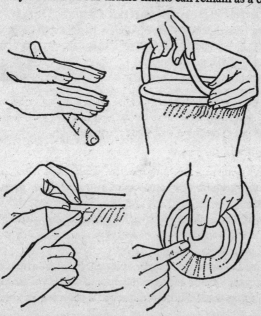

feature or you can smooth the surface with a spatula, stone or stick. To ensure that the coils do not come apart in the firing, you can coat the inside of the pot with slip. Either apply the slip with a brush or allow the pot to dry a little, then fill it with slip, wait a few moments and pour it out again.

If you have made pastry, you can make slab pottery. All you need is a rolling pin, two slats of wood about 1 cm thick, a ruler, an old knife, a pot of slip and a brush.

Press out a lump of clay on a dry table. Place a slat of wood on either side to control the thickness and roll the clay with the rolling pin. Use the ruler and knife to cut out pieces for the pot. Brush slip on to all the joins and press them together. It is easiest to begin with square slab pots, but you can make cylindrical ones.

If you shape a cylindrical pot round a tin or jar, be sure to remove this at once as all clay shrinks a little on drying, and pots must allow for this shrinkage.

Because they present large plain surfaces, slab pots lend themselves to incised or impressed decoration.

Throwing

Throwing is perhaps the most difficult pottery technique to master and the one most likely to frustrate the beginner. There is only one way to learn how to throw pots and that is to do it and keep on doing it. Once you have mastered it, you will find it the most practical and elegant way to make pots by hand.

Start with a lump of clay the size of your fist. When your hands are dry the clay should feel fairly soft but not sticky. Make sure the wheel-head is dry and smack the clay down as near to the centre of the head as you can.

Start the wheel in motion and work up to a moderate speed. Wet your hands and sprinkle a little water over the clay. Rest your forearms on the front edge of the wheel tray, cup both hands over the spinning clay, keeping your elbows well to your sides, press downwards gently but firmly and towards the centre of the wheel. When the clay revolves smoothly and without kicking, you will know that it is centred.

Begin to pull the clay upward to make a lighthouse shape and then flatten again. Do this two or three times and then, starting from the ball shape, press both thumbs steadily into the centre of the clay. You will need to wet your hands continually. Work your thumbs firmly

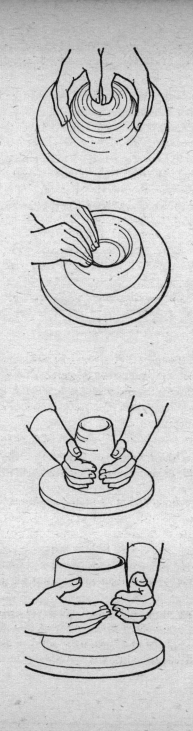

outwards, squeezing the wall of clay between your thumbs and forefingers at the same time. At this stage the shape to aim for is that of a dog dish.

The next shape to form is the cylinder. Lean over the wheel with one hand inside the pot and the other outside, and draw the clay upwards. With practice you will be able to shape the cylinder and make it thinner.

Use a pin mounted in a cork, as a handle, to trim up the top edge. Use a small sponge held in a cleft stick to remove excess water from inside the pot. If you wish to smooth the outside of the pot as it rotates, use a flat piece of wood or rubber. You may also make incised decorations at this stage.

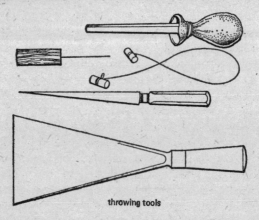

throwing tools

Lubricate the wheel-head with water and cut off the pot with a cheese wire. Slide the pot gently on to a flat board held flush with the head.

Remember that in throwing, all your movements should be slow, steady and deliberate.

The kiln

The kiln is the most important part of the potter's equipment. Essentially it is a device for heating the clay to the point at which it begins to melt and fuse together. With earthenware this happens between 900°C and 1000°C. At temperatures above 1200°C earthenware pots will collapse into shiny puddles of vitreous substance on the kiln floor. This need not deter you; the problem with small kilns lies in achieving a temperature that is high enough.

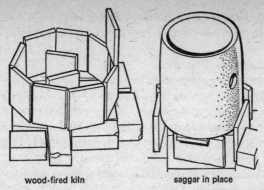

wood-fired kiln   saggar in place

The simplest kiln is wood fired. The most primitive way to make a wood-fired kiln is to surround a heap of pots with a large pile of brushwood and set it alight. You can make very serviceable pots in this way, but you cannot glaze them. Most glazed earthenware is fired twice and to ensure a smooth surface after the second firing you need a kiln with an enclosed firing chamber. The first firing bakes the clay hard, at temperatures between 700°C and 900°C; the second firing fuses the glaze at a temperature between 900°C and 1000°C.

To build a wood-fired kiln you will need fireclay or ready-made fire bricks and a quantity of ordinary house bricks for use away from the hottest part of the kiln. Some heavy bars of cast iron on which to build the fire are useful but not absolutely necessary. Their inner chamber, called a 'saggar', can be made from fireclay by the coiling method. Make it with a separate lid and a spyhole in one side. When it is dry enough to move you can begin to construct the kiln as in the picture. The fire bricks should be 'luted', or cemented together with mortar made from fireclay and water. Before a proper firing you must allow the kiln to dry out thoroughly. In the later stages you can speed up the drying by lighting a gentle fire in the fire pit.

For the first firing, pack the chamber with 'green' (unfired) ware. You can stand smaller pots inside larger ones provided they are not too tight a fit. (All pottery shrinks further on firing.) Shelves made from thin fireclay and supported on fireclay pillars should make it possible for you to fill the chamber completely.

Start the firing slowly on the first day, banking up the fire late in the evening and stopping most of the draught so that the kiln retains its heat overnight.

On the second day, build up the heat steadily so that by evening the inside of the chamber is glowing a dull red. Shut down the fire by sealing off the flow of air.

If you can resist the temptation to examine the results, leave the kiln alone for two to three days.

When you remove your pots they should be 'biscuit' fired and have a definite ring to them when they are tapped.

The 'glost' or glaze firing should follow a similar pattern, but this time you must pay more attention to the temperature. You can do this in one of two ways. Craft suppliers sell specially prepared cones that are graded to melt at particular temperatures. If you mount three or four of these in a lump of clay in the saggar – where you can see them through the spyhole – they will ensure that you achieve the right temperature and shut down the kiln at the right time. Alternatively, you can make little rings of clay each with a dab of glaze on it and at intervals during the peak of the firing hook them out through the spyhole using a long, thin iron bar. If they are ready, so are the pots.

Try to resist the temptation to remove the glazed pots too soon. A sudden drop in temperature will craze the glaze.

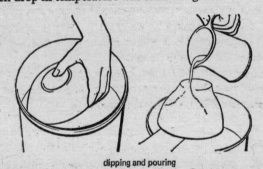

dipping and pouring

Glazes

All pottery glazes are a form of glass, basically silica and alumina melted together with the aid of a flux. Most traditional glazes used lead as the fluxing agent, but we know now that this is far too toxic a substance to use on pottery that is intended for food or drink. It is much better to use glazes with fluxes based on soda, borax or potash. Unless you are prepared to spend a great deal of time experimenting, it is best to buy a ready-made glaze that is free from lead and suitable for the maturing temperature of your clay.

Your glaze base will give you a clear glaze; it can be varied greatly by adding different oxides for different colours. Tin oxide will make the glaze white and opaque; cobalt will make it blue; copper will make it green; iron will make it red or brown.

You must mix the dry glaze with water. Take care to avoid lumps. It is a good idea to run the glaze through a fine phosphor bronze sieve, with about a 100 mesh, to make sure that there are no small lumps. Pour the glaze over the biscuit ware, or dip the pots in it. Make sure the pots are coated evenly but not too thickly. The ware should be quite dry before it is fired.

An even simpler method for glazing, used mainly by German potters from the fifteenth century, is to use salt.

Salt glazing is still used today in the manufacture of drain pipes. It gives them their characteristic 'orange peel' texture.

Remove the saggar from the kiln and construct a temporary floor in its place, leaving gaps for the combustion draught and for the circulation of vapour from the salt.

Only one firing is necessary. Pack the kiln with green ware and follow the same procedure as for biscuit firing. The temperature must exceed 1100°C and, if the clay can stand it, 1200°C is even better.

At the peak temperature, throw handfuls of common salt into the kiln chamber, using about 1 kg for every 0.75 cubic metres of kiln chamber. You may need to repeat this six or seven times. After salting, close down the kiln in the usual way.

The disadvantage of salt glazing is that it does not penetrate inside tall or narrow-necked vessels very readily; it may be necessary to coat these vessels beforehand with another glaze.

Leather

When it dries, the skin of an animal becomes stiff and brittle. Soaked in water, it may dissolve. When it is wetted by tanning, it is converted into a supple leather that does not change its character. Literally, this involves impregnating it with tannic acid, traditionally derived from oak bark. The complete process is long and complex. It is unlikely that a family or small group of people would wish to embark upon it. There is no reason at all, however, why a larger community or village should not make its own leather from the skins of the animals it kills.

Materials

Hides are the skins of fully grown large animals, such as bulls, cows, oxen and horses. Kips are the skins of the young of the large animals

– calves, younger oxen, young horses. Skins are the skins of small animals such as sheep, goats, pigs or, if you live near the coast, seals.

Hides are used mainly for the soles of shoes and boots, and for heavy harness leather. Kips are used for the uppers of shoes and boots. Skins are used for shoe uppers, gloves, upholstery, saddle seats, book bindings and handbags.

You will need a number of pits or vats in which to treat skins, kips and hides. How many depends on the extent to which you plan to open a full-time tannery with continuous processing. A commercial tannery may have thirty or more pits; you can probably make do with one, in which skins are treated in batches from start to finish, changing the solutions in the pit rather than moving the skins from one pit to the next. A second pit will mean that you can treat skins at the same times as you treat the more difficult hides and kips.

You will also need: a 'beam', or horse, which is a robust working surface set at an angle so that one end is higher than the other; a large, very sharp knife and a number of blunt knives, one of which can be made from a piece of slate; a heavy roller and a sheet of metal to protect the leather from the roller; tallow, or refined mutton fat; oak bark, and some method for crushing the dried bark into a fine powder; linseed oil, extracted from crushed linseed, which is the seed of flax (see

page 33 for growing flax). The linseed contains between 33 and 43 per cent of oil by weight, so you will need between 2 and 3 times the weight of linseed to extract a given quantity of oil. (The crushed linseed remains are fed to livestock as a protein feed.)

Whenever an oak tree has been felled, score round the trunk at intervals of about 500 cm, then make vertical slits, so that large semi-cylindrical sections of bark can be removed. Stack them to dry; tannin is very soluble in water, so if the bark gets wet you will lose tannin from it. When it is dry, grind it to a fine powder. It is now ready for use.

Cleansing

The hides, kips or skins must be cleaned thoroughly in clean water. All traces of blood must be removed, since this stains the leather. Soak the skins in clean water for two or three days to soften them.

Dehairing and fleshing

Mix slaked lime with water to form lye. Start with a very weak solution. Lime is fairly insoluble in water, so most of it will be in suspension. A weak solution holds all its lime in suspension, while stronger solutions accumulate a layer of precipitated lime at the bottom.

Soak the hides for a day or two in the weak solution; add more lime and soak for a day or two longer; then add more lime again. For hides that are to be used for sole leather, a soaking of 8 to 10 days in the strong solution is sufficient; for softer leathers you will need a longer soaking in a rather weaker solution: harness leather should soak for 12 to 14 days, very soft leathers for anything up to 6 weeks. The hides may be suspended in the pit from bars or allowed to float free.

Remove the hides from the lime pit and place them over the beam, flesh-side down. Use a blunt-bladed knife to remove the hair. The lime will have loosened it, so it should come out easily. Do not throw the hair away: it is a useful additive for mortar (see page 159).

Turn the hide over and remove the flesh, scraping and cutting it away with a sharp knife carefully so as not to damage the hide.

Now thoroughly wash the hides in clean water. Remove excess lime from heavy hides by 'scudding' – scraping them with a slate-bladed knife, or just a piece of slate with a smooth edge.

Mastering

Light hides, kips and skins are not washed or scudded after dehairing and fleshing. Instead they are placed in another pit, the 'mastering pit'. This contains a mixture either of hen or pigeon dung and water, or of warm water and dog excrement. The acid of the mastering pit removes the lime, but do not leave the skins there too long or they will begin to dissolve! In a pigeon or hen 'bates', 10 or 12 days should be long enough, but in a dog 'drench' a few hours will do. After mastering, wash the skins thoroughly in clean water.

Rounding

Cut the hides into parts. If you immerse them in the tanning solution complete, the coarsest parts of them will absorb the best tannin. Cut with a sharp knife. Remove the cheeks, the forepart including the shoulders and the two sides of the belly. What you are left with is called the 'butt', and it is the best part of the hide.

Wash again.

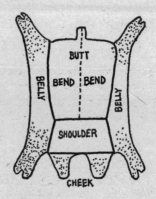

Making the tanning liquor

You have ground up your dried oak bark. If you cannot obtain oak, you can also tan with chestnut wood, hemlock, larch, oak galls or acorns: the last two can be ground up and added to oak bark. Add cold water to the ground bark and leave it to soak for several weeks. The resulting liquor is diluted before use.

Tanning

Leather is tanned by being suspended in a solution of tanning liquor that is made progressively stronger. Commercially, this involves moving the leather from pit to pit, but the same effect can be achieved by strengthening the liquor in a single pit.

Suspend the leather in the solution, making sure that no two pieces touch. Start with a very weak solution and make it stronger each day for 10 days.

Remove the leather pieces and lay them flat. Do not proceed to the next stage until all creases have disappeared.

Now lay the leather pieces flat in the pit. Strengthen the tanning solution every 2 or 3 days. For the first few days turn the pieces over at least twice a day to ensure penetration. Use a long stick to stir up the solution and keep adding more ground bark – as bark now, not as solution.

This process may take 6 to 8 weeks. At the end of it, remove the leather, lay it flat on a bed of ground bark, cover with more ground bark, add a second piece of leather, more bark and so on, to make a stack. Now pour tanning liquor over the stack and leave it alone for about 6 weeks. Take the stack apart, remake it with more ground bark, pour more liquor over it and leave it again. This process can go on for months or even as long as three years.

Drying

When, at last, you remove the fully tanned leather from the stack, wash it in a weak solution of tanning liquor and brush off loose particles with a stiff brush. You can place the pieces over the beam and use a blunt knife to draw the liquor from them; alternatively, use a smooth stone.

Wipe over the grain of the leather with a thin coat of linseed oil. This prevents too-rapid drying, which will lead to a hard, brittle leather – too slow drying will lead to the formation of mould.

Dry in the dark in a well-ventilated room, with the leather hung on racks. After a week or 10 days, remove the pieces and pile them, still damp, in heaps, separated by sacking. Beat them with a heavy pin and then place the stack on a level surface, cover it with a sheet of metal for protection, and pass a roller over it. Hang the pieces again, oil them, roll them. As soon as they are completely dry, the tanning is complete.

Currying

Currying is the final finishing process for leather. The leather is softened by soaking in water, then scoured by being laid on an inclined board and scraped with a blunt knife while hot water is poured over it. The knife must be very blunt indeed or it will damage the leather.

Stack the pieces between sacking again until they are partially dry, then wet them again, lay them flat, grain-side down, and use a blunt knife to scrape and stretch them.

Finally, with the leather slightly moist, use a hard brush to apply a generous coating of oil or tallow. When the leather dries completely, some of the harder fats from the tallow will be left on the surface of the leather and can be scraped off.

Dyeing

Use a mixture of lampblack and soap to blacken the underside of the leather.

To blacken the grain side, first brush all over with urine or soda dissolved in water. Then brush on a mixture of ferrous sulphate and logwood. Turn grain-side down and shave the underside with a sharp blade. Turn grain-side up again and rub with tallow, then a blunt blade, then a wooden (it should be mahogany) board, and finally with your bare forearm.

Alternative tanning processes

Alum The oldest method for tanning is much simpler and quicker. Make up a mixture in the following proportions:

For every 100 g of hide to be treated, 8 g of alum, 8 g of salt, 3 to 5 g of flour and 2 to 4 g of egg yolk.

Add all the ingredients to the water in the pit and soak the hide in it for about two hours, keeping it moving all the time. Then remove, drain and dry.

This will give a satisfactory finish to light hides.

Chrome Modern leathers are usually tanned by this method, which requires chemicals that may not be easy to obtain. Compounds involving chromium are highly polluting and must be treated with great respect. There are two methods, using one or two baths.

Double-bath method: Pickle the hide in sulphuric acid and common salt. Then place into a bath containing 6 per cent bichromate of soda, 4.5 per cent hydrochloric acid or 1.75 per cent sulphuric acid. Keep the hide moving in the solution until it has turned bright yellow. Remove, drain carefully and leave it stretched out for 24 hours. Then immerse it in a second bath containing 15 per cent sodium thiosulphate, 7.5 per cent hydrochloric acid or 3 per cent sulphuric acid. Keep the hide moving until the colour changes from bright yellow to a bluish green. When mixing the solution for the second bath, first dissolve the sodium thiosulphate, then dilute about one-third of the acid and add it. Stir and wait for the solution to become cloudy. Add another one-third of the acid and, after about an hour, the remainder.

Single-bath method: For every kilogramme of hide, use half a litre of water at between 85° and 95°C, and 150 g of chrome alum. Dissolve the chrome alum in the water. Prepare a solution of 16 g of soda ash or 60 g of washing soda in 250 cl of hot water. When the chrome alum is dissolved, add this solution cautiously. When all has been added, stir thoroughly.

Now prepare a second solution. Dissolve the bichromate of soda in a little water and mix with the concentrated sulphuric acid, then add the remainder of the water and glucose. Use (still for each kilogramme of hide) 1 litre of water, 200 g of bichromate of soda, 200 g of 95 per cent sulphuric acid, 50 g of glucose.

Keep the hide moving and add the second solution cautiously to the first until the colour of the leather changes from bright yellow to bright bottle green. Then remove, drain and dry.

When using strong acid mixtures you should use a lead-lined bath.

Shoemaking

Nowadays, shoes are made from a wide variety of materials. Rubber soles and heels replaced – to some extent – leather ones and these in turn have been replaced by composition materials made from plastics. Uppers are also often made from plastic. The traditional material, however, for making strong, hard-wearing boots and shoes is leather. You need nothing else.

The leather that wears best is cut from cattle hide. The tanned hide (see page 257) is cut down the centre to make it easier to handle and the two pieces are called 'sides'. On a side you will find leathers of varying thickness. The thinner leather is used for the uppers and the thicker leather for soles and heels.

You can also make uppers that are softer from pigskin, calf or kid, which is taken from goat hide. If you can obtain tanned horsehide you can take from it cordovan, a very heavy, tough leather that will last many years. Suède is usually made from cattle hide, calf or kid, by buffing the inner surface to create a napped finish.

The traditional village shoemaker used more tools than most crafts-men. Most of these tools, if not all of them, can be improvised from

263

commonplace tools. You will need several very sharp knives, suitable for cutting leather. Two or three Stanley knives with a range of blades should suffice. You will need awls for making holes of several sizes – for stitching and for eyelets, for example; rasps for finishing the surfaces where several thicknesses of leather have been used together, as in the sole and heel; irons that can be heated for shaping, especially around the heel and toe; and needles. You will need several lasts, and of two kinds. The first is used to shape the upper of the shoe or boot. It must be made the exact shape of the inside of the finished shoe, so you will need as many of these lasts as you have feet to shoe. You might make a last by taking an old shoe worn by the foot that is to be re-shod, filling it with plaster of Paris and then cutting the shoe away, very carefully. Grease the plaster and place it into a vessel containing more wet plaster. When that sets, remove the first 'foot' and you will be left with a mould that you can use to make a last of a more durable material – fired clay, perhaps. The advantage of using an old shoe to begin with is that it will retain and transmit the exact shape of the foot that wore it. You will need other lasts for soling and heeling. These are usually made from iron and are not difficult to buy from second-hand shops or even to find lying around rubbish tips and scrapmetal yards. You will need a hammer that has one flat face for hammering nails and one round face for shaping the leather, plenty of strong waxed thread, polish, and nails.

Making the shoe

Take another old shoe and dismantle it carefully so that you can lay out all its constituent parts. It will consist of a heel, a sole, an inner sole, an upper, a lining, a counter (which strengthens and helps to shape the heel), possibly a toe box to strengthen and help shape the toe, and welting.

Cut out pieces of leather to correspond to each of these pieces and begin by stitching together the upper.

The complete upper now lies more or less flat and is ready for shaping over the last. This is the most skilled part of the operation. Place the inner sole on the bottom of the last, the counter around the heel, and place the upper loosely over the last. Wet the leather and, using hot irons, stretch the upper tightly over the last and fasten it to the inner sole. It is important that the inside of the upper corresponds exactly to the shape of the last if the shoe is to be comfortable to wear.

When the upper is finished and attached securely to the inner sole, transfer the shoe to the other last for soling. The sole is made from two or more layers of thick leather, stitched to the upper all round.

Now make the heel from a further three or more layers of leather and fasten it by nailing through the sole to the inner sole. The nails must have large heads to prevent them from slipping through the leather. If you cannot obtain suitable nails you might use metal washers.

The shoe is now ready for finishing. Cut away surplus leather from around the heel and sole and use rasps to smooth down the edge. Fit eyelets to the lace holes or buckles if the shoe is to be fastened with a buckle. Then polish.

Cut a 'sock' from a piece of soft leather and glue it above the inner sole to protect the wearer from the turned-over nails.

Now make the other shoe!

Decorating leather

An impression made with a tool on wet leather will become permanent when the leather dries out.

Draw a pattern on the dry leather. Wet the leather and work the pattern into the surface by pressing firmly with a metal tool (such as a Dresden tool) that is of an appropriate shape. Work on a firm surface, damping the leather whenever it begins to dry. When you have finished, leave the leather to dry.

Decorations of this kind form attractive embellishments on bags and belts.

Laundering
Bleach

Bleach for use in the laundry used to be called 'buck'. It is simply a lye (see page 259) made from wood ash.

Take a quantity of wood ash. Place a forked stick of hazel or maple across the top of a large tub, or 'keeler', and use the stick to support a wooden bowl with curved sides, the bottom of which is pierced with many small holes so as to act as a strainer, or 'leech'. Place the wood ash – the whiter the better – into the leech and pour cold water over it until the quantity of liquid in the keeler is sufficient for your needs. Pour the liquid from the keeler into a bucket, this time straining it through muslin to remove particles of ash.

Use this lye for bleaching whites before washing. If you also spread the bleached garments on the grass in the sun, stains will fade still more and the washing will be easier.

Soap

You need a stronger lye than for bleach. Make a board with a channel to carry liquid from one vessel to another and stand on it a barrel without a bottom. Place some straw in the barrel, then some lime, then fill the barrel with wood ash. Pour cold water into the barrel, a bucketful at a time, at intervals of three or four hours on the first, third and fifth days. Have another vessel at the other end of the channel to catch the lye. When it is thick enough to float an egg, heat grease to its boiling point and add it to the lye. Stir it for five minutes every day until it forms soap. If nothing has happened after a week, add a bucketful of soft water. The proportions are: for each kilogramme grease, 0.5 litres lime and 14 litres water.

The leaves of soapwort (*saponaria officinalis*) which is found in hedgerows and beside streams, are an effective substitute for soap.

Starch

You can make starch from old potatoes that are not fit to eat. Grate them coarsely under water. Leave the mash for twenty-four hours, strain off the dirty liquid and set the deposit on a tray to dry. The resulting powder is a strong starch.

Lighting
Rush lights

Rush lights were the only source of light in rural England for many centuries. The best rush for the purpose is the common soft rush, *Juncus conglomeratus*, which grows in wet pastures, by streams and in ditches. They are in their best condition in mid-summer but are quite usable into the autumn. As soon as they are cut they must be placed in water to prevent them from drying out. Remove the rushes from the water and peel off the bark, or rind, leaving a single, even, narrow strip of pith from top to bottom. This is difficult, but the knack can be acquired with practice! Then set the rushes out on the grass to bleach and to take the dew for several nights. Then they must be dried in the sun. Prepare scalding grease (pork or bacon fat is excellent for this purpose; mutton fat is less so). Dip the rushes in it one at a time. The proportions are 6:1; 6 measures of grease will coat

1 measure of rushes. A full-length rush, about 70 cm, will burn for nearly an hour.

Candles

These can be made in moulds or by dipping. If a rush light is dipped repeatedly in the grease and is left to cool again each time, layer builds upon layer until eventually it is the shape of a candle. The dipped candles are hung up by their wicks and cut to length as required. Candle moulds are not difficult to make with plaster of Paris, provided you have a few bought candles to start with! A mould should make several candles at a time. Make a wick of string (*not* nylon), soak it in a boracic solution and then dry it. Place the wick in the mould and pour in molten fat. The candle is made tip down. You can use tallow, which gives a poor light, beeswax, which gives an excellent light (but is so difficult to obtain in sufficient quantity that bought beeswax candles were used only at court and by the very wealthy), or a composite mixture of the two.

Rope

Rope can be made from any coarse fibre. Of old it has been made from hemp or jute, but you might try nettles as well. The fibres are prepared and spun in the usual way (see page 109), but the equipment for rope making needs to be larger and heavier than for spinning wool or flax.

The spun yarn is then twisted into rope using a jack. This is a cogged and geared wheel worked by a handle. Each of its spokes (usually there are four) has a hook, and the ends of the yarn are fastened to the hooks. The thickness of the rope is determined by the number of threads twisted into it.

The rope must then be polished. It is passed through water, washed and scoured until the scum and waste are removed, then passed through a size made from flour and water, and finally through a bath of paraffin wax. It is then hung on posts set at intervals along a 'rope walk' to allow it to dry.

Ropes are coiled, but strings and twines are balled.

Commun-
ities

Who's an escapist?

People who seek alternative lifestyles alone or as members of communities are often accused of escapism. The accusation is not a new
one; members of religious communities have been called escapist for
many years, perhaps for centuries. It is not true of them and it need
not be true of you.

We have some right to choose how we should live. We cannot alter
the world, impose our will upon it to make it into the kind of world we
would like. Belief that 'mastery' of this kind is possible is the real
escapism of our age; it is the escapism that has led to most of the
problems we face today. We cannot do this, but to some extent at least
we can choose whether we will live alone, working out our own lifestyle in our own way, or as a member of a nuclear family, or as a
member of an extended family of relatives or like-minded friends.
Escapism is not involved in this choice, any more than it is involved
in the choice to live in one part of the country rather than any other.

Perhaps we should be more precise about 'reality'. Man has always
lived as a member of a family, an extended family, a clan or a village.
These are fundamental social units. Even great cities like London are
based on a village structure, although the villages have merged and
lost much of their separate identity. In some countries the subdivisions
of cities are called 'communes'. If we choose to live in one of these
basic social units, then we are returning to – or, if the critics insist,
escaping to – reality, to the traditional kind of organization that has
worked successfully for many generations. If any kind of social life is
natural for man, it is one organized in this way. A determined attempt

to live a more natural life cannot be called escapist; escapism is departing from this lifestyle.

We may try to do more. We may find that living becomes a full-time occupation – living as distinct from making a living, which becomes of secondary importance. We may seek to experience directly the struggle for survival, the effort to get by, to change and adapt and improvise. The living that we make comes from the quality of the life we lead, alone or with one another. Does this sound grim and earnest? It need not be so, for if we are free to adapt easily to changing circumstances we can live better in changing times than can the 'organization man' who must accommodate himself to a rigid system on which he is entirely dependent for his security. Should the system fail he may need to be hospitalized, medically or socially, for his conformity has sapped his natural resilience and adaptability.

So we are seeking a more real life, free from the straitjacket of security, a steady job, a regular guaranteed income, a contract of employment and an investment in the company pension fund. The security afforded by such an apparently protected life is illusory. How much safety did it provide when, during the Cuban missile crisis, the world teetered on the brink of thermonuclear war? How much safety would it provide were the company to go bankrupt? Would a 'survival' kind of alternative provide more security? Well, a dispersed population is less vulnerable to attack than one that is concentrated in a few areas of high density; if one grows one's own food, a depression may make the surplus difficult to sell, but at least one will not starve.

The cycles of development

Human history is the story of a never-ending alternation between two phases of growth and social development. One phase is civilization, or the kind of life associated with city cultures. The other phase is one of non-centralization, or dispersal, within which people develop independently, free from the rigidity of city life. Of the really important advances in human knowledge and experience most have occurred either in societies that were politically weak and tolerant and able to exercise but little control over the behaviour of their members, or among rebellious members of societies that are politically domineering and intolerant. At its height, the civilization of weak, divided Ancient Greece was original, innovative; at its height, the civilization of Rome was centralist, consolidating, oppressive. Today we are at the point of change between one kind of civilization and the other.

269

We are witnessing the decay of that part of our culture that goes back into our ancient history and that has to do with precious metals, bronze, iron, fossil fuels and now the apparent security of ferro-concrete, which will disintegrate if it is subjected to a vibration resonant with either iron or calcium.

Overgrowing this aspect of our culture, there is another that has to do with survival for its own sake. We adapt ourselves and our behaviour so that we may get by, no matter what may happen. We turn our backs on part of the memory of our race and obey those instincts which, if we can hear them clearly, are as sure a guide for us as they are for many other species. We think again of the things we actually need – food, clothing, shelter, companionship – and of how they are obtained. We are acting out a reflex that is conditioned not only by memories of the past, but on our knowledge of the future. This is less absurd than it may sound. A bird will build its nest in spring, before the leaves open that will shelter its young and hide them from hungry predators. The bird does not wait for the leaves to open before it builds its nest.

Right motives

Yet, even though the movement itself may not be escapist, we may be. We may seek a different lifestyle in order to escape not from a way of life that is insecure, but from things within ourselves that will go with us. When an idealistic young man told Goethe of the fine new life he planned to build in America, the land of freedoms and opportunities that Europe could not offer, Goethe replied, 'If America is anywhere, it is here.'

Motives are important. Man is motivated in all he does. Every act he performs aims to satisfy some appetite. If today we seek to survive, then the appetite we aim to satisfy is an appetite for life itself. A 'survival' lifestyle can offer us no more than life and it is useless to seek from it anything else. We must convince ourselves that we can do something more than wait passively to die.

Are communes right for you ?

There are no hard and fast rules, no convenient yardsticks by which you can measure yourself to discover whether, psychologically, you are suited to live in a small community or commune. Monks, nuns, leaders of expeditions and people who have spent months on end on board ships at sea will agree that life is full of surprises. People you might think quite unsuitable may blossom in a communal environment, while others, apparently ideally equipped for this kind of life, find it an intolerable strain. During the Second World War psychopaths did well, while people who were normal but rigid broke at the seams and fell apart. Remember, though, that if you are mad already then you cannot go mad. If you are too sane, too correct, then take care. You may lack the necessary adaptability. Life in a small community involves a great deal of tolerance, of give and take, of willingness to muck in, to do your share or more than your share of the work, and to do things the way others like them, at least some of the time.

Do you need a leader?

We are all in the world together and we must sink or swim together. In a commune, or in the world, there is no room for inner circles, for ideas of blood being thicker than water, for formal hierarchies and pecking orders. If someone wants to be a leader, then let him prove his worth. Fair's fair and he must be fairer than most. If he isn't fair, then avoid him. There will be competition for the leadership. Unless you want to join in and aim for the role yourself, then sit back and let them work it out for themselves. Let the best win. Watch the candidates, though, for certain qualities. Your leader should be well mannered: does he help himself first or does he offer you a share? Does he do his share of the chores or is he simply decorative? Does he set a good example? Is he considerate of others? Does he enjoy himself? This is an excellent quality, provided that in doing it he doesn't prevent others from enjoying themselves as well. Avoid people who are so tolerant they can't stand your personal brand of intolerance, or so pie they can't stand your piety, or so good at everything you can't bear it.

It is our weaknesses that make life possible. It is through the chinks in our armour that contact can be made; they are what make us human. The most important qualities of all are the capacity for enjoyment and a sense of humour.

Whom should you accept as a new member?

This is a problem that will begin as soon as you have arrived at your communal home and the word has gone round that a new establishment has opened its doors. People will simply arrive, usually unannounced and certainly uninvited. Sometimes they will be passing through, sometimes they will want to stay. Some of them will be an asset to you, others will be a pain in the neck. How do you decide which are which?

The problem is not new. In some African tribal societies it was the custom to greet visitors on the first day with a meal and a bed; on the second day they were given a hoe.

Beware the too sane, the too balanced, but choose your rogues with care. So far as possible, let them choose themselves. Start as you would wish your relationship with them to continue. Make no concessions to them: do not alter your routine or your lifestyle in any way in order to accommodate them, and do not expect them to put themselves out for you. Treat them casually, in the rough and ready fashion you would treat them if they had lived with you for years. In other words, expose them to your lifestyle as it is and as it will be for them if they decide to stay. If you make a special effort to impress them, they will be lured under the false pretence of a style you cannot sustain. If they cannot stand it, they will drop away. Others may leave but return. Some may not leave at all. Give them time, do not try to push them around, and except in extreme circumstances, do not try to push them out. Do not try to force them to conform to your pattern. In their own time they will either join in or go. Do not give them that kind of emotional support that will encourage them to latch on to you without making a contribution.

Remember the first rule of a Zen monastery: a day of no working is a day of no eating.

What conflicts will there be?

Communes do fall apart, either from internal feuding or simply from boredom. A commune must be a group of people living together for a purpose, and the operative phrase is 'living together', rather than living separately but in the same place. The relationships within it are symbiotic: individual members are different and behave differently, but the behaviour of each contributes to the welfare of all. It begins as soon as the casual people drifting through your life begin to do some of the chores without being asked, buying some of the food, helping to make the establishment run smoothly.

Allow people to be different. Some people like to serve. Let them. Some people like to entertain. Let them. Give and take means that some people give and others take; some give more than they take while others take more than they give. This is as it should be. If everyone were to give five pounds and to take five pounds no one would gain anything. Avoid at all costs a situation in which people mind their own business, wash up after themselves, cook their own food, buy their own drink. Break this habit by forestalling them and cooking or washing up for them, or buying them drink: it is easier sometimes to persuade people to take than to give and what is important is to end their separatism.

Mutual aid means the division of labour. Someone has to provide a lavatory; someone has to keep it clean; someone has to provide lavatory paper. In one commune there was a rule that the oldest male member had to empty the Elsan. Once this chore has been done the rest is much easier.

Families must each have a private territory into which they can retreat and within which they can care privately for their children. On the whole, men are large, affable creatures who tend to get along easily with one another, if necessary agreeing from the start to differ but to put up with one another in a kind of subdued hate!

Do not worry about the men, but structure the commune around the needs of the women. Like robins, women need a territory, their own privacy to rear their families in their own way. Let each woman have this, and let each woman have her own man. Remember that women menstruate. Pre-menstrual tension can make sparks fly. Each woman must have her own sphere of influence, though the borders may be invisible.

Unless you have this kind of organization, the children will become monsters. They will behave uncontrollably, their mothers will side with them and the quarrels that begin among the children will end by driving the adults apart.

By keeping the mothers and children apart and letting the men muck in together you can make into a kind of preventive detention what otherwise might be a mixed slum.

Religious belief

A ligature is that which holds things together. A common religion can do just that for a commune. You may even go so far as to say that a common religion is the *sine qua non* of a successful commune. This does not mean the religion must be formal. It need have no name. It is some basic outlook that is held in common, or some common purpose that may seem vague to an outsider but that is real to those who share it.

The best religion you can have is one that aims to serve not only the members of the commune itself, but the world outside as well. Nurses may weep and scream at one another in the nurses' home. They can hate sisters and devise infernal torments for matrons. Yet the girls have a common purpose. The community survives and flourishes.

Perennial communes as well as religious orders are held together by a prayer routine. This is a sacramental ritual which has an outer form, such as formal prayers that are said in unison, but also has an inner reality. The unification of the physical activity brings a mental unity as well and creates a kind of cooperative healing session. Everyone who participates leaves the session affected by it – invariably. It is as though the members of an orchestra were all playing their instruments, each satisfying himself by playing the tunes he liked best. Then the conductor arrived and their activities become coordinated to achieve together more than they could have achieved separately. This is the reality of religion. You may care to go further, to think and speak of a living God or of some being, state, force or higher reality within which everything is embraced and known.

Beware, though, of any fancy religion that entails submitting your personal judgement. Even Jesuits, sworn to a spiritual discipline that binds them to obey their superiors, may disobey if the command they receive offends their conscience. Even military law is no excuse for evading your personal responsibility to obey your conscience: the Nuremberg war crimes trials established that. Yet you will need personal self-discipline to prevent freedom from becoming self-indulgence.

Communal living

Monasteries

Despite the large number of communes that have come into existence in the last few years we know little about communal living. Most of the communes are short-lived. We may determine the causes of dissolution and become aware of some of the more obvious snags. But we know far less about what makes successful communes work, simply because there are too few examples.

Yet within our culture there have always been ways of life that are based on communities rather than on individuals. Military establishments, prisons, monasteries and convents are all communes, in the sense of self-sufficient communities living in only partial contact with the world around them. There is little we can learn from military establishments or prisons, because they are fundamentally different from the modern concept of a commune. They are cells within a highly centralized organization. One prison, one barracks is much like another, and so is the lifestyle within it. The pattern on which each unit is built is determined centrally. Religious communities, on the other hand, are highly decentralized. They have much in common with modern communes, they have encountered and solved many of the problems that divide and finally destroy secular communes and they have survived over long periods of time.

Decision making

A community of any sort needs many ways of expressing its common vision and ideology and of bringing them to bear on practical decisions. If this does not happen, and if it is not felt to happen, members cease to belong to, relate to, the whole.

It is often thought that this common ideology is laid down for monks in a rigid book of rules. In fact, however, the rule that is adopted most widely by western monks, that of St Benedict, written in the fifth century, is as much descriptive as prescriptive, inspirational as regulating. It insists that decisions and the way of life must be at the initiative of the local existential community, and in particular in the person of the abbot.

Lifestyles

There are four main constituents of the daily life of a monk: work, study, leisure and prayer. They are related to one another closely, and should their mutual balance be lost, the quality of life is endangered.

Work can be undervalued, thought of as no more than a hobby or a way to fill time. Then life loses its essential roots in creation. Or it can be overvalued, as a sort of idol, so that everything becomes subservient to it. Members then seek achievement and visible fulfilment.

Study can be over-academic and cerebral, so that learning and cleverness take over from that wisdom and reflective quality that has characterized monastic life through the ages; or it can be neglected under the pressure of other work, and then prayer, the search for God and life, awareness of the world, all suffer profoundly.

Leisure can be undervalued if, for instance, life becomes too masculine, orientated to work and achievement, and loses its feminine quality. Or leisure can slide into laziness and lack of discipline. Meals have always been highly valued in monastic life; they are second only to liturgy as special moments of community life and growth. Deep symbolism is attached to them.

'Let all guests that come be received like Christ himself ... As soon as a guest arrives let him be met with all charitable service ... Let the greatest humility be shown and let Christ be worshipped in them, for indeed he is received in their persons.'

Prayer, perhaps the most vulnerable of the four, becomes unbalanced if it is seen as the only thing in life that matters, rather than as interpreting and summing up all the rest of life, each part of which matters; or if it is seen merely as a support operation for the rest of life, rather than supremely as an end in itself, with the same quality of 'play' as games should have; or if it is seen primarily as a routine duty which will somehow carry the monk, rather than calling him to constant renewal of life.

BRAD

BRAD, short for Biotechnic Research And Development, was established in March, 1972, based on the ideas of Robin Clarke, a science journalist. A group of seventeen people was formed to provide an alternative way of life, human in scale and ecological in emphasis, for people wishing to live in harmony with their environment, in peace with their neighbours, and in control of their lives and their technology. Four of the members – Robin and Janine Clarke and John and Maria Clemow – purchased a dilapidated 43-acre farm in the Welsh hills. The attrition of the original group began as reality replaced the romantic view. During the summer and autumn of 1972 others joined the four, and meetings among themselves and with an Australian architect, Peter Bynon, were used to thrash out their views of the physical shape of communal living, which they planned to incorporate in the 750-cubic-metre extension to the small stone farm cottage. Work began on April Fool's Day, 1973.

After eighteen months BRAD was self-sufficient in most foods. It still buys condiments, tea, coffee and sugar (but is experimenting with sugar beet). It also buys hard fruit, because the orchard had been neglected for fifteen years. The vegetable garden is 900 feet up on a north-facing slope usually considered fit only for average pasture, but spread with compost it produces all the usual vegetables in profusion, as well as a few exotica such as tobacco and outdoor tomatoes. The unheated greenhouse produces green peppers and aubergines. The herb and flower gardens flavour and decorate the table. The community grinds its own flour for bread, makes its own wines, jams, butter and cheeses.

The livestock includes two Jersey cows, their heifer calves, a couple of piglets, four breeding geese, a couple of dozen hens and a cock, bees and about seventy sheep. Since the first harvest in the autumn of 1974, no feedstuffs have been bought in: oats, barley and wheat are all home-grown, as are fodder crops and hay. The only outside purchases are mineral licks and one day these will be replaced by herbal leys.

Care of the animals is mostly pleasant and rewarding, though time-consuming. Animals are less often criticized for apparent inefficiency when they are known and named characters, part of the total way of life. The community is not vegetarian, though the diet has moved naturally and pleasantly far from urban diets dominated by meat. Mutton and lamb – with incredible taste – are the main meats, with occasional pork, chicken, goose or jugged roadside hare. The members find they can kill their own meat, though without relish.

There have been many positive achievements, especially in the development and application of alternative technologies. As a social community, the group has come to experience the reality of freedom. Ironically, this has created problems. In the words of one member, Philip Brachi:

'In one sense Eithin-y-Gaer is a very free place. Gone is the need to play roles to gain respect from one's neighbours, business associates, partner or family; instead one is free to be simply oneself. Perversely, that is perhaps at first the very hardest thing of all. (It is not that we sit around the big sycamore dining table and shred one another's psyches; on the contrary, there has never been any such structured or formal encounter and delving among us here – though experience now tells us that this should be included in future.)

'Upon introspection we find that most of our life is lived out in the form of roles, many and various. Gradually, usually humanely, this place has a way of exposing such nonsenses, enabling one to transcend such constraints and become more truly and fully oneself. Which, of course, poses forcibly such basic and utterly personal questions as: Who am I? What do I really hold dear? Why in relationships do I think and act as I do? What do I most wish to do with my life? With its deliberate lack of hierarchy, a wary eye for the charismatic leader, and an absence of the structured time one became so used to in the cities, Eithin is a natural setting in which to seek and share the answers.

'With the freedom, though, come modest but time-consuming obligations. Our sole "rule" is that whoever has not cooked for longest washes up tonight and cooks tomorrow. Beyond that, each animal or group of animals has one person responsible for its wellbeing; likewise the broad areas of the farm, the wood supply, the kitchen garden, the building work, and AT [alternative technology] research. But this is not the same thing as the old bogy of urban specialization, for all the actual work is shared and done by all or any, according to preferences.

'As people are enabled to grow in freedom, sexist roles may be broken or blurred: a man becomes a cook or child-minder, a woman becomes car mechanic or joiner. Tangible, occasionally joyous evidence of personal evolution, this can be hard to handle when it occurs at different rates within a couple. Old patterns are smashed and as one grows outward to the group the other may feel neglected and turn away to seek security or solace. Such a situation requires an openness and honesty quite antithetical to middle-class upbringing; unless there is a willingness to dig a little beneath the surface of statements and appearances, true community may never be experienced. One's own frustrations, hang-ups and presumed inadequacies are taken out on others and games, shallowness, role-playing and mistrust abound. The alternative, calling for truthfulness and gentle understanding from everyone, leads to relief, unburdening, and a real comprehension of that over-used word "together". "Love thy neighbour as thyself" seems a good basic tenet for any community, but first each person must love and accept him- or herself fully, warts and all. It is not an easy state to reach, but group support can be a great help. Some people will have none of it. Hale and hearty for the most part, they denounce such evolution, which they see as mere distraction from the real life of physical teamwork, the men pulling together, the good, inebriate times. No synthesis is possible for them; the real communal experience is refused. Eventually some deeper trouble or doubt intrudes, but is not shared; on one pretext or another, often amicably, they leave the community.

'The essential message from BRAD seems to be that building a solar roof, a windmill, one's own house even, is child's play compared to open, honest, joyous communal living therein. But we think the effort worthwhile.

'The Visitor Problem requires capital letters! It is a problem endemic to all communes, it seems. While we were still building, living in tents, caravans and barns, and with little communal feel to the place, the longer-term visitors were a huge source of energy and the day-trippers hardly affected us. It was in 1974 that the Problem became acute. From May till November there was not a single day without visitors and for all but a week or two there were visitors staying as well. Almost without exception, each was pleasant enough and some were fine folk whom we shall see again and again, but this was forgotten in the sea of faces, changing, coming and going without even knowing your names, requiring food and bedding; and questions, the same endless questions about our income, politics, sex-life, decision-making, and all this in our *home*! Neither the visitors nor the "zoo" gained much from this experience and now we try to have a "visitor-free week" once a month and anyone who does not contact us first by letter or telephone is liable not to be well received.

'We have discovered that "one person, one room" is necessary, even if two people consider themselves a couple, although of course they may choose to sleep in one room and use the other as a sitting room. The option is there, to be apart when necessary. Privacy is indivisible. This belated discovery limits the number we can house, but we feel that eight adults, plus children, is about the right number.

'The sharing of income is an "unproblem". Each member, or couple if they work like that, earns whatever they can, keeps back what they think they need, and puts the rest into the communal kitty. Though we have not yet been faced with this, a person unable to earn any money ought to be able to draw a little each week from the kitty. There have been huge inequalities in both capital inputs and earning abilities, but provided no corresponding hierarchy is allowed, this simple system of trust has worked extremely well.

'The degree of communality of sharing personal belongings is also based on trust and individual choice, rather than on any rules. One puts into communal use what furniture, books, kitchen equipment, tools, records one wishes. It is true that communal items are not so well cared for as individual possessions, but it is also interesting that those who put least into the communal pool, and so perhaps made Eithin less their home, are the same people who have now left for one reason or another. Vehicles have always been pooled, or sold to raise communal capital.

'A commune venture such as ours cannot be directed, but rather evolves. We could not say now where we shall be – even if we shall exist at all – in a year's time. This lack of any specific direction causes problems for some who may enter with a firm blueprint in mind for the community.' [*Editor's note:* since this was written, the BRAD community has dispersed.]

Education

Children must be educated. This may sound obvious, but it is a point you could forget in planning a lifestyle for a community that begins with no children but several young couples.

When children reach school age, the simplest way to educate them is to send them to the village school. If there are no schools anywhere nearby, then those among you with training and/or aptitude for teaching must cope as best you can.

Meanwhile we have a situation in which schools exist but there exist also children who prefer not to go to them and parents who prefer to find other ways of educating their children.

The law provides parents with some clear obligations, but also with a basic right. The Education Act (1944), Section 36, says: 'It shall be the duty of the parent of every child of compulsory school age to cause him to receive efficient full-time education suitable to his age, ability and aptitude, either by regular attendance at school or otherwise.' In other words, parents do have the right to educate their children 'otherwise', that is, other than at school. You don't have to send your children to school if they don't want to go and if you don't want to force them. You can still carry out your legal responsibilities.

You should begin by buying a copy of the Education Act (1944) from Her Majesty's Stationery Office or by borrowing a copy from a public library.

If you embark on an 'otherwise' educational programme, either by yourself or together with other parents, you will have to arrange it and pay for it yourselves. Exceptions to this rule are made only when the local education authority cannot provide a school place for a child or when, for some compelling reason such as chronic poor health, a child is unable to attend school regularly. In these cases you will receive official help and, probably, a teacher to act as a tutor.

You will have to submit your 'otherwise' plans to your local education authority and the authority will have to approve them. (If you live in the Inner London area you will be given a form DO/35, 'Parents' statement of arrangements made for education of child'.) Whether you receive a form or not, you will be required to give your name and address, the name and qualifications of the person who is to do the teaching, and the 'programme of educational work and activity' that they will provide. Having submitted all this information in writing you will then be interviewed either at the education offices or at your home, and if the plans are accepted that is all there is to it. You will be in charge of your child's education, but you will also be responsible for it under the Act.

The wording of the Act is not very precise when it describes what it means by 'education', but when they interview you the education authorities will be looking for certain specific points: qualifications, timetable and curriculum, written work and other activities.

Qualifications

Ideally the person teaching the children should be a qualified teacher. However, this is not absolutely necessary. Most education authorities will accept some basic academic qualification, the higher the better. Even A levels and technical qualifications have been accepted in the past, and there have been one or two cases of persons with no academic qualifications at all being accepted by their local authority. All the same, if you have no qualifications it will help if you can enlist the support of someone who has and who is willing to act as a tutor, and it is better still if your 'otherwise' programme includes other people from the start. It is surprising how many qualified teachers there are who are not working in schools and who might be willing to help. You can advertise in local papers or shop windows, or you can look for sympathetic contacts at playgroups and adventure playgrounds. There may be a community newspaper or an advice and information service in your area which might help.

The essential points are that there is no legal requirement for a person teaching children in an 'otherwise' programme to have any formal qualifications; nonetheless, the support of a qualified person will help; and it will be easier still if the scheme involves a number of families rather than just one.

Timetable and curriculum

Education officers do not expect a person providing an 'otherwise' programme to be able to offer the full range of facilities and opportunities that one finds in state schools. They do expect to find parents or people working to provide regular and varied learning opportunities. They expect the basic skills of reading, writing and arithmetic to be covered.

The law does not define 'full-time' education. 'Otherwise' programmes have been accepted in the past on the basis of anything from three to eight hours a day. Some formal teaching is required. Regularity is more important than quantity. You would do best to keep a full record of all your activities, formal or not, so that when the education officer contacts you there is a timetable to show him that indicates regularity and variety in your teaching programme.

Written work

At all times you should encourage your child or children to do written work and drawing. You should keep this work, or copies of it, in workbooks or folders, because quite apart from your own interest in it, the education officer will certainly wish to see it. Education officers will not be impressed by educational programmes that contain little or no written work.

Other activities

Education officers will want to know about the physical and recreational activities in which your child or children participate. They will want to know how much contact your children have with other children, both in learning situations and casually. It is not a good idea to keep children at home all the time without easy contact with other adults and children. Of course, if your 'otherwise' programme involves other parents and other children right from the start, this problem will not arise.

In the end much depends on how well you get on personally with your education officer. This will involve many factors: the personality of the officer and your own personality, the underlying attitude of the officer, your own confidence, your determination to persevere even if the authorities are at first unsympathetic. The law is so vague that, as well as genuine differences of opinion, it is open to different legal interpretations and you must be prepared for this and, if necessary, prepared to argue your case. Your chances of acceptance will be much greater if you yourself live in an organized home, with an 'educated' lifestyle, especially if there are books on the shelves. If you have the support and active involvement of qualified teachers then your problems will be considerably reduced.

If your child simply fails to attend school and if you present no plans for an alternative education system, then eventually you will be taken to court. If you are found guilty under the Act you will be fined or, after a third conviction, possibly sent to prison. Your child or children may be taken into care or even sent away to an approved school (now called a community home) or, if other offences are involved, to Borstal. Attitudes are changing; the authorities and magistrates are less likely than they were to equate truancy with delinquency, but these penalties are still sometimes imposed and this is a risk you will run. In short, if you do not wish your children to attend school, you *must* find an alternative within the law.

Advantages of a Tuition Scheme

1 A Tuition Scheme differs from a school in that tuition can take place anywhere, at any time. Central and comprehensive premises are not required, although any project needs a base.

2 It involves local people, qualified or not, who are thus more likely to be known to the children and the neighbourhood.

3 It necessarily involves parents and helps to break down the usual barriers separating education from the home.

4 Learning takes place at the level of the children's experience and needs.

5 It is adaptable; it can serve as many children as need tuition at any time, and can involve as many tutors as are available.

6 By involving local children and local adults, it helps to bring together families who have been trying to cope in isolation at home.

7 It can concentrate on the particular difficulties, needs or interests of the children involved.

8 A Tuition Scheme allows children to participate for as long as they want to; for some this will be longer than for others. It can also serve long-term needs, and in particular can encourage children to specialize in those fields of interest which are not encouraged in normal schools.

9 Children generally like a Tuition Scheme, because it is flexible and can respond to their interests. If they don't like a part of it, then they can be involved in changing it to suit their special needs.

The Centre of Living

Two years ago, John Seymour wrote a book called *Self Sufficiency* which brought him more than a thousand letters from people who wished to take up a piece of land in the country, become self-sufficient in food and 'do their own thing'. Many of these correspondents have since obtained their land. Some have evolved a good lifestyle, others have failed and given up. Without exception, the failures failed because they did not know how to do it, and you can't learn everything from a book, not even from this one.

To help such people, John Seymour wishes to expand his existing 62-acre farm by the purchase of at least one other farm nearby and to establish a Centre, or School, of Self-Sufficiency. People will be able to come and stay, for a year if possible, while they learn the arts and disciplines of self-sufficiency, in return for their labour, which will be used to produce the food everyone will eat, to develop land and buildings, to establish crafts and industries, and to produce a surplus of high-quality produce which will be sold to the public. As a few examples, the Centre will not sell milk to the Milk Marketing Board as its commercial neighbours do, but will produce high-quality semi-soft cheese of the Brie, Camembert or Port Salut type, which will be sold for the sorts of price at which such cheeses sell. The whey will go to the pigs, which will not be sold as fat pigs but as high-quality 'continental'-type smoked sausage and sweet-pickled ham. The Centre will not sell its wool as wool, but as high-quality cloth or as garments. Timber will not be sold as timber, but as finished furniture or other products. Hides will not be sold as hides, but as finished leather products. Such things would be quite impossible on a commercial farm which paid standard agricultural wages, but with intelligent, willing, well-directed volunteer labour, they will be possible, and the labourers will be mastering skills which will be useful to them when they, in turn, get their land and become self-sufficient.

Contact will be maintained with ex-students. They will be given help when they need it and they will help others. Everyone will be expected to help new settlers to become established and so a growing network of self-sufficient people will spread over the country. Eventually it is hoped that more Centres will be established in other places.

The reason for the desirability of this development is that in the future it will be necessary for these islands to be self-sufficient in food, and to achieve this without the help of a lot of oil-derived chemicals. An agriculture with a much better input-output ratio will be needed.

It will be highly labour intensive, but very moderate in its demands for imported oil and chemicals. We must prepare for this now by replacing machines and chemicals with men and women, and they must be men and women who have been trained so that they know what they are doing.

Partners in the Centre will have to produce between them enough capital to buy extra land and buildings. Each partner will own his own house and a piece of land, but he will also have a share in the land, buildings and equipment owned by the Centre. He will be expected to help with the work of the Centre, but in return he will share in the produce of the Centre and in its community and social life. The aim is not to make money, but to work hard, with fresh air, good food, fun and a good life for everyone. The money investment will be secure and arrangements will be made to enable anyone to withdraw his investment if necessary.

John Seymour and his family have been practising self-sufficiency in food and many artefacts for more than twenty years with some success, and they know a great deal about it. All the same they will call on expert help from outside whenever they need it. The aim is to achieve the highest standards possible in every activity, not merely to muddle along.

The Seymours are not vegetarians, have no politics, and believe every man's religion is his own concern. The only thing the partners at the Centre will hold in common is a belief in what they are doing and a capacity for hard work.

For further information, write to John Seymour, Fachongle Isaf, Newport, Dyfed, Wales. [*Editor's note:* since this was written, the Centre has opened and is now a reality.]

Communicating

During the Dark Ages, monasteries became repositories for knowledge. Not only did they store books and manuscripts, so preserving the culture of previous ages, but they produced their own, conducted their own research – or what we today would call research – and played a major role in the education of the young, whereby the cultural legacy was transmitted down the generations.

The modern community is existing in a much less extreme situation, but there are parallels. Your experiences, your successes and failures, and most of all the results of your own applications of technologies that are still fairly new, may be of the greatest help to others – and you, in turn, may derive benefit from information that reaches you from other groups.

BRAD agreed from the first to be open to others. This caused problems with visitors (see page 279) but these can be foreseen and overcome by others who learn from BRAD's experience. BRAD has also been the subject of numerous items in newspapers, magazines and on television, and the BRAD team have worked with the Open University's second level technology course team. They have accepted many personal invitations to talk, to show slides and films of their experiences to groups as diverse as universities and colleges, Women's Institutes and the Royal Institution. More recently, they have also been able to share with others their experience of the personal and social problems that arise when people live in communal fashion.

The importance of maintaining and developing contacts of this kind cannot be over-emphasized. In the words of Philip Brachi of BRAD: 'Reality is rarely optimal. BRAD has made a start at living out the consequences of alternative technology and sharing the experience with others. Living (let alone living as a commune) under a solar roof is different from developing one on a laboratory bench in Birmingham; other demands by the community, the farm, the animals, mean that development time is lengthened and refinements postponed. Explaining the less than theoretically ideal, maximally efficient nature of alternative technology when practised as part of a total way of life, to the "stick up a Savonious and unplug the mains" brigade, has been a small, positive achievement.'

Entertainment

You will need to provide yourself with forms of entertainment. This is not difficult and the equipment you require is minimal. It is possible, though, to hire professional entertainers. The Arts Council provides support for many individual entertainers or small companies who tour rural areas. All you need to do is contact the one of your choice (see page 311), provide some kind of space, indoor or outdoor, where the performance can take place, and find an audience. It is possible, too, for groups of professional entertainers to live in this way, as a specialized kind of commune that is largely self-sufficient but that also practises its craft for the benefit of others.

Foot's Barn Theatre is one such group. Formed in 1971 – in the barn owned by Oliver Foot – the idea was to create grass-roots theatre related directly to the people in whose area the company would work.

The group works from a 2.8-hectare farm that is the home, rehearsal space and workshop area for a total of 17 people: musicians – who work in a group called 'Touch the Earth', actors, technicians, poets, painters and mechanics. No member of the company receives any wages. Food is bought in bulk and a certain amount is grown on the farm – most vegetables in season, ducks and chickens.

The company has no hierarchy and people are not given set jobs. Everybody sets up and takes down the show and plays are written by the company, almost always following a majority decision as to which of the ideas presented will be performed. The actors then take the idea and begin to improvise with it until it is built into a complete performance. There is no script until the play has been rehearsed fully and, often, performed once or twice.

All major decisions are taken by the group, but administration is delegated to one person. In addition to its private bookings it makes at least three tours a year in its area – Cornwall – which are open to everyone. The company handles all its own publicity, and the usual admission charge is 40p for adults and 25p for children and old age pensioners. As its experience grows, the company adds to its list of halls, greens, friends and people who deal in booking halls.

The shows often have local flavour, being based on items of news or history, or legends that are familiar to the audience. The result is that Foot's Barn plays to packed houses – although the halls are often small. In Port Isaac, a tiny fishing village, 151 people packed a hall to see the Christmas show. The company decided to take its shows to the people who prefer a warm pub to a cold hall on a winter's night and now pub shows are a regular part of their programme. In addition to the original Cornish plays, which include the story of Tristram and Iseult and the life of a nineteenth-century eccentric, John Tom, the company has also presented plays by Chekhov, N. F. Simpson, Beckett, Ionesco and Albee. Like all good craftsmen, the Foot's Barn company believe in training their successors, and they run workshops and classes in mime, movement, mask-making and -using, street theatre and clowning.

Trading

One of the greatest dangers for any small community is that it may lose contact with the world outside, turn inward upon itself and eventually become irrelevant – if it survives at all. It is very important to maintain contact and good relations with the larger society within which the community must live. You may need the wider society outside as a guarantee of your own survival in other ways. Should this or any other country become chaotic, with industry at a standstill and starvation in the cities, you would not be able to defend your small patch of land against invaders searching for food or valuables – at least, not for long. If the society outside your own boundaries is under stress, local people may change their attitude from one of mute distrust to open hostility and attack you. After all, you are strangers to them, seeking to live differently and in ways that might represent a threat to the established values they wish to preserve, in a time when everything is changing, nothing is dependable. If you make friends locally, however, you may be able to integrate yourself into the wider community so that invaders from other regions meet a totally hostile and united population. This is the best defence you can have. So try to enter into the life of the society around you. Drink in the pub to meet people, be hospitable and generous, ask for help and advice if you need it, but do not criticize openly or seek to change traditional ways.

You will need the economic support of outsiders as well, for no matter how self-sufficient you become, you will need some money – how else will you pay the rates ? You will need to sell your surplus produce or your skills or, ideally, both.

You should have little difficulty selling food products, but some are easier and more profitable than others. Forget about selling grains or milk (it is illegal to sell unpasteurized milk). Vegetables can be sold if they are clean and presentable. Eggs can be sold. Herbs can be sold, tied in attractive bunches – but the return is small when you calculate the time it will take you to cut, sort and tie them. Mushrooms will sell, although it is a waste of time to collect wild fungi for sale – it takes too long. Honey always sells and has the added advantage of keeping indefinitely.

If you are beside a road that is used – especially if it is used by tourists – you can open a stall. Remember, though, that the stall must be kept well stocked. It need not be manned the whole of the time. If produce is pre-packed in some way and priced clearly, customers can leave their money in a box – and do, by and large. But if you border only a narrow country lane, the roadside stall is hardly practicable. You will need to move into the nearest market town. Try taking a stall at the weekly market if you can get together sufficient produce to keep you in business all day and pay the rent. Sell bread – made from your own grain perhaps – to help out the fresh produce. If you are really daring, try selling your own cheese. If there is no market, or if you cannot find a pitch at one, then fall back on the local shops – especially the health food shop, of which there is bound to be at least one in the area.

If you wish to be more ambitious than this, but still not sell to the ordinary commercial dealers – who may not be interested in your produce if the quantity is small and delivery irregular – then Organic Farmers and Growers Ltd may be the firm for you. Formed as an offshoot of The Soil Association, they deal only in food that has been grown organically. Basically this means that no imported artificial fertilizers or chemical sprays have been used, but the reality is more complex than that and they will be glad to send you the list of standards that is used to define organically grown food (see page 305). If you import nothing to help grow your food it is almost bound to qualify. At present this cooperative venture is based in Suffolk, but it is establishing regional branches as quickly as it can, each of which will be largely autonomous, bound by the broadest of policy guidelines laid down at the head office. They will accept as a member any farmer or grower with half a hectare of land or more, and once he satisfies them that his produce conforms to their standards he is entitled to use their mark to identify it as 'organically grown'. They will take even small amounts of produce and find a buyer, sometimes at a better price than it would fetch if sold privately, but sometimes worse. It depends on the produce, its location and its quality. The cooperative does more than that, however. It provides an advisory service that can answer questions and give help in growing food, duplicating many of the services provided by the Government's Agricultural Development and Advisory Service (ADAS). There is a price, of course. Each member has to buy one share in the cooperative, which costs £1, and to pay an annual subscription of at least £10. The cooperative requires a guarantee, initially for three years and then from year to year, that all surplus produce will be sold through its auspices, and it takes a 2 per cent commission on total turnover, plus $\frac{1}{2}$ per cent commission on all produce using the trademark but which the cooperative is unable to market.

If you can sell processed goods, however, you will earn more than you can from the sale of primary produce. The Centre of Living (see page 284) plans to sell hides as finished leather goods, wool as finished cloth and milk as cheese. If your craftsmen can produce surpluses, most hand-made goods can find a market provided they are well made.

You may be able to trade with other groups like yourselves. Most groups find they have surpluses of some things and are short of others. The bartering of surpluses is a sensible way of equalizing such imbalances, while at the same time facilitating the flow of information and ideas between groups.

Health

Mental illness

The first rule in recognizing the symptoms of mental illness or distress that may need professional help is to know your own limitations. Don't start diagnosing one another with fancy labels. All of us, without exception, can be labelled and there is no great virtue in being a Normal Norman. If you must typecast yourselves, divide yourselves into those who are excitatory and those who are inhibitory. Then call the wildly excited ones hypo-manics and the withdrawn ones schizoid. Call yourselves neurotic and live with it, but know the difference between neurosis and psychosis. Psychosis is insanity and the insane person is a danger to him- or herself and to others. Temporary insanity through drugs or drink doesn't count. Diabetes can make you insane temporarily if you can't get your insulin. The withdrawal of a drug or alcohol if you are an alcoholic can send you off your rocker. Try to cool the situation and do as little as you can to aggravate it: it is tricky. Most problems pass, so try to ride out emotional storms by playing for time. Tomorrow is a new day, there is a new life to be led, a new today in which to build on the wreckage of yesterday.

Don't think you can get people certified. You can't. If they want to see a doctor, fine, let them. There's nothing to stop them but his dragon of a receptionist. If you think someone is past helping him- or herself, then you can see a doctor. Be definite with the patient, though. Tell him or her that you are calling a doctor and then do what you say.

You must act if there is a threat of suicide or violence, even if you think the chances are that the threat will not be carried out. You must act if there is drug-pushing going on, or if you yourself are at risk. By all means take the attitude that you don't mind what people do so long as they don't frighten the horses, but you must know what is a private and what is a community matter. If a man breaks a leg he will limp. If he has a nervous breakdown he may do anything irrational – and that's *anything*.

There is, however, method in madness. It is rare for people to be so barmy that they do not know, in the last resort, how to preserve something of themselves – if only their good opinion of themselves. Suicides are trying to attract attention – which they need. The golden rule is to take an interest in the criminal and the crime will take care of itself.

Drugs

The taking of non-therapeutic drugs by any member of a commune is *out*. Let those who take such things form their own kinky set-ups, but do not mix drug-takers with others or you will all end up tarred with the same brush. A single offender will get the whole commune a bad name and while the law remains, observe it. Chain-smoking, drug-dependence, alcoholism – all are equally non-therapeutic drug taking. Social drinking, occasional smoking and self-medication are acceptable, but even the regular taking of sleeping pills is out for commune members: it is the commonest cause of poisoning, not only of the taker but of others, such as children. Do not try to play God and draw lines. If you allow pot, why not acid? If you allow acid, how long will it be before you have a hard drug on your premises? And unless communes as a whole have self-discipline they will all be labelled as kinky.

Sexuality

Sharing sexual partners is better than nothing, but it has its snags. Polyandry, where one woman has to share or satisfy several men or, if you prefer, where several men share one woman, is, by and large, a custom in poor communities. It was often necessitated by the dire consequences that would ensue were the meagre family property to be shared among several sons on marriage – so they all married the same wife. Polygamy is the use of several women by one man. This is found in affluent societies. The pattern among North American Indian women, followed by modern Americans and now exported for more general adoption, is for one woman to have a number of men in sequence, one at a time, one after another.

This idea of variety devalues sex when compared with the variations on a single theme that are possible in a maturing monogamous relationship. The 'one flesh' concept does have objective validity, and ignorance of this makes the sharing of sexual partners hazardous, not only physically but also psychologically. Happiness is a by-product of making others happy, and you can rarely achieve this by sleeping around with somebody else. If you do, be discreet, save face, and do not talk about it.

Be realistic about the snags. Soap bubbles lose their iridescence when they burst, and relationships and marriages, once broken, can only be patched. Kids feel confident if they know where their parents are, especially if they are in the same bed.

Sexually transmitted diseases

The occurrence of sexually transmitted diseases varies from time to time and from place to place. Ports are the prime source of distribution, as immunity develops within a closed population.

The gonococcus of gonorrhoea is as common as the common cold, but at the wrong end. And as with a cold, the purulent drip is the sign. It is a mild infection that clears up with a series of injections of penicillin or the like. It is not all that serious in a man if it is treated properly immediately it has been contracted.

Where such mild infection abounds, the much more serious but rare syphilis may also occur. It's safe to say that everyone who sleeps around will contract gonococcal infection unless he's exceptionally lucky. Syphilis, on the other hand, is the disease of the professional. There is an old saying that the ways of the sinner are hard, and so are his inguinal glands. This is due to syphilis. It starts as a tiny sore at a crack in the skin where the spirochaete enter by direct contact, flesh to flesh. Then there is a rash, and neither the original sore nor the rash may be noticed. The next thing is a gumma, which is an ulcer with a sheer edge, like a tiny lunar crater. Later in life you may get an aneurism, or blow-out, of a blood vessel. Worst of all, you may develop tabes, or insensitivity of the spinal nerves, and finish up as a G.P.I. – with general paralysis of the insane.

Apart from all these snags exchanged just for a bit of pleasure, there is the risk of transmitting this kind of thing to your innocent partner. Even worse, children can be infected. With the gonococcus in the female birth canal, the eyes of the newly born baby may be infected, which is why drops of disinfectant are put in babies' eyes immediately on birth as a routine. The love bug of syphilis can infect the unborn child across the placental barrier, and inherited syphilis is only too common.

There are many other sexually transmitted diseases, such as non-specific urethritis, lice, and other pests that can step from one lot of pubic hair to another.

Try to avoid such intimate activity with persons unknown to you, but if needs must, avoid kissing sores, and avoid unhealthy-looking playmates.

If you do identify a sexually transmitted disease, the place to go to is the nearest large hospital centre where they have a special genito-urinary out-patients' department. This is not something to be dealt with locally as too much is at risk for things to remain utterly confidential. Go to the inquiry desk and ask for the special department that deals with sexually transmitted diseases. You will be seen by an expert in conditions of the strictest confidence and privacy. You may have to disclose information about the suspect from whom you may have contracted disease. This information will be treated properly and a health visitor will follow up your contact and each person involved will be treated properly. Do not put off all this, but act, and, until you do so, lay off other people entirely.

Injuries and common ailments

The best treatment for accidents is prevention. Accidents do not happen by themselves, they are caused. People who are accident-prone may have something on their minds, for example. Protect them by removing causes of injury or disease if you can.

Small children can drown in 15 cm of water. Make sure it is possible to escape quickly in case of fire. Lock up and label poisons. Keep first-aid equipment where it can be found and used quickly. In the event of injury, speed may be vital. Keep plenty of antiseptic, such as peroxide, handy for each and every break of the skin surface.

If someone who feels ill has fever, pain or other acute symptoms, or seems very unwell, call a doctor. If not, put the patient to bed and nurse him or her yourself. Remember that shock is a killer and any person who has been injured may also be shocked. Shock must be treated at once. Cold is more dangerous than high temperature, especially in the very old and the very young.

Allow the sick person to rest and keep him or her warm inside as well as outside. Keep windows open, but not doors. See that the person gets hot, clear fluids to drink, especially in cold weather, and that he doesn't become constipated.

Do not play doctor – it is a dangerous game. Use old-established methods of treatment. There are many herbal remedies that are effective. Keep a doctor informed, however, and call him in if you are in the slightest doubt about what you are doing.

Once you have called in the doctor let him get on with his job in his own way. He will decide what needs his care and you can assume that antibiotics, drugs, surgery or hospitalization will be used if he thinks they are needed. He has no time to try out unorthodox treatments and his professional reputation is based on rules of thumb that dictate standard procedures for one and all. He will not often be wrong. (If he is, change your doctor quickly!)

First aid

There are a few simple rules for dealing with an accident or emergency:

Keep calm and take charge
Do first things first, quickly, quietly and methodically
If breathing has stopped, start resuscitation
Control bleeding
Guard against shock
Do not remove clothes unnecessarily
Do not attempt too much – do what is essential to save life and to
   prevent the conditions from becoming worse
Do not allow people to crowd around
Send for professional help if you think you need it

Resuscitation

Lie the patient on his back, support the nape of the neck and press the top of his head backwards to ensure a clear air passage to the lungs. Open your mouth wide, take a deep breath, cover his mouth, pinching his nose shut, or cover his nose, holding his jaw shut, or, in the case of a small child, his nose and mouth. Blow gently until his lungs are filled, then stop and remove your own mouth. Watch the chest movement and then repeat until normal breathing recommences. Give at least four inflations to saturate the blood with oxygen.

If there is no response, if the pupils are dilated widely, if the victim is blue or blue-grey in colour (check his lips and finger nails) and if there is no pulse in the carotid artery in his neck, then his heart has stopped beating.

Strike his chest over the heart sharply. This may start the heart beating again. If it doesn't, kneel beside him, place the heel of your hand over the lower part of his sternum (breast bone) keeping your palm and fingers off his chest, cover this hand with your other hand, straighten your arms, and rock forward and press down. In an adult the lower part of the sternum can move inwards by about 45 mm. In adults repeat this pressure once per second; in children up to 10 years of age the pressure of one hand is sufficient and the rate is 80 to 90 times a minute; in infants the pressure of two fingers is enough and the rate is 100 per minute. The pressure must be firm, controlled and regular. If it is erratic or violent it may make matters worse. Give the victim one inflation of the lungs to about six or eight depressions of the sternum.

If you suspect the victim has been poisoned by gas, cut off the source of the gas and ensure plenty of fresh air. If the victim is drowning and you take him from the water, begin resuscitation as soon as your feet are on firm ground. Do not wait until you are ashore. If the victim has choked, remove any obstruction you can reach (take care you don't push it farther in) and if he still cannot breathe strike him hard three or four times between the shoulders. If the victim is a child, turn him upside down either across your knee or, if he is small enough, by holding him by the feet.

Control of bleeding

If you can see the cause of the bleeding – from a wound, for example – grasp the sides of the wound and squeeze them together firmly. You may have to hold the wound in this way for up to 15 minutes. If you have a dressing, apply it directly to the wound, press it down firmly and cover it with a pad of soft material. Make sure that the dressing extends well beyond the limits of the wound. Bandage it in place if necessary, but do not bandage too tightly. If bleeding continues do not remove the dressing, just add more pads.

You may not be aware of internal bleeding but if you suspect it, there are signs you may look for. If the bleeding is slight (a loss of up to 10 per cent of blood) the victim may faint but there will be no other symptoms. If 30 to 40 per cent of blood has been lost, the victim may feel light-headed, he may be pale, cold, sweating, and his pulse and breathing rates may increase. If he has lost more than 40 per cent of blood he will feel very cold, especially at the extremities; his pulse will be rapid and shallow and his breathing rapid and gasping, he will feel thirsty, restless and he will ask for doors and windows to be opened to give him more air; he will become less sensitive to pain and eventually he will become apathetic. Keep the patient quiet and warm. Loosen tight clothing, reassure him, try to make him relax physically and mentally, and get help fast.

Shock

Shock is a state of collapse which, if not controlled, will kill. It is associated with severe injury, burns, heart attack, abdominal emergencies, loss of body fluid (through recurring vomiting, for example, as in sea sickness), some bacterial infections or a strong emotional stimulus, such as a bad fright.

The victim may feel giddy, his vision may blur, he may actually collapse. He will be pale, his skin will feel clammy and cold, and he may sweat. His breathing will be rapid and shallow, perhaps gasping. When he gets over his first fright he will become anxious. His pulse will normally beat faster, but in cases of emotional shock it will beat more slowly.

Reassure the patient. Make him comfortable. Do not move him unless you must. Keep him warm, but do not overheat him. Heat causes blood vessels to dilate and if he has lost blood this may make his condition worse.

Bruises

Cover with a cold compress or ice bag.

Muscle strain

Massage the affected part, support with a bandage if necessary, encourage the victim to move the muscle.

Sprain

Rest the injured joint. Beware of too much movement, as it may be dislocated. Place a good layer of cotton wool around the joint and above and below and bandage firmly. If it is the wrist, elbow or shoulder that is sprained, use an arm sling.

If the joint is dislocated, support it in the most comfortable position for the victim.

Fractures

Immobilize the fractured bone, including the joints above and below the fracture. Do this by binding the injured limb to a wooden splint or by binding it to a sound limb (one leg bound to the other, for example), or to the trunk. Always separate skin surfaces with soft padding to prevent chafing. Never apply a bandage directly over the site of a fracture. Always tie knots on the sound side. If both legs are injured, then tie knots above and between them. Check at regular half-hourly intervals to see that bandages do not interfere with circulation as the injured tissues swell. Splints should be long enough to immobilize joints above and below the fracture; they should be well padded, and if they are wide so much the better.

If face or jaw bones are fractured, check that airways are not obstructed. Shock is not usually severe in these cases, and bleeding can usually be controlled by direct pressure.

If the spine is fractured, prevent the victim from trying to get up, find out whether he can move his toes and fingers, and do not move him by picking him up by his head and feet. If he must be moved,

support the whole length of his body and use padding on the stretcher to support the natural curves of the body.

If the ribs are fractured, place the arm on the injured side in a sling, lay the victim down with his head and shoulders raised and his body inclined towards the injured side. Use a folded blanket against his back to support him in this position.

If the collar bone is fractured, place a good-sized pad of soft material in the armpit, hold the arm on the injured side across the chest so that the finger tips lie on the opposite shoulder, and use a sling to bind the arm in this position.

If the pelvis is fractured, lay the victim in his most comfortable position; if he wishes to bend his knees, support them on a folded blanket. Tell him to try not to pass urine. If he must be taken on a

rough or long journey, place two broad bandages around the pelvis, overlapping by half, with their centres in line with the hip joint on the injured side. Tie the feet together with a figure-of-eight bandage and place a broad bandage round both knees.

Burns and scalds

If these are severe, the victim needs urgent medical treatment. Lessen the spread of heat and alleviate pain by immersing the injured part in cold water, then keep it dry and clean. Do not apply any lotions, ointment or oil dressings. Do not prick blisters. Remove anything constricting, such as rings, bangles, belts and boots: it is easier to do it straight away than when swelling has started. If the burn or scald may get dirty, cover it lightly with a sterile or clean dressing. A washed and freshly ironed handkerchief is fairly sterile.

If the injury is caused by a corrosive chemical, flush the area of the injury with running water and remove contaminated clothing, but be careful not to contaminate yourself.

Unconsciousness

If a person is unconscious, check that the head is not injured. If it is, regard the injury as serious and send for help at once. Place the victim in the coma position (on his side, with a bolster under his neck to prevent his tongue from being swallowed). This position prevents the obstruction of air passages, especially by inhalation of vomit. Check that his mouth is empty (remove his false teeth if he wears them), and loosen tight clothing. Give him plenty of fresh air, keep him warm but do not overheat him. When he recovers do not allow any drinks until you are sure his condition is improving. Ask him simple questions about what happened to check his level of consciousness and clarity.

Convulsions or fits

Take what steps may be necessary to prevent the victim from injuring himself or others and reassure him when he begins to recover. Seek medical advice.

Diabetes

Find out whether any member of the group is being treated for diabetes and make sure that he and you know how to deal with emergencies that may arise from too much or too little insulin. If in doubt, ask a doctor.

Poisoning

Try to eliminate or dilute the poison. If the victim is conscious try to find out what the poison was. If it is non-corrosive, try to make him vomit by tickling the back of his throat or by giving an emetic – two heaped tablespoons of common salt in a quarter of a litre of tepid water. If he has swallowed a corrosive poison – an acid or alkali – dilute it by giving copious fluids or soothing drinks. Barbiturate plus alcohol is extremely dangerous and if you suspect this mixture you must send for medical help at once, as you must for all forms of poisoning.

Heat and cold

If you are out of doors under cold conditions beware of hypothermia, or exposure. The victim may be unaware of the symptoms. If he moves or thinks more slowly than usual, if his behaviour is unreasonable or he is irritable, if he has difficulty with speech or vision, stumbles repeatedly or complains of cramp or shivers, then you must stop. Improvise some kind of shelter. Warm the victim – with your own body if necessary. If he is conscious, give him tepid to warm sweet drinks. Do not heat him too quickly or the sudden dilation in his blood vessels could cause a surge of blood away from deep tissues, leading to a sudden and fatal drop in temperature and blood pressure.

If he has frostbite, the affected parts – usually fingers, toes or the face – will be white and quite numb. Thaw them slowly by rubbing in snow or placing them in cold running water. If you go out alone for long periods in the snow, always carry a pocket mirror and use it to check for frostbite in ears and face from time to time. If you are in a party, check one another.

If the weather is unusually hot, you may suffer from sunstroke or heat stroke. Place the victim in the shade, lay him down until he regains consciousness if he has fainted, and give him a drink containing half a teaspoon of salt to the half-litre. If you suspect heat stroke – which can kill quickly – strip the victim and wrap him in a cold, wet sheet to reduce the surface temperature quickly.

The medical chest

You must have medical equipment on hand for first aid. It should include a good medical guide, designed for home use. A book on herbal remedies for humans and animals is useful. The chest should contain:

a thermometer
a set of plasters
an antiseptic powder
a bottle of peroxide
plenty of vitamin C
a few large wound dressings
a few large and plenty of small bandages
a pair of scissors
some sterile gauze and lint
some kaolin dressing
some pain killers – tablets containing aspirin
a barrier cream against radiation
some mild sedative
some burn dressing, such as tulle gauze
cotton wool
antihistamine salve and tablets
oral antibiotics or injections
sterile, disposable syringes
plaster bandages
salt tablets
disinfectant
surgical spirit
laxative
antacid

Reproductive system

Pregnancy

Pregnancy is the key to healthy mothers and babies. It is useful for one community member to read up on it, and on 'natural childbirth'. But delivery, especially of a first child, requires expert help if possible. Emergency advice is given below.

The mother needs to be given special care throughout her pregnancy. Even so, there are times of special stress, such as when her third missed period is due: she is likely to miscarry then if she is stressed unduly. The seventh month is a critical time for the kidneys: they are overloaded with excretion from the foetus as well as from the mother. It is important to have the delivery on time as there are hazards with either late or early delivery.

During pregnancy the mother must eat well, especially of foods rich in iron and calcium, though she should not get fat. Extra fruit and milk is a good idea. Plenty of vitamins, minerals and proteins are essential to a normal pregnancy.

The emotional diet counts, too. A peaceful atmosphere, adequate physical rest and confidence in the outcome are the foundation of good health for the mother and child.

Childbirth

When the baby is born let the father cope with the top half of the mother, if he is around, while you cope with the other end as best you can. Complications in delivery are most often caused by neglect during pregnancy; a woman should be seen by a doctor at least two or three times before delivery. She should know who the person is who will be with her when she comes to term.

To make delivery as painless as possible, get the mother to let her breath go. This makes her relax. If she concentrates on her breathing, the delivery will look after itself.

Can you deliver a baby? Yes, of course you can. Babies have a habit of coming, no matter what. They are active participants in the matter of their birth, pushing themselves into the world and coming up like deep sea divers from the great pressure in the birth canal. Your job is to be around. Do not leave the woman on her own. Do not panic. 'If in doubt, then do nowt.'

When the baby is born you will have to cut the umbilicus. This is a slippery tube, about the size of a gas pipe, that joins the baby to the afterbirth, or placenta, which follows it out after about a quarter of an hour. Tie off the umbilicus with secure knots in two places. Take a sterilized (boiled!) pair of scissors, and cut the cord between the knots. One snip and the job is done, with two blood-tight stumps. If you have any disinfectant, dab it on the stump that sticks out of the baby. If you have a bit of tulle gauze, put that on and wrap it round the stump.

The best thing to do with the baby is to wrap it in a warm shawl or blanket. Lay it down with its head below the level of its body, and its mouth and nose placed where the air passages can clear. If the baby is blue and won't breathe, you must clear these passages of mucus. One way is to hold the baby up by its feet – but be careful. It is very slippery and on no account must you drop it. When it makes its first cry you can be satisfied.

Now turn to the mother. She should have the cord dangling out of her with your knot on the end. If nothing much happens after half an hour, place your hand on her tummy and *very gently* massage the uterus until you feel it contract into a hard lump. This should squeeze out the afterbirth and when this has happened all will be well.

If you need help, or think you will, make sure it is there before the birth begins. Once you have started on your own you are very committed – once begun you must see it through until the baby breathes and the afterbirth is delivered. It will all happen quite naturally if you let it. Above all, be sure of yourself. This will calm the mother who needs the assistance only you can give – simply by being there.

Contraception

Contraception can be practised with the sheath, which also prevents the spread of sexually transmitted diseases.

Women can be fitted with caps and spermicidal jels, they can employ continuous abortion by means of the coil (IUD), or they can take the pill.

There are many methods of natural birth control, such as the ABC (African Birth Control). This is based on observation of the albumin secretion that begins after the menses have dried up. During the dry post-menses phase there is relative sterility. The fertile phase is from the start of albumin secretion until two days after the ovum is shed. This is marked by a change in the albumin, which becomes slimy, like egg white. The Africans use this method and it works. It helps to have a simple thermometer to detect the change in body temperature associated with ovulation. After being steady for six days, the temperature rises by half a degree Fahrenheit for three days, indicating that ovulation has occurred. Women can learn to recognize mid-cycle pain on ovulating. There is no absolute security against conception from the time the menses begin until two days after ovulation is ended.

The needs of the young

A baby is a tube, dry at one end and wet at the other. Keep the dry end wet, and the wet end dry and the basic needs of the very young are catered for. Prior to birth the baby hears a heart beat which it finds comforting, so it needs to be cuddled. Babies need the sound of parental voices and they need to feel secure – they are better wrapped up, packed up, tucked up, than simply sprawling. They need air. This is our first biological need and we will last for about seven minutes without it. In a town, the lower the level of air the more polluted it will be. Don't let babies spend all their time in basements. Wrap them up and put them out of doors, preferably not near a busy road. Along with dogs, babies in small prams and pushchairs are at just the right height to receive the full blast of car exhausts in the street.

Small children need to play. Without this means of self-expression they do not develop properly, and physical dexterity and mental development go together. It is not for nothing that we talk of 'grasping' ideas and concepts as well as hammers.

Children must feel they belong. Nobody's kid is a forlorn kid, and if you visit an orphanage you may find that each child wants you for his or her parent alone. Parents cannot be shared. Moreover, two parents are better than one: the child's relationships develop and mature from one parent to the other. Siblings can take the place of parents and nothing is more cruel than separating brothers and sisters. Marriage creates problems as well as solving them and probably the ideal arrangement would be one in which a smaller number of families had larger numbers of children. One child may cement a marriage, only to create a one-child problem. A second child solves that problem, but then there is the first child, who was something of an experiment, and the second, who is always the baby. So a third child is needed to provide an intermediate one.

Although children need their parents, they do not need to be with them all the time. In many societies, the children spend much of their time with grandparents, while the parents get on with the business of supporting the old, the young and themselves. For the rest of the time the children run in a bunch, which is also good for them.

Children need to be fed regularly and fairly frequently – a little and often. They need plenty of sweet things as they use up more energy than do adults, having a larger surface area compared with their volume and so having to burn more fuel to maintain body temperature. They are less able to adapt to changes of temperature so you can economize on food by ensuring that they are properly clothed. The next food economy is made by dispensing with processed foods. For slightly older children, the first rule of cooking is don't. Let them eat as much raw food as they can. Grate and sieve vegetables, boil up bones and extract the marrow for them and see that their food is fresh and that it has been grown properly. Let them eat anything and everything, and let them please themselves rather than forcing them to eat food they don't want or like, but cultivate in them a taste for bitter and savoury foods as well as for sweet ones. Give them one good cooked meal a day, one raw meal and snacks in between to keep them topped up. Give them an apple each after meals, or a carrot, to clean their teeth. Use raisins, dates, honey, wholemeal bread, black treacle, syrup, moist dark brown sugar, and avoid coloured crystals of sugar, even if they are brown.

The needs of old people

Old people eat – do they eat! They often have little other pleasure in life, nothing much to look forward to but the next meal. They must be kept warm with proper heating outside and proper food inside. Give them hot, clear fluids every few hours. Give them a flask of a milky drink as a nightcap and leave some in the flask for them to repeat the dose during the night if they feel like it. If they have trouble sleeping, spirits are better for them than drugs as a sleeping draught. Give them a tot of whisky to cheer them up. Let them have their fags and fancies. Make an effort to find out what they really want and then get it for them. They like variety, a little often enough to whet their appetites and make them want more. Serve food well, and let them enjoy good company while they eat, but don't let them argue while they are digesting their food. Try having someone reading while they eat as an entertainment and distraction. It is important to prepare them for eating by making something of a ritual of the preparation of the table and of getting them settled down and waiting to be fed. They must not wait on table and eat as well: those who wait on them should eat somewhere else and afterwards.

Old people need personal dignity and attention. They need people to have time for them, to care for them, to listen to them and to talk to them. They need to be kept in touch mentally as well as physically, as with a steadying hand on their arm when they get up from a chair. It is the tone of the grasp that counts, as with children. Behave as though you had all the time in the world and when you have to go, go. You must have such comforts as hot water bottles and mufflers on hand.

In an emergency, play children's games. At all times encourage the relationships between the very young and the very old. Don't separate the young and old into two discrete groups, but let them mingle at will. They need one another and the relationships will develop naturally. If the old folk like to look after the kids, let them, but don't force them.

References
and suppliers

Land

Books

The New Vegetable Grower's Handbook by Arthur J. Simons, revised by Brian Furner (Penguin Books)

The Kitchen Garden by Brian Furner (Pan Books)

Food Crops from your Garden or Allotment by Brian Furner (Pan Books)

Organic Vegetable Growing by Brian Furner (Macdonald)

Self Sufficiency by John and Sally Seymour (Faber)

Information, advice, services

The Soil Association, Walnut Tree Manor, Haughley, Stowmarket, Suffolk IP14 3RS. Telephone Haughley 235

The Henry Doubleday Research Association, 20 Convent Lane, Bocking, Braintree, Essex. Telephone Braintree 1483

The Good Gardeners' Association, Arkley Manor, Arkley, Barnet, Herts. Telephone 01 449 3031

The Viticultural Research Station, Rockfield Road, Oxted, Surrey.

Organic Farmers and Growers Ltd, Longridge, Creeting Road, Stowmarket, Suffolk LP14 5BT. Telephone 2845

Vegetable seedsmen

Sutton Seeds, Hele Road, Torquay TQ2 7QJ

Thompson and Morgan Ltd, London Road, Ipswich, Suffolk

Carters Tested Seeds Ltd, Raynes Park, London SW20

Farm seedsmen

Hunters of Chester, Chester

Chase Compost Seeds, Benthall, Saxmundham, Suffolk

Food
Books

Food for Free by Richard Mabey (Collins and Fontana)

Larousse Gastronomique (Hamlyn)

Good Things by Jane Grigson (Michael Joseph and Penguin)

English Food by Jane Grigson (Macmillan)

Herb Gardening by Claire Loewenfeld (Faber)

Pan Book of Winemaking by B. C. A. Turner (Pan Books)

The Simple Science of Wine and Beer Making by H. E. Bravery

Home Brewed Beers and Stouts by C. J. Berry (Amateur Winemaker)

Scientific Wine Making Made Easy by J. R. Mitchell (Amateur Winemaker)

Plants Unsafe for Wine-Making by T. Edwin Bolt (Amateur Winemaker)

Farmhouse Fare (Countrywise Books)

Suppliers

Springhill Farms (Dinton) Ltd, 38 Buckingham Street, Aylesbury, Bucks HP20 2LH. Telephone Aylesbury 89825. Suppliers of grain mills, hand- or power-operated (see page 88)

Textiles
Books

Weaving by Nell Znamierowski (Pan Craft Books)

The Art of Weaving by Else Regensteiner (Studio Vista)

Techniques of Rug Weaving by Peter Collingwood (Faber)

The Use of Vegetable Dyes by Violetta Thurston (Dryad Press)

Your Hand Spinning by Elsie Davenport

Hand Spinning, Art and Technique by Allen Fannin (Van Nostrand Reinhold)

Equipment

Dryad, Northgate, Leicester. Dryad is one of the main mail-order suppliers of all kinds of craft equipment.

Frank Herring and Sons, 27 High West Street, Dorchester, Dorset

Harris Looms, North Grove Road, Hawkhurst, Kent

Boddy's Bookshop, 165 Linthorpe Road, Middlesbrough, Cleveland

Peter Teal, Mill House Studios, Parracombe, N. Devon.
Mr Teal makes spinning wheels of a very high quality and restores antique wheels. He also gives lessons in spinning.

D. J. Williamson, Timber Top Tables Ltd, 97 Lonsdale Road, Thurmaston, Leicester LE4 8JJ. Mr Williamson also makes spinning wheels to order.

Buildings

Books

Building Construction by Mitchell (Batsford). This is a standard text book on building, published in several volumes.

Architectural Building Construction by Walter Jaggard and Francis Drury (Cambridge University Press)

The Thatcher's Craft published by COSIRA, the Council of Small Industries in Rural Areas (35 Camp Road, Wimbledon Common, SW19 4UP)

The Pattern of English Building by Alec Clifton Taylor (Faber)

Illustrated Handbook of Vernacular Architecture by R. W. Brunskill (Faber)

Equipment

Most of the equipment and materials you need for building must be bought locally from tool shops and builders' merchants.

The Clivus dry toilet was imported to this country in very small numbers. There may be one or two left at *The Ecologist*, 73 Molesworth Street, Wadebridge, Cornwall.

The Mullbank dry toilet is available from Conservation Tools and Technology Ltd, PO Box 134, Kingston, Surrey.

Energy

Books

All the following books are obtainable from Conservation Tools and Technology Ltd, PO Box 134, Kingston, Surrey:

New Energy Sources (bibliography)

Solar Power

Solar Energy for Man by B. J. Brinkworth (Compton Press).
The best-selling textbook on solar energy yet published in the English language.

Wind Power

Methane – Fuel for the Future

Hydropower Manual

The Owner-Built Home by Ken Kern

Information

Conservation Tools and Technology Ltd, PO Box 134, Kingston, Surrey.

BRAD's solar roof: plans and detailed instructions, including costs and materials required, from Conservation Tools and Technology, or The National Centre for Demonstration of Alternative Technology, Machyrlleth, Montgomeryshire. Price 30p plus stamped addressed envelope.

Northern Water Power Society (Secretary, R. Swinn), Scugdale Hall, Swainby, Northallerton, N. Yorks

National Association of Water Power Users, PO Box 27, Exchange Chambers, 10(b) Highgate, Kendal, Cumbria LA9 4SX

Land and Leisure Recreation Services, Quarries Cottage, Meldon Hill, Chagford, Devon

Commercial solar collectors

Stellar Heat Systems, Upper York House, 30 Upper York Street, Bristol. Cost about £50 per square metre double-glazed aluminium collector plate. Nicely finished, but expensive.

Sunheat Systems, Barn House, Kemerton, Nr Tewkesbury, Glos. Cost about £36 per square metre glazed or £20 unglazed. Reflector surfaces in ABS plastic.

Solarcyl, Wyvern House, Anchor Road, Bristol. Cost about £30 per square metre. Rather pricy, unglazed converted radiator.

A. T. Marston & Co (Calor Sol), Lancaster Road, Harlescot Grange, Shrewsbury, Salop. About £46 per square metre, glazed with plastic. With a full set of ancillary fittings, a panel 3 metres by 1 metre costs £138.

Air Distribution Equipment, 64 Whitebarn Road, Llanishen, Cardiff. About £50 per square metre. Its 60 × 60-cm double-glazed panels are very handy for building. It is well made and effective.

Drake and Fletcher, Parkwood, Sutton Road, Maidstone, Kent. About £40 per square metre. Makers of 'Warm Swim' solar panels.

Solar Water Heaters, Pillar House, 21 South Parade, Doncaster, S. Yorks. About £38 per square metre. Uses blackened water as an indirect heat system to provide heat transfer liquid. Glazed in plastic.

Solar Heat Ltd, 99 Middleton Hall Road, Birmingham 30. About £38 per square metre. Not very well made, unglazed, but good for the tropics. This is Britain's longest established solar heater.

Robinsons of Winchester, Robinson House, Winhal Industrial Estate, Winchester. About £20 per square metre. Unglazed swimming-pool panel in rigid ABS. Framed and glazed version extra. This one is good value.

Distrimax Ltd, 88 The Avenue, London NW6. About £30 per square metre. Unglazed metal collector from Israel. Features special selective surface.

Solar Centre, 176 Ifield Road, London SW10. A shop featuring most makes of solar collector, including their own 'Sunstor' swimming-pool collector.

Conservation Tools and Technology Ltd, PO Box 134, Kingston, Surrey. About £15 per square metre. Unlovely, but cheap and effective PVC collector for factories, swimming pools and homes – in that order.

Water power

Pelton water wheels are available from Small Hydroelectric Systems, PO Box 124, Custer, Washington 98240, USA. A 45-cm wheel costs about $350 FOB Custer and can be used either to generate electricity or to do work directly.

Larger glass-fibre waterwheels made to the traditional design are supplied by Trago Mills, Twowatersfoot, Liskeard, Cornwall.

Crafts

Books

General

The Craft Industries by Geraint Jenkins (Longman)

Whole Earth Catalog and *Whole Earth Epilog*

Do-It-Yourself magazines
Reader's Digest Complete Do-It-Yourself Manual

Crafts for All by Karl Hills (Routledge and Kegan Paul)

Pottery

A Potter's Book by Bernard Leach (Faber)

Pottery by Jolyon Hofsted (Pan Craft Books)

Carpentry

The Technique of Furniture Making by Ernest Joyce (Batsford)

Boats

Boat Building by Howard Chappelle (Allen and Unwin)

Make Your Own Sails by R. M. Bowker and S. A. Budd (Macmillan)

Toys

The Puppet Theatre by Jan Bussell (Faber)

Brushes

The Story of Brushmaking, a Norfolk Craft by Mervyn Jones. Available price 20p from Briton Chadwick Ltd, Wymondham, Norfolk

Brush up on Brushes by Mervyn Jones. A more technical booklet, supplied free on request.

The Directory of Brush and Allied Trades (Wheatland Journals, 157 Hagden Lane, Watford WD1 8LW) gives the only comprehensive list of suppliers of materials and equipment.

General information and supplies

The Rural Industries Bureau, COSIRA, 35 Camp Road, Wimbledon Common, SW19 4UP

Communities

General information

The Centre of Living, c/o John Seymour, Fachongle Isaf, Newport, Dyfed, Wales

BIT, 146 Great Western Road, London W11. Telephone 01 229 8219. BIT operates a round-the-clock information service for those attempting alternative lifestyles and it also collects and publishes information on communes.

The Children's Rights Workshop, 73 Balfour Street, London SE17. Telephone 01 703 7217. Provides information and guidance on all forms of education outside the official 'system', including a comprehensive bibliography of books on the subject, available on request.

Books

First Aid (published in association with the British Red Cross and the St. John Ambulance Association) is the standard reference for first aid. *New Essential First Aid* by A. Ward Gardner and Peter J. Roylance (Pan)

Entertainments

For details of theatrical groups in your area or for information on the arts generally:

The Arts Council of Great Britain, 105 Piccadilly, London W1V OAU. Telephone 01 629 9495

Index